P9-CLD-921

Co-Active Coaching

CO-ACTIVE
COACHING

NEW SKILLS FOR COACHING PEOPLE TOWARD SUCCESS IN WORK AND LIFE

2ND EDITION

LAURA WHITWORTH ▪ KAREN KIMSEY-HOUSE
HENRY KIMSEY-HOUSE ▪ PHILLIP SANDAHL

Davies-Black Publishing • Mountain View, California

Published by Davies-Black Publishing, a division of CPP, Inc., 1055 Joaquin Road, 2nd Floor, Mountain View, CA 94043; 800-624-1765.

Special discounts on bulk quantities of Davies-Black books are available to corporations, professional associations, and other organizations. For details, contact the Director of Marketing and Sales at Davies-Black Publishing: 650-691-9123; fax 650-623-9271.

Copyright © 2007 by Laura Whitworth, Karen Kimsey-House, Henry Kimsey-House, and Phillip Sandahl. All rights reserved. No part of this book may be reproduced, stored in a retrieval system, or transmitted in any form or by any means, electronic, mechanical, photocopying, recording, or otherwise, without written permission of the publisher, except in the case of brief quotations embodied in critical articles or reviews.

Davies-Black and its colophon and Strong Interest Inventory are registered trademarks of CPP, Inc. Adobe, Acrobat, and Reader are registered trademarks of Adobe Systems, Inc. DiSC is a registered trademark of Inscape Publishing. MetaSkills is a trademark of The Coaches Training Institute. Myers-Briggs Type Indicator and MBTI are trademarks or registered trademarks of the Myers-Briggs Type Indicator Trust in the United States and other countries. StrengthsFinder is a trademark of The Gallup Organization. Team Diagnostic is a trademark of Team Coaching International.

Visit the Davies-Black Publishing Web site at www.daviesblack.com.

11 10 09 08 07 10 9 8 7 6 5 4 3 2 1
Printed in the United States of America

Library of Congress Cataloging-in-Publication Data
Co-active coaching : new skills for coaching people toward success in work and life / Laura Whitworth ... [et al.]. — 2nd ed.
   p. cm.
Includes index.
ISBN-13: 978-0-89106-198-4 (pbk.)
1. Self-actualization (Psychology) 2. Mentoring. 3. Motivation (Psychology)
4. Success—Psychological aspects. I. Whitworth, Laura.
BF637.S4W484 2007
158′.3—dc22

2006030970

SECOND EDITION
First printing 2007

This book is dedicated to the clients and coaches
whose lives we have touched
and whose lives have touched us . . .
and to the clients and coaches to come.

Contents

PART I

Co-Active Coaching Fundamentals

PART II

Co-Active Coaching Contexts

PART III

Co-Active Coaching Principles and Practices

About the CD

The accompanying CD contains audio files introducing and demonstrating the co-active coaching model. Brief introductions highlight the contexts and skills emphasized in the sample coaching dialogues.

The CD also contains PDF files of the forms and exercises in the Coach's Toolkit, which you may download and print out for use with clients. Please note: To read and print the PDF files, you will need Adobe® Acrobat® (version 5.0 or newer) or Adobe® Reader® installed on your computer.

The contents of the CD are listed below.

AUDIO

1   The Co-Active Coaching Model
2   Introduction to Demonstration 1
3   Co-Active Coaching Demonstration 1
4   Introduction to Demonstration 2
5   Co-Active Coaching Demonstration 2
6   Conclusion

THE COACH'S TOOLKIT PDFS

Discovery Forms and Checklists

For Use with Individual Clients

1 Individual Client Discovery Checklist
2 Coaching Agreement
3 Personal Information Fact Sheet
4 Wheel of Life Exercise
5 Primary Focus
6 Individual Client Interview
7 Strategic Planning Checklist
8 Completion Log
9 Coaching Preparation Form

For Use with Corporate Clients

10 Corporate Client Discovery Checklist
11 First Meeting Checklist
12 Corporate Client Profile
13 Alternative Client Profile
14 Performance Awareness Appraisal
15 Job Performance Wheel
16 Management/Leadership Wheel

Additional Coaching Forms

17 Co-Active Coaching Definition
18 Wheel of Life Exercise
19 Priorities Wheel
20 Management Competencies Wheel
21 Blank Wheel
22 Goals and Commitments
23 Daily Habits
24 Daily Habits Tracking Log
25 Action and Planning Log
26 Saboteur Clarification
27 Saying Yes—Saying No

Coaching Exercises

Coaching Resources

Preface

Welcome to the second edition of *Co-Active Coaching*. It is an extraordinary experience to look back and see how much the world of coaching has changed in just a few short years. Back in 1998 when the first edition was published, if you told people you were a coach, their automatic response would likely have been, "Oh? What sport?" Today, the profession of coaching as we know it is widespread, familiar to most, and growing continuously. In our view, it is the demand and desire for coaching that is pulling the profession ever more deeply into the world.

As we survey the landscape of coaching today, we see the profession's dramatic growth, and data from the International Coach Federation (ICF) help illustrate it. The ICF is the largest association for professional coaches worldwide. In 1998, the ICF counted fewer than 2,000 members, and less than 140 of those were outside North America. Seven years later, the ICF is still growing, supporting more than 8,000 members; of those, more than 2,000 are outside North America, representing every major country in the world.

The growth is not just geographic; coaching continues to become more diverse in its reach as coaches specialize in a wide variety of demographic and interest-related niches. Nearly every age, occupation, and personal passion has a coach waiting to answer the call.

In the corporate world, where coaching was once the exclusive perk of executives and rising stars, it is becoming a standard part of the organizational toolkit to help employees, managers, supervisors, and, yes, executives in their personal development and achievement.

Organizations have learned that highly motivated and fulfilled employees at all levels produce high-performance results for the organization. In fact, many organizations are now bringing coach training into the organization, so that coaching skills and the coaching context are developed in-house.

In a related way, the past few years have seen the emergence of a new branch of coaching: team coaching. It is a complementary approach to individual coaching, not a substitute. In a world that is increasingly aware of the power of teams inside organizations, team coaching is on the rise. Coaching for relationship systems is expanding as well, and not just for romantic relationships, but for families, business associates, and other close partnerships.

Even the definition of "coach" is widening. The first edition of the book was aimed primarily at individual coaches working as individual practitioners. Today, we see consulting companies offering coaching services, and a wide variety of professional service providers are adding coaching or coaching skills to their current practice. More and more, for example, we see consultants offering ongoing coaching to help ensure that changes and new skills take hold and grow.

We also see an emerging emphasis on coaching as an essential skill set for leaders. Coaching is widely recognized as one of the fundamental leadership styles that top leaders need in order to operate effectively.

In the first edition, we talked about co-active coaching as not only a set of professional skills but a unique way of communicating. The nature of the relationship and what is honored are different in a coaching relationship compared to other relationships, in which there is often a strong identification with who is dominant and who is not. Today, we see this "coach approach" spreading from professional coaching relationships into general use. We see teachers using coaching skills and a coaching style when these are called for. We see managers, parents, customer service representatives, and health care workers using coaching skills and a coach approach.

In the years since the first edition, the profession has grown along with our own understanding of what makes coaching work. Since the publication of the first edition, we have trained literally thousands of coaches in public workshops and inside organizations around the world. We have learned that the co-active coaching model crosses all of the usual boundaries: geographic, cultural, and demographic. It has been an exciting and provocative learning experience. Training others has given us more clarity about the principles, contexts, and skills of co-active coaching, better ways of articulating the material, better descriptions and distinctions, and better examples. We are now ready to share what we have learned in this second edition.

One of the first things you'll notice is that we present a broader application of coaching and coaching skills. Whereas the first edition emphasized one-on-one, life coaching examples, the second edition uses a variety of coaching situations, including dialogue samples and corporate scenarios, to illustrate the material.

Another important change is our increased emphasis on an attribute we consider essential in co-active coaching, what we call "dancing in the moment." Dancing in the moment is the coach's ability to be flexible and unattached, to stay curious about the unfolding conversation and adjust instinctively. This quality has been so much a part of the way we coach that it is like the air we breathe—and because we take it for granted, it didn't receive enough attention the first time around. Readers of the first edition will note that we have removed the designed alliance from the co-active coaching cornerstones and replaced it with dancing in the moment.

Making this change in the four cornerstones turned out to be simple enough. In the first edition, the essential work of designing an alliance between coach and client appeared as a cornerstone and was also part of the coaching model. Designing an alliance is still emphasized as an essential component of the model, and dancing in the moment is given its rightful place as a cornerstone of co-active coaching. Chapter 1 provides a detailed description of the model, including the cornerstones.

Other changes: We added a chapter that integrates the three core coaching principles and describes the artistry of choosing the coaching direction, in the moment, in a way that will best serve the client. We also emphasize the role of the coach in having the courage and confidence to take charge of the coaching and call forth the client.

In this edition, you will find three new appendices:

- Appendix A presents a compelling case for the underpinnings of co-active coaching for organizations.
- Appendix B describes organization and relationship systems coaching and the ways in which this form of coaching differs from mainstream individual coaching.
- Appendix C presents the International Coach Federation's ethical guidelines for coaches.

We also revised and updated the Coach's Toolkit to reflect the broader scope of coaching. You will find more materials related to corporate, organization, relationship, and team coaching.

Finally, one very practical addition to the second edition is the accompanying CD. On the CD you will find audio files of sample coaching dialogues as well as printable versions of the tools in the Coach's Toolkit in PDF file format. (Please note: To download and print the files, you will need Adobe® Acrobat® [version 5.0 or newer] or Adobe® Reader® installed on your computer.)

Creating this second edition has been very gratifying on a number of levels. It has been gratifying to look back and see the growth of the profession and the ongoing commitment of coaches to professionalism. It has been gratifying to clarify what we have learned in the intervening years. It is very gratifying to be able to put in your hands our most up-to-date understanding and clarifications for co-active coaching. And it has been especially gratifying to see that the model is strong, durable, and more than flexible enough to be viable as the coaching profession continues to grow.

Laura Whitworth
Karen and Henry Kimsey-House
Phillip Sandahl
Spring 2007

Acknowledgments

We owe an enormous debt of gratitude to so many people who have supported, encouraged, and championed this work.

We want to especially acknowledge the pioneers who were with us in the beginning as the coaching profession found its way in the world, especially Thomas Leonard, John Whitmore, Julio Olalla, and Frederic Hudson.

Coaching training played an enormous role in spreading the power and possibilities of coaching as a profession. The faculty and staff of The Coaches Training Institute have been at the forefront of the mission to prepare new coaches, maintain high professional standards, and keep the co-active coaching material up-to-date. Their commitment to the essence and the particulars has helped us continuously refine what we present, and that commitment shows in this second edition. We particularly want to thank those who reviewed early drafts: Elaine Jaynes, Eric Kohner, Caroline Hall Otis, Steven Filante, Craig Carr, Jil Windsor, Hope Langner, Andrea Sigetich, and Marcia Dorfman.

Coaching has spread around the globe in the years since the first edition was published. There is something in the world itself that is pulling coaching into organizations, relationships, and individual lives on every continent. And it would not be happening without the vision and initiative of very determined people willing to take on the challenges of language and culture for the sake of coaching. We especially want to acknowledge the early visionaries of our own work, in particular Hide Enomoto in Japan, Kathy Lasher and Linda Taylor in the United Kingdom, and Jeroen Schüssel and Ann Elin Schüssel in Norway.

To the thousands of coaching students we have trained, to our clients, and, yes, to our own coaches, we are thankful beyond words. And finally, to the clients who are and always have been our most important teachers, this acknowledgment is for you. You are the reason we do this work

Laura Whitworth
Karen and Henry Kimsey-House
Phillip Sandahl

Introduction

In today's world, coaching is both a growing profession worldwide and a growing communication style adopted by leaders in organizations, teachers, counselors, parents, and others. This book describes a particular approach to coaching and the coaching relationship, which we call co-active coaching because it involves the active and collaborative participation of both the coach and the client. It is the underlying beliefs of co-active coaching that make it both powerful and adaptable.

The co-active coaching model is a proven approach based on many years of experience working with clients and coaches worldwide. This book describes the model in detail, defines the skills and techniques of co-active coaching, and offers samples of coaching conversations as well as practical exercises that will enhance your understanding.

The co-active coaching model was the starting point and is still at the core of the training we do through The Coaches Training Institute (CTI). CTI was founded in 1992 by Laura Whitworth and Henry Kimsey-House, who were joined a year later by Karen Kimsey-House. Today, CTI is one of the largest coach-training organizations in the world, delivering courses in North America, Europe, the Middle East, and Asia. CTI offers a comprehensive training program for coaches as well as a highly regarded certification program, a unique leadership development program, a curriculum designed specifically for organization and relationship systems coaching, courses in coaching mastery and business development, a diverse online network through which coaches may engage in special-interest dialogue, and a strong presence as a visionary force in the field of coaching.

GETTING TO THE CORE

This book is not just about skills and a description of the model. It is about the nature of a coaching relationship—specifically, a co-active coaching relationship. We look at the nature of a co-active coaching conversation and at what makes this so different from other conversations. This book gets to the core.

What is different about a co-active coaching conversation? In our view, coaching is not about solving problems, although problems will be solved. It is not primarily about improving performance, attaining goals, or achieving results, although all of that will certainly happen in an effective coaching relationship. We believe that coaching is chiefly about discovery, awareness, and choice. It is a way of effectively empowering people to find their own answers, encouraging and supporting them on the path as they continue to make important choices.

Coaching is a form of conversation with unspoken ground rules regarding certain qualities that must be present: respect, openness, compassion, empathy, and a rigorous commitment to speaking the truth. There are certain assumptions underlying the conversation as well. We assume strength and capability, not weakness, helplessness, or dependence. We assume a deep desire to give the best and achieve potential. A coaching conversation has certain beliefs built into it: that every situation has possibilities and that people really do have the power of choice in their lives.

In our view, coaching is a way of being in relationship and being in conversation that might be unique in human history. Coaching is a style of communication that has risen organically from an urge within the human community—it was not somebody's great marketing idea. How else can we explain coaching's rapid spread around the world, essentially by word of mouth? There is a tipping point behind this phenomenon that has to do with what people believe and how they relate to one another. It reflects a change in consciousness: consciousness of choice and a clearer commitment to choosing based on values of integrity.

In the profession of coaching, this unique style of co-active communication shows up in how a coach listens, not only to the words but also to what is behind the words, and even to the spaces between the words. A coach is someone who is in tune with the nuances of voice, emotion, and energy, who is intent on receiving everything the client communicates—someone who listens to the very best in others, even when they can't hear it in themselves.

A coach is someone who cares that people create what they say they want, that they follow through when they choose. The coach is there to hold people accountable and keep them moving forward toward their dreams and goals.

In our view, one of the most important qualities of a coach, and something clients can count on in a co-active coaching relationship, is truthfulness. A coach is someone who will absolutely tell the truth—the truth about where clients are strong, for example, and where they hold back and give up, deny, or rationalize.

With this book, you will learn how to discover and promote your client's mission, purpose, and specific agenda. You'll find effective ways to rigorously hold others to account and do it with a light hand. You'll learn the co-active coaching approach to values, setting goals, life balance, and self-management.

You'll also learn coaching strategies for addressing the self-limiting behavior that often shows up strongest just when people need the courage to take risks for the sake of change. These proven strategies help clients stay on track and overcome actions that sabotage desires, plans, and dreams.

This book emphasizes information and exercises for professional coaches, yet the skills and insights it offers can be applied in almost any relationship—at work, with family and friends, in volunteer and community settings—because coaching skills and the nature of the relationship are not limited to professional coaching sessions.

HOW THE BOOK IS STRUCTURED

Part One presents an overview of the co-active coaching model. The first chapter outlines the five contexts of co-active coaching: listening, intuition, curiosity, forwarding action and deepening learning, and self-management. The chapter also describes the three principles—fulfillment, balance, and process—that together form the client's agenda at the heart of the model. Part One also explains how to design the alliance between coach and client, the foundation on which the entire coaching relationship is built.

Part Two describes each of the five contexts in detail and presents descriptions and examples of the coaching skills in action. Here we provide sample coaching conversations as well as exercises that bring the skills to life.

Part Three covers the three core principles: how to coach the client's fulfillment, balance, and process. In the last chapter, we describe the integration of these three principles into the artistry of coaching.

The Coach's Toolkit, immediately following Part Three, is an extensive section of forms and exercises that coaches can use with clients, while the three appendices provide information on co-active coaching in organizations, relationship and organization systems coaching, and ethics in coaching.

In summary, this book offers a comprehensive approach to coaching and coaching skills. It provides a systematic structure reinforced with real-life examples and practical exercises for developing your coaching abilities. It is a book for those who want to expand their knowledge and develop their capacities as professional coaches and those who wish simply to add a coaching approach to important conversations using the unique model we call *co-active coaching*.

Co-Active Coaching Fundamentals

From day one, coaching focuses on what clients want. People come to coaching because they want things to be different. They are looking for change or they have important goals to reach. People come to coaching for lots of individual reasons. They are motivated to achieve specific goals: to write a book, to start a business, to have a healthier body. They come to coaching in order to be more effective or more satisfied at work. They hire a coach because they want to create more order and balance in their lives. Sometimes people want more from life—more peace of mind, more simplicity, more joy. And sometimes they want less—less confusion, less stress, less financial pressure. In general, they come to coaching because they want a better quality of life—more fulfillment, better balance—or a different process for accomplishing their life desires. Whatever the individual reason, it all starts with the client.

Part One explains what the coach brings to coaching in response to the client and shows what the process looks like from a co-active coaching perspective. In this part of the book, we outline the elements and convey a sense of how they fit together in a comprehensive model. In later chapters, we expand on these major components to provide more depth and offer examples from coaching conversations.

The Co-Active Coaching Model

The term "co-active" refers to the fundamental nature of a coaching relationship in which the coach and client are active collaborators. In co-active coaching, this relationship is an alliance between two equals for the purpose of meeting the client's needs.

FOUR CORNERSTONES

There are four cornerstones that form the foundation of co-active coaching:

- The client is naturally creative, resourceful, and whole.
- The agenda comes from the client.
- The coach dances in the moment.
- Co-active coaching addresses the client's whole life.

Naturally Creative, Resourceful, and Whole

The primary building block for all co-active coaching is this: Clients have the answers or they can find the answers. From the co-active coach's point of view, nothing is wrong or broken, and there is no need to fix the client. The coach does not deliver answers; the coach asks questions and invites discovery.

Sometimes clients don't think they have the answers. They'd rather believe someone else—an expert—has the answers for them, which can lead to a natural desire to buy the answers in a packaged program rather than doing the work that needs to be done to find their own solutions. All too often, what people end up with is a prepackaged answer that doesn't fit their unique needs.

In some cases, people have a powerful sabotaging voice, a judgmental voice we call the "Saboteur," that tells them they don't have the answers. But co-active coaching stands on the certainty that clients really are naturally creative, resourceful, and whole and capable of finding the answers they need. When they look inside, with the help of a coach, they'll find they know themselves, their strengths, and their limitations. They'll also discover what they want, what they fear, what motivates them, and what holds them back, their purpose and their vision, and where they betray themselves. They may never have sought the answer before the coach asks the question—the question that creates the channel for self-discovery—but the answer is there. Clients do know how to find their way, especially with the help of their coach. Years of experience using the co-active coaching model confirm it. This is why we say that the coach's job is to be curious, not to be an expert. We have found that clients are more resourceful, more effective, and generally more satisfied when they come up with their own solutions. And because they choose the solution, they are more likely to follow through with action. When what they need *really* is expert advice, they will have the motivation to find that, too.

The Client's Agenda

In a co-active coaching relationship, the agenda comes from the clients, not the coach. This is one of the most important distinctions of co-active coaching. The relationship is entirely focused on getting the results clients want. They set the agenda. The coach's job is to make sure the agenda doesn't get lost. So while clients focus on the ongoing changes they are making in their lives, the coach holds on to the agenda. The coach ensures that clients are always steering toward fulfillment and balance and are able to engage in the process of their lives. "Holding the client's agenda" is such an important role for the co-active coach that you will see the phrase used over and over in this book.

This way of working with an agenda is different from consulting, as the consultant brings specialized expertise and very often sets the agenda for the relationship. Co-active coaching is not about the coach's expertise, advice, or solutions. In co-active coaching, the coach's expertise is confined to the coaching process. The coach's job is to help clients articulate their dreams, desires, and aspirations, help them clarify their mission, purpose, and goals, and help them achieve that outcome.

Dancing in the Moment

A coach in the midst of a coaching session is constantly choosing. Every response from a client provides information about where to go next with the coaching. This awareness of the shifting currents and themes becomes second nature to experienced coaches; they are constantly sensing what is most important and choosing a question or skill based on what just showed up. This is the art of dancing in the moment. This is listening at a very deep level—underneath the words and story, underneath the content or logic of the issue being presented. This is listening with intuition tuned to a high level. Sensing and adjusting in this way require great flexibility, the willingness to fly instantly in a new direction, the willingness to accept paradox or apparent contradiction and keep going. We call this coaching agility "dancing in the moment."

In practical terms, dancing in the moment is also about responding to the client's agenda. At the beginning of a coaching session, the coach needs to be ready to respond to whatever the client has determined is most important that day. The issue a client brings is rarely a complete surprise; after all, this is an ongoing relationship, and there is typically a major issue coach and client are working on, with some form of accountability. Even so, coaches need to be ready to change course, to dance in the moment as clients do their discovery work in the moment.

Addressing the Client's Whole Life

Co-active coaching recognizes what may seem obvious: the decisions we make are interconnected. Clients don't live their lives in discrete compartments; there are links between all of the pieces. A career choice can affect health, family, and friends. Choices about finances affect plans for vacation, education, and retirement, and vice versa. Nearly every choice exists in a system of possible choices stretching into other areas of life. Even when a coaching session focuses on one particular facet of a client's life, there is an awareness of the ripples that are set in motion. Flexibility is one of the strengths of the co-active model. The underlying principles and contexts make it possible for co-active coaches to work with clients in every aspect and virtually every corner of their lives.

CLIENT'S AGENDA AS HEART OF THE MODEL

The ongoing relationship between coach and client exists only to address the client's agenda—and so the client's agenda is at the center of the diagram in Figure 1. There are two ways to think about this agenda. The first is at the level of the big picture for the client's life. Every day, people make dozens, even hundreds, of decisions to do or not do certain things. The choices we make during the day, no matter how trivial they may seem, contribute to creating a life that is more (or less) fulfilling. The decisions we make move us toward or away from better balance in our lives. The choices contribute to a more effective life process or to a process that is less effective. And so at one level, the client's agenda is wrapped in these three core principles of fulfillment, balance, and process. They are principles because they are fundamental to the liveliness of life. In the same way that oxygen, fuel, and heat are neces-

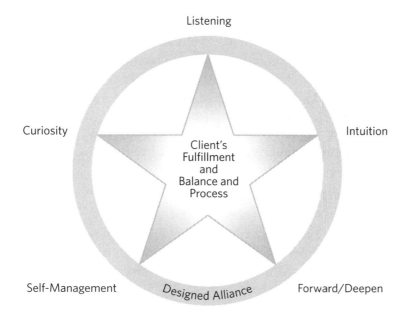

FIGURE 1 **The Co-Active Coaching Model**

sary for fire, these three principles combine to create an ignited life. In our model, we often refer to this big-picture agenda as the *Big-"A" agenda*.

The second way we look at the client's agenda is through specific issues that the client brings to his or her coaching sessions. Clients bring all sorts of agenda items to their coaching, and yet, whatever the specific issue, there is a way to link it to a more fulfilling life, life-giving balance, or better process. This specific issue is often referred to as the *little-"a" agenda*.

Fulfillment

The client's definition of fulfillment is always intensely personal. It may include, especially at first, outward measures of success: a great job, enough money, a certain lifestyle. Eventually, the coaching will progress to a deeper definition of fulfillment. It's not about having more. It's not about what fills the client's pockets or closets—it's about what fills the client's heart and soul. A fulfilling life is a valued life, and clients will have their own definitions of what they truly value. If they value risk taking, is there enough adventure in their lives? If they value family, are they shortchanging themselves by caving in to the demands of work? What are the personal values they want present in their work? Sorting out values is a way of sorting out life choices, because when the choices reflect the client's values, life is more satisfying and often feels effortless. Achieving a certain goal can be very fulfilling—especially as a benchmark—but most clients find that fulfillment is not the finish line. At its deepest level, fulfillment is about finding and experiencing a life of purpose. It is about reaching one's full potential.

Balance

Today, with so many responsibilities, attractive options, demands, and distractions, balance may feel like an impossible dream. It's especially elusive for most of the people who come to coaching. They tend to be dissatisfied with functioning at some minimum standard of being alive: they want more from life and want to give more back. They can be passionate about the things that matter to them, focused in their commitment, and so intense that sometimes one corner of their lives is a model of excellence while the rest is in ruins. They understand the value of balance and have probably made attempts to achieve it—with good intentions to exercise more, take time off, or reconnect with friends—and found that weeks or months passed without any change. Life is out of balance.

People often seem resigned to being out of balance, as if that's just the way life is. That's the real world, given the circumstances. There's only one way of looking at it, and it looks bad. Coaching for balance, however, focuses on widening the range of perspectives and, therefore, adding more choices. Ultimately, balance is about making choices: saying yes to some things and no to others. This can be challenging. Clients often want to say yes to more in their lives without making room for it by saying no to something else. This impulse leads to an overwhelmed feeling—and lives that are out of balance.

Balance is a fluid state because life itself is dynamic. Therefore, it makes more sense to look at whether clients are moving toward balance or away from balance rather than to offer them "balance" as a goal to be achieved. Like the seasons of the year, balance is best viewed over the long haul. It is also a perennial issue, one that coaches will see, in some form or another, many times over in the course of a coaching relationship.

Process

We are always in process. Sometimes it looks frantic; sometimes it looks graceful. Because coaching is effective at achieving results, both clients and coaches can get drawn into the "results" trap—focusing entirely on the destination and losing sight of the flow of the journey. In fact, process is often compared to a river. As life flows, there will be fast periods of onrushing, white-water progress as well as days of calm, steady currents. But there will also be times of drifting, being stuck in job eddies and relationship whirlpools, and backsliding into treacherous swamps. There will be flooding and drought. The coach's job is to notice, point out, and be with clients wherever they are in their process. The coach is there to encourage and support, provide companionship around the rocks, and escort clients through the dark waters as well as to celebrate their skill and success at navigating the difficult passages. Coaching allows clients to live more fully in a deeper relationship with *all* aspects of their lives.

Co-active coaching therefore embraces this whole picture of the client: fulfillment, balance, and process. These are the core principles at the heart of the coaching model. Together they create the heat and light of a life that is fully alive.

DESIGNED ALLIANCE FOR AN EMPOWERED COACHING ENVIRONMENT

With the client in the center of the co-active coaching model (see Figure 1, p. 7), we encircle the client and the client's agenda; we name this protective circle the *designed alliance*. In co-active coaching, power is granted to the coaching relationship, not to the coach. Client and coach work together to design an alliance that meets the client's needs. In fact, clients play an important role in declaring how they want to be coached. They are involved in creating a powerful relationship that fits their working and learning styles. The relationship is tailored to the communication approach that works best for them. The process of designing the alliance is a model of the mutual responsibility of client and coach. Clients learn that they are in control of the relationship and, ultimately, of the changes they make in their lives.

THE FIVE CONTEXTS

Visually, the coaching model illustrated in Figure 1 represents a five-pointed star. Each point of the star is a context that the coach brings to the coaching. Each is a point of contact with the client. The coach consistently draws from these contexts in the practice of coaching. In time, and through training, the coach develops these the way a musician develops musical technique. The five contexts are always in play. We present them in one order here in the book, but they are a constellation, not a sequence—essential elements of a complete coaching approach—like a spotlight that is always shining, illuminating the client's life.

Listening

Of course, the coach listens to the words that come from the client, tracking the content of the coaching conversation. But the most important listening of coaching takes place on a deeper level. It is the listening for the meaning behind the story, for the underlying process, for the theme that will deepen the learning. The coach is listening for the appearance of the client's vision, values, purpose. The coach is also listening for resistance, fear, backtracking, and the voice of the Saboteur, who is there to object to change, point out the client's shortcomings, and bring up all the reasons why this idea, whatever it is, won't work.

The coach listens at many levels simultaneously to hear where clients are in their process, to hear where they are out of balance, to hear their progress on the journey of fulfillment. The coach is listening for the nuance of hesitation, too, for the sour ring of something not quite true. (In Chapter 3, we look in depth at the three levels of listening.)

Intuition

By listening below the surface, the coach finds the place where the hard data and soft data merge. Intuition is a kind of knowing that resides in the background and is often unspoken. It remains in the background because, for many people, it's not easy to trust. Our culture doesn't validate intuition as a reliable means of drawing conclusions or making decisions, so we hesitate to say what our intuition tells us. We hold back because we don't want to appear foolish. And yet it is one of the most powerful gifts a coach brings to coaching.

As coaches, we receive a great deal of information from the client and then, in the moment of coaching, combine it with previous information as well as experience, not only of coaching, but of operating in the world. Add to this one more factor: information that comes from our intuition. We may not call it "intuition." We may consider it a thought, or a hunch, or a gut feeling. Regardless of how we define it, the impulse emerges from our intuition. For most coaches, intuition is a skill that needs practice and development. It is enormously valuable because, time and again, it synthesizes more impressions and information than we could ever analyze consciously.

Curiosity

One of the fundamental tenets of co-active coaching is that clients are capable and resourceful and have the answers. The coach's job is to ask the questions, to lead the discovery process. The context of curiosity gives a certain frame to the process of uncovering answers and drawing out insight. Curiosity is open, inviting, spacious, almost playful. And yet it is also enormously powerful. Like scientific curiosity, which explores the deepest questions of matter, life, and the universe, curiosity in coaching allows coach and client to enter the deepest areas of the client's life, side by side, simply looking, curious about what they will find.

Because the coach is not an inquisitor but is really on the client's side in this exploration, the coach can ask powerful questions that break through old defenses. When clients learn to be curious about their lives, it reduces some of the pressure and lowers the risk. They become more willing to look in the dark places and try the hard things because they are curious, too.

Forward and Deepen

The products of the work the client and coach do together are action and learning. These two forces, action and learning, combine to create change. Because the notion of action that moves the client forward is so central to the purpose of coaching, we often make "forward" a verb and say that one of the purposes of coaching is to "forward the action" of the client.

The other force at work in the human change process is learning. Learning is not simply a by-product of action; it is an equal and complementary force. Learning generates new resourcefulness, expanded possibilities, and stronger muscles for change.

One of the common misunderstandings about coaching is that it is simply about getting things done—performing at a higher level. Because of this misunderstanding, coaching has been compared to hiring a nagging parent who will make sure your bed is made and your homework is done. In some organizations, it's the image of a schoolteacher with a ruler, poised to measure your failure and provide the punishment. But coaching is not just about getting things done; it is just as importantly about continuing to learn, especially to learn how the action is or is not contributing to the core principles. This connection between action and learning and the core principles is key. Gandhi is quoted as saying, "There is more to life than increasing its speed." In the same way, there is more to life, at least in the co-active model, than increasing action.

Self-Management

In order to truly hold the client's agenda, the coach must get out of the way—not always an easy thing to do. Self-management is the coach's ability to set aside personal opinions, preferences, pride, defensiveness, ego. The coach needs to be "over there" with the client, immersed in the client's situation and struggle, not "over here," dealing with his or her judgments and thoughts. Self-management means giving up on the need to look good and be right. In this way, the coach also models an ability to manage the judgment and opinions of self and others.

THE COACH'S ROLE IN THE MODEL

The coach is a kind of change agent, entering the equation for change without knowing what the outcome will be. Goals and plans, new practices, new benchmarks, achievements of every kind are all part of the client's ongoing work, facilitated by the coaching interaction. The coach is a catalyst, an important element in the process of accelerating change.

But this is more than a passive role. We see coaching, especially the form presented here, as a role of service that requires commitment and presence on the part of the coach. Whether the coach is working with individual private clients or has been hired to work with clients inside an organization, a sense of purpose, even a higher purpose, is definitely an underlying element. In the world of co-active coaching, we would say that coaching exists to serve the client's higher purpose. When we aim for this higher purpose, we create the means for transformative change in clients and, by extension, in families and organizations. The ripples of change in a client's higher purpose move out into the world.

2

The Co-Active Coaching Relationship

Coaching is not so much a methodology as it is a relationship, a particular kind of relationship. Yes, there are skills to learn and a wide variety of tools available, but the real art of effective coaching comes from the coach's ability to work within the context of relationship. Every client is unique, with a unique set of circumstances, unique goals and desire for change, unique abilities, interests, even habits of self-sabotage. We can talk in very general terms about focus areas that clients often pursue—career change, life transition, performance improvement, health and wellness issues—but only in the broadest terms. Add to this picture the fact that goals change over time as clients clarify what is important, as they dig deeper into what motivates them, and as they produce results (action and learning). There is no authorized universal reference manual with standardized diagnoses and coaching solutions neatly defined. Coaching is inherently dynamic; that is one of the fundamental qualities of coaching and a reason for its power as a medium for change. Coaching is personal; coaching creates a unique, empowered relationship for change.

In co-active coaching, we also emphasize the peer relationship—that coach and client have equal, though different, roles. They are co-active in the relationship, so they are co-creators, collaborators, in a way. This makes sense when we look once more at the cornerstones of co-active coaching:

- Clients are naturally creative, resourceful, and whole. So of course clients have full responsibility, make contributions, and exercise authority.

- The agenda comes from the client; clients know what they want to work on.

- Coaches are adept at dancing in the moment—an especially important ability, given the understanding, even expectation, that clients will take charge of the agenda and direct the coaching where it needs to go to support them.

- Coaching can address any area of the client's life; clients are empowered to choose.

We can picture this relationship as a triangle (see Figure 2). The coach grants power to the coaching relationship. The client also grants power to the relationship, not to the coach. Clients are in turn empowered by the relationship—empowered to take charge of their lives and the choices they make. In this figure, all the power of the relationship exists to serve the client.

In fact, the co-active coach must make the shift from "I am powerful" to "the coaching relationship is powerful." Powerful coaching is not about being a powerful coach; it is about the power the client experiences. Imagine that the coaching relationship is a recharging place where clients tap into the source of energy they need to get over the hurdles in their lives. They can't get the work done if the energy level is low. The power comes not directly from the coach, however, but from the relationship—the synergy of energy clients bring in the form of desire and motivation and the energy coaches bring in the form of their commitment, skills, and understanding of human change.

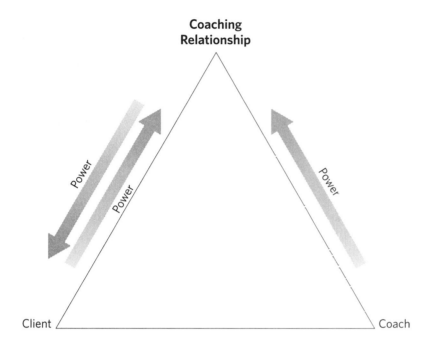

FIGURE 2 **The Coaching Power Triangle**

THE COACHING ENVIRONMENT

At its most fundamental, a coaching session is a conversation between a coach and another person or—in team, partnership, and systems coaching—a coach and two or more people. But this is no ordinary, everyday conversation. An effective coaching conversation gets to the heart of what matters. It is a focused, concentrated conversation designed to support the client in clarifying choices and making changes. The environment in which the conversation takes place is crucial.

By "environment," we mean both a physical environment and a relationship environment made up of ground rules, expectations, and agreements. In co-active coaching, we talk about two core characteristics of an effective coaching environment: one, it is safe enough for clients to take the risks they need to take, and two, it is a courageous place where clients are able to approach their lives and the choices they make with motivation, curiosity, and creativity. By the way, "safe" does not necessarily mean "comfortable." Significant change may be highly uncomfortable, and yet there are ways to ensure that the experience is safe. Like the rock climber ascending the cliff face, striving for the summit, clients may find the process exhilarating, exhausting, and scary. But knowing that there is the equivalent of a belay team literally holding their rope, ensuring their safety, gives them the confidence to keep climbing.

Certain qualities characterize an environment that is safe and courageous for clients. These qualities give shape to what might be called the "container" for the coaching relationship.

Confidentiality

Making change means disturbing the familiar and well-established order of things. It may be deeply satisfying, maybe exciting, to embark on that change and yet still feel risky. Even if the client and the client's world are completely committed to and supportive of the change, change by its nature is an unknown. If clients are going to risk making significant change, they must be able to risk talking freely with their coach. Disclosure is crucial because it leads to the discovery that is necessary for action. Without the safety and reassurance that confidentiality provides, the coaching will be tentative, and there will always be an undercurrent of wondering about what is being withheld.

Coaches who work with clients inside organizations have to deal with a more complex environment. Confidentiality between coach and client is still a key condition for safe and courageous conversation, but because the organization has a vested interest in the result, it usually requires some form of reporting on the coaching. Often clients are the ones who take responsibility for reporting the nature of the coaching work, which allows them to disclose what is most relevant to the organization while preserving confidentiality between themselves and their coach.

Trust

An agreement to hold the coaching conversation confidential is one key component in building trust. Trust is also built over time as both client and coach learn they can be counted on and the client learns that the relationship delivers results. Trust is built from small things like being punctual for coaching sessions and from a pattern of reliability. Because trust works both ways, it is as important for the coach as it is for the client. The coach must be trustworthy in his or her action.

Relationship is also built and trust expanded by coaches simply believing in their clients. We live in a culture that, for the most part, demands that people prove themselves, demonstrate their worthiness by performing to some standard, before they are accepted into the circle. The culture creates relationships in which the emphasis is on proving, explaining, justifying. A coaching relationship built on the premise that clients are naturally creative, resourceful, and whole and are capable of making the best choices is a relationship founded on basic trust in the client's capacity and integrity. Clients see that they have a person in their lives who believes they can do what they say they can do, who believes they can be the people they say they want to be.

It is a paradox that coaches believe completely in their clients and, at the same time, hold them accountable. But by "accountable" we do not mean a context of judgment, as in "prove it to me," but simply accounting for their promise of action and the insight of learning. Clients see that the coach is really on their side, respecting their vision and their action plans but also willing to be honest and direct for their sake.

Speaking the Truth

We could also call this attribute of a coaching environment "getting real." A safe and courageous space for change must be, by definition, a place where the truth can be told. It is a place where clients can tell the whole truth about what they have done, and not done, without worrying about what the coach will say. This is an environment without judgment, and it is a place where the coach expects the truth from the client because truth carries no consequence other than learning, discovery, and new insight. Clients expect the truth from the coach because that is precisely the perspective for which the coach has been hired. Clients are often so close to their own situations, so wrapped up in their own histories and habitual patterns, that they are sometimes unable to see the truth accurately. This may be one of their reasons to seek out coaching. They rely on the coach for the acuity that sees through the chaos and fog. This should be one relationship in which clients can count on straightforward and honest interactions.

Truth telling doesn't have to be confrontational, although it may confront. It can be handled with sharpness or softness, but it confronts the usual tacit acceptance of the client's explanations. Truth telling refuses to sidestep or overlook: it boldly points out when the emperor is not wearing clothes. There is no inherent judgment in telling the truth. The coach is merely stating what he or she sees. Withholding the truth serves neither the client nor the coaching relationship. A real relationship is not built on being nice; it's built on being real. When the coach has the courage to tell the truth, the client gets a model of the art of being straight. And in the process, more trust is built between coach and client.

Openness and Spaciousness

One of the qualities that makes the coaching relationship work is spaciousness. This is a place where clients can breathe, experiment, fantasize, and strategize without limitation. It is another world, a place of wide-eyed dreams. It is a space in which they can vent their anger, troubles, spite, perceptions of injustice. It is a place where failure is acknowledged as a means for learning, where there are no absolutes and few rules.

For the coach, spaciousness also means complete detachment from any particular course of action or any results clients achieve. The coach continues to care about his or her clients, their agendas, their health and growth, but not the road they take to get there, the speed of travel, or the detours they might make along the way—as long as they continue to move toward the results they want. Ultimately, coaching is not about what the coach delivers but about what clients create. A coach may propose a course of action to get the results a client desires. That is fine. Brainstorming is part of coaching and can make a valuable contribution to the client's process. But in order to preserve openness in the relationship, the coach must not be attached to whether clients take his or her suggestions. The spaciousness of the relationship requires that clients have many channels open to creative inspiration and not be restricted to the coach's good ideas, no matter how sound or grounded in experience. In this way, clients are able to explore the widest range of possibilities.

THE DESIGNED ALLIANCE

So far we've been talking about this relationship between client and coach as if it were conceptual. Actually, we believe it is important for client and coach to consciously and deliberately design their working relationship and continue to redesign it as necessary up through and including its completion. The designed alliance surrounds the coach and client in the co-active coaching model (see Figure 1, p. 7) and represents the container within which coach and client do their work.

The form of the design will be different for different coaches and unique to each coach-client relationship. The conversation that creates the design focuses on the assumptions and expectations of coach and client. The purpose of this intentional conversation is to clarify the process and expected outcomes and provide a forum for negotiating the design of a relationship that is as powerful as possible for both client and coach.

In simplest terms, the design of the alliance looks at questions such as *What are the conditions that need to be in place for the two of us to work together effectively? What are the obstacles or potential obstacles? What fundamental questions need to be answered in order to get the most out of this process?* And as the coaching continues, there will be ongoing questions: *What is working and what is not? What do we need to change in order to make the coaching relationship more effective or have more impact?*

In one way, the strength of a client's ability to make changes in his or her work and life is a measure of the strength in the coach-client relationship. And the strength of that relationship is measured by the commitment and open, fearless design of their alliance.

COACHING FORMAT

Over the past decade, coaching as a practice and as a profession has taken root in a myriad of forms, and the variety of environments in which we find coaching and coaching skills being used continues to expand. Today you will find coaches working from home offices and inside institutions and organizations, from prison cells to corporate cubicles. Some coaches work as employees within organizations, often with other job duties in addition to coaching. Others combine coaching with consulting work in order to provide ongoing implementation support and follow-up. Many coaches work with private, individual clients. Some specialize in working with teams, people in relationship, or organization systems. Coaching today is global and cross-cultural. Coaches and clients cover dozens of demographic categories: age, income, education, ethnic background, job position. Many coaches specialize in a select interest or career area and focus on working with CEOs, immigrants or expatriates, artists and musicians, parents and their teenagers.

The environment within which coaching takes places is equally varied. Many coaches work with clients by telephone, with regularly scheduled, often weekly, appointments, although there are many variations. Some coaches and clients prefer in-person coaching, whether at the client's site, at the coach's office, or off-site. Coaches may contract with clients for a fixed period of time, such as three months, six months, or a year. Other coaches establish ongoing, open-ended relationships with clients. Coaching takes place in paneled board rooms, inner-city homes, and mountain retreats.

Within that framework, coaches bring their coaching training and experience and a wide variety of tools and assessment instruments (see the Coach's Toolkit for examples). The permutations of forms and environments continue, inspired by the imagination of coaches and the interests of clients. And yet, no matter what form the coaching takes, we believe that it will be most effective when coach and client create a safe and courageous space for the work and when both parties consciously design their working alliance.

GETTING STARTED

Coaches typically begin a working relationship with an initial process that is part client orientation and part self-discovery work for clients. This foundation-setting process familiarizes clients with the coaching process, provides an opportunity to design the alliance, and begins the work of clarifying client issues and goals. There is no standardized form for this. With some coaches, it is a brief interview or a page or two of basic questions, all handled in the initial coaching session. Other coaches might use several sessions, assessments of various kinds, and interviews with the client's co-workers, direct reports, or family members. Or this discovery process might be done as visioning work at a retreat center. (Chapter 11 contains further discussion of formats for this discovery work, with variations for private clients and clients in organizations. Appendix A discusses coaching within organizations.)

In this initial work, clients learn what to expect from coaching. It is also a time for them to clarify where they are, where they're headed, the strengths they will use to get there, and the obstacles that often interfere.

The coach typically covers these four areas:

- Logistics
- You are here. Where is here?
- Designing the future
- Orientation to coaching

Logistics

One of the first, obvious elements in getting started is communication and agreement on fundamental ground rules and administrative procedures. Settling such details as appointment schedules, cancellation policy, and payment arrangements is part of getting under way, but it is also key in creating relationship. Clients will begin to set expectations of their coach and the coaching based on the coach's handling of these administrative procedures. How coaches "handle the details," especially in the area of getting agreement, sets a tone and creates a particular environment.

You Are Here. Where Is Here?

This discovery phase focuses on where clients are today and how they got there. It's a conversation about where they are and the issues at hand, what is at stake, what moves them, what blocks them. The conversation might address such issues as life purpose or mission, values, principles, or personal beliefs. Often, the coach will make an overall assessment of satisfaction in the significant areas of the client's life using a tool like the Wheel of Life (see Figure 3) or a version of the wheel created specifically for a client's situation. (See the Coach's Toolkit for more information on using this and other tools for discovery.)

Clients and coach might talk about previous disappointments and successes in order to get an idea of what does and doesn't work, where clients are fulfilled, and the strategies they use to handle obstacles and derailment. In this phase, client and coach are beginning the process of really getting to know this person, the client, from the inside out: the bright places, the dark places, the effective places, and the not-so-effective places.

The coach may use assessment tools or exercises, but at the heart of the discovery process are answers to simple, powerful questions: *Where do you want to make a difference in your life? What do you value most in your relationship with others? What works for you when you are successful at making changes? Where do you usually get stuck? What moti-*

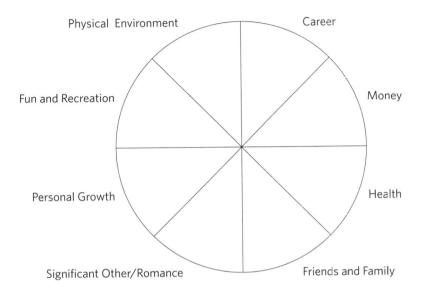

FIGURE 3 **Wheel of Life**

vates you? How do you deal with disappointment or failure? How are you about doing what you say you'll do?

The answers also point very clearly to the design of the most effective coaching relationship. For example, the question *Where do you usually get stuck?* leads to a logical next question, *How would you like me to respond as your coach when you're stuck?* In that exchange, clients experience and contribute to the design of the alliance.

Designing the Future

A third area of this initial work involves the outcomes and desires clients bring to coaching. Here the focus is on having clients describe what they want to change or what they want to achieve. Most clients have one or two primary areas of focus. Chances of success are better when clients concentrate on one or two key points of change, so part of the foundation-setting conversation is designed to clarify those key areas. These future outcomes will be the result of achieving goals, ful-filling commitments, changing habits, and bringing a compelling vision to life. The initial conversation also explores who the client will be in order to create that new future.

Desired Outcome and Goals. Clients bring a desire for change to coaching. The results they have in mind may be vaguely defined or crystal clear, but in either case, clients have not yet been able to achieve the results they want. Desired outcomes may be as specific as a partic-ular goal, or clients may want to move toward a certain state of being, such as "balanced," "living well with a life-threatening illness," or "more fulfilled with my work." Part of the initial process will be devoted to clarifying outcomes and, in many cases, refining broadly stated desires into specific goals: What will happen? By when? And how will clients know they have achieved the results they want? Coach and client work together to clarify the goals as well as develop strategies for achieving them. Just as important to achieving results is putting new practices in place. Eliminating life-draining habits while implementing sustaining, life-giving practices is another important focus of the coaching process.

Compelling Vision. We can be pushed down the road by deadlines and expectations and to-do lists. We can be driven by the desire for money or accomplishment or by the promises we make. Or we can be pulled down the road by the gravitational force of a compelling vision, like water running downhill. You can feel the difference between these two forces: pushed or driven on one hand, or pulled irresistibly on the other. Discovering what draws us has the power to overcome the bonds of lethargy and fear. Finding the compelling vision can take any goal, action, or outcome and invest it with new power. An important ele-ment in the initial discovery work with clients is uncovering or ignit-ing this vision.

Who You Need to Be. The classic definition of "crazy" is to continue to do things the same way and expect different results. The truth is, if nothing changes, nothing changes. Very often, something new on the outside, like a new outcome, includes the creation of something new on the inside. In order to achieve the results they want, clients very likely will need to change attitudes, paradigms, or underlying beliefs. The beginning of a new coaching relationship is an ideal time to peel back the accumulated layers of identity and old roles to uncover the authentic person within.

Orientation to Coaching

Another outcome for the foundation-setting process is to orient the client to coaching. Even clients who have worked with a coach before could use the opportunity to talk through assumptions and expectations. A clear, forthright conversation helps reinforce frank, unrestrained, and hence co-active, groundwork.

HOMEOSTASIS

Part of the orientation to coaching ought to include a few words about homeostasis, a natural, often subconscious resistance to change. "Old habits die hard," as the saying goes. So do old beliefs and old ways of relating to others. Particularly in the middle of change, when the old way is undone and the new way not yet embedded, there is a strong pull back to the familiar, the known, even if it didn't get clients the results they wanted. Change requires the expenditure of energy, and continuing the process of change requires sustaining energy. Some change will be easy; other change will not be so easy. There will often be a tendency, or a temptation at least, to backslide. It's better for clients to be aware and prepared, so that if the temptation appears, it does not feel like they are failing. Homeostasis, the natural tendency to keep things just as they are, is also inherent in the system. Every individual, private client or organizational client, lives within a system, and the system itself often contributes to the resistance to change. Again, an awareness of the system's power can help clients as they move through changes.

And finally, there is a specific counterreaction to change that appears fairly consistently with clients, which might be called "the dip."

For coaches who work with clients on a weekly basis, it often shows up between weeks three and eight, either because change is not happening fast enough or because the initial euphoria of commitment has worn off. Clients realize that talking about action is one thing and actually taking action is quite another. Many coaches start clients with a three-month commitment to help them get past the dip.

THE BIGGER PICTURE

In order for coaching to work, there must be commitment: commitment on the part of the client to exploring, changing, learning, taking risks; commitment to persevering even when it is difficult; commitment to investing the time and energy. Clients must be willing to go beyond their comfort zones and step into the unknown for the sake of change. Without this commitment, coaching drifts and devolves into chitchat or to-do lists that often don't get done. Fortunately, most clients are energized and willing when they start. This is the perfect time for clients to clarify and declare their commitment.

Coaches, in turn, need to be clear about their commitment to their clients. It is a commitment to dig deeply and courageously, to listen intently to the words spoken and those unspoken. Coaching with this level of commitment can be exciting and inspiring. It will not be trivial. The coach who is committed to clients and their ultimate goals is willing to challenge, incite, motivate, encourage, and sometimes insist that clients take charge. When coaches bring 100 percent of their effort and expertise and match the client's commitment with their own, that makes theirs a truly co-active relationship. And it is this mutual commitment and the designed alliance between client and coach that create the safe and courageous space in which clients can do the important work of their lives.

Co-Active Coaching Contexts

One of the easiest ways to see and understand the application of coaching skills is to view them within the five contexts of coaching:

- Listening
- Intuition
- Curiosity
- Forward and deepen
- Self-management

The following five chapters present detailed explanations of the contexts as well as the definitions of specific coaching skills. Each chapter also contains coaching conversations that illustrate the skills in action and a number of exercises you can use to develop the skills.

3

Listening

To be listened to is a striking experience, partly because it is so rare. When another person is totally with you—leaning in, interested in every word, eager to empathize—you feel known and understood. People open up when they know they're really being listened to; they expand; they have more presence. They feel safer and more secure as well, and trust grows. This is why listening is so important to coaching and why it is the first of the five contexts we discuss.

Listening is a talent each of us is given in some measure. People who become coaches tend to be gifted listeners to begin with. But listening is also a skill that people can learn and develop through training. Masterful coaches have taken their abundant gift and brought it to a high level of proficiency. Indeed, they use it with the same unconscious grace an athlete uses in a sport or a musician in a performance.

Most people do not listen at a very deep level. Their day-to-day occupations and preoccupations don't require more than a minimum level of listening—just as most of us never acquire more than an average level of physical fitness. We don't need the muscles because we are not world-class athletes. In everyday listening, we listen mostly to the words. The focus is on what you said and what I said. Think of all the arguments in which the crux of the fight was the precise words that were used: "That's not what you said." "It's what I meant." "But it's not what you said." Or we hear the words and then disconnect from the conversation while we process the words internally. We start thinking about what we'll say next. We look for a comparable story—or one that's just a little more dramatic: "You think that was scary, let me tell you about the time I . . ." We get caught up in our own feelings; we take things personally; we listen at a superficial level as we evaluate and judge what the other person is saying.

Most of us would say that our friends are generally good listeners because they are willing to suspend their judgment of us and sometimes will even be quiet and hear our stories. And yet, too often, when we really want just to be listened to, our families, friends, and co-workers, with the best intentions in the world, want to solve the problem or take care of the feelings. Masterful coaching requires masterful listening, attuned and adept, and the ability to maximize the listening interaction. "Interaction" is the right word, too, because listening is not simply passively hearing. There is action in listening.

AWARENESS AND IMPACT

There are two aspects of listening in coaching. One is awareness. We receive information in what we hear with our ears, of course, but we also listen with all the senses and with our intuition. We hear, see, and experience sounds, words, images, feelings, energy. We are attentive to all the information we draw in from our senses. We are multifaceted receivers with many receptors of various kinds, all of which are taking in information: we notice the breathing on the other end of the phone, the pace of the delivery, the modulation of the voice. We sense the pressure behind the words—the voice might be soft or hard edged, tentative or enraged. We listen not only to the person but, simultaneously, to everything else that is happening in the environment. In person, we see body language. Over the phone, we sense emotion and imagine the clenched jaw or the head bowed in sorrow. It's all information. We are aware.

The second aspect is what we do with our listening. This is the impact of our listening on others—specifically, the impact of the coach's listening on the client. As an experienced coach, you need to be conscious not only of what you are listening to but of the impact you have when you act on your awareness. Most of the time, this consciousness occurs just below the surface while your attention is still on the other person.

Think of it this way: Imagine you're in a fencing match. All of your attention is focused on the opponent as you instantaneously make choices and respond, parry, thrust. Your attention is not on the choices you are making—that would break your concentration, with disastrous results. Once the match is over, you can recap the action and review the choices you made. When you listen like this, you are not thinking about what you take in or what you're going to do with your awareness. Your listening is hyperconscious and unconscious at the same time.

What you do with your awareness, the choices you make, will have an impact. For example, imagine you're in a crowded room and you smell smoke. There might be a fire. Your attention is drawn to the smoke. You notice it. That's the first aspect of the awareness. Then you decide what to do with this information. You might yell "Fire!" or you might mention it casually to the host. You could grab a fire extinguisher and shoulder your way through the crowd to heroically fight the blaze, or you could slip quietly out the side door. Each of these choices will have a different impact. There will be different consequences depending on what you did with your awareness.

Clearly, listening is not passive, especially in the coaching relationship. In our listening model, we describe three levels of listening. These three levels give the coach an enormous range and, ultimately, the ability to listen at a very deep level.

Level I—Internal Listening

At Level I, our awareness is on ourselves. We listen to the words of the other person, but our attention is on what it means to us personally. At Level I, the spotlight is on "me": my thoughts, my judgments, my feelings, my conclusions about myself and others. Whatever is happening with the other person is coming back to us through a diode: a one-way energy trap that lets information in but not out. We're absorbing information by listening but holding it in a trap that recycles it. At Level I, there is only one question: *What does this mean to me?*

Many times this may be entirely appropriate. When traveling alone to a different city, you are likely to be operating at Level I most of the time. As you arrive at the airport, you're thinking about where to check in, whether you remembered your ticket, how much time before the flight, the fact that you hate flying, your opinion of airline food, your awareness that the person in the seat behind you keeps kicking you. All of your attention is on yourself, as it should be. Another indication that you are operating at Level I is a strong desire for more information. You want answers, explanations, details, data. The internal conversation might sound like this: *The flight is delayed? But I'll be late. When will we leave? When will I eat? How can I let people know I might be delayed? Is there another flight? Did I bring enough to read?* The purpose of information gathering at Level I is to meet your own needs.

Another typical setting for Level I is a restaurant. Your awareness is self-directed, and the impact of Level I listening is all about you. The consequences affect your pleasure, your health, your satisfaction, and your wallet: *Do I want a beverage before ordering? What are the specials today? Is the chair comfortable? Is there a draft? Am I too close to the kitchen? How are the prices? Can I afford it?* You are conscious of your thoughts and feelings. The decisions, choices, and judgments you make are all about you. You love certain kinds of fish—but not if they serve the whole fish with those dead blank eyes staring up from the plate. You think about the weight you want to lose, so you decide to order the low-fat dressing on the side. Your internal mind chatter is at maximum here. Even though you are sitting in the restaurant across the table from someone you are madly in love with, your awareness is entirely at Level I until you have ordered.

Level I informs us about ourselves and what's going on around us. It's where we figure things out and understand. It's very important. Clients need to be at Level I. That's their job: to look at themselves and their lives—to process, think about, feel, understand. But it is definitely not appropriate for the coach to be operating at this self-absorbed level for any length of time. Coaches, being human, will naturally have moments of losing focus on the client and being at Level I. The practice for coaches is to return to connection with clients at Levels II and III as quickly as possible.

Level I Dialogue

Client: *The new house is a mess. I've got boxes everywhere. I can hardly get from the front door to the bathroom—and I've got the biggest proposal of my career to finish by Friday.*

COACH: *I went through the same thing last year. The key is to make sure you've got your long-term vision in sight.*

Client: *That's sort of the dilemma, though. Because I traveled so much last month, my wife's past the point of patience. I'm really not pulling my weight at home.*

COACH: *That'll work out. The mess is temporary. Don't let it distract you from the real issue—maintaining momentum.*

Client: *This feels like more than a little distraction.*

COACH: *I'm sure you can explain why this is so important. In the meantime, let's get back to your proposal.*

Client: *Okay. If you're sure . . .*

Clearly, the coach is listening at Level I—paying more attention to his own judgments and opinions and driving his own agenda. The point of this example is not which course of action is correct for this client but where the coach is focusing his attention. In this case, the coach's attention is on a problem and his preferred solution rather than on a client with a dilemma.

Level II—Focused Listening

At Level II, there is a sharp focus on the other person. Sometimes you can see it in each person's posture: both leaning forward, looking intently at each other. There is a great deal of attention on the other person and not much awareness of the outside world.

Let's go back to the restaurant scene and our two lovers. Dinner has been ordered, the menus taken away. Now their eyes are focused on each other and nothing else. Their desire is to be so close that they become one. They are so oblivious to the outside world that this scene of complete romantic isolation has become a caricature used in commercials. It's as if they're living in their own bubble.

When you, as a coach, are listening at Level II, your awareness is totally on your clients. You listen for their words, their expressions, their emotions, everything they bring. You notice what they say, how they say it. You notice what they don't say. You see their smiles or hear the tears in their voices. You listen for what they value. You listen for their vision, for the unique way they look at the world. You listen for what makes them come alive in the coaching session and what makes them go dead or withdraw.

Energy and information come from the client. These are processed by the coach and reflected back. At Level II, the impact of awareness is on the client. The coach is like a perfect mirror that absorbs none of the light; what comes from the client is returned. At Level II, coaches are constantly aware of the impact their listening is having on their clients—not constantly monitoring the impact, but aware.

Level II listening is the level of empathy, clarification, collaboration. It is as if there is a wired connection between coach and client. At this level, coaches are unattached to self, their agenda, their thoughts, or their opinions. At Level II, coaches are so focused on the client that the mind chatter virtually disappears and coaching becomes almost spontaneous. As a coach, you are no longer trying to figure out the next move. In fact, if your attention is on trying to come up with what to say next—what brilliant question to pose to the client—that should be a clue that you are listening at Level l, inside your own experience.

As a coach listening at Level II, you not only hear the client speak but notice all that is coming to you in the form of information—the tone, the pace, the feelings expressed. You choose what to respond to and how you will respond. Then you notice the impact of your response on the client and receive that information as well. It's as though you listen twice before the client responds again. You listen for the client's initial conversation, and you listen for the client's reaction to your response. You receive information both times. This is listening at Level II.

In describing Level II listening, we tend to use illustrations of one coach and one client, but Level II listening is about the focus of the awareness. For coaches who work with partners, couples, or even teams, it is entirely possible to listen at Level II to more than one individual.

Level II Dialogue

Client: *The new house is a mess. I've got boxes everywhere. I can hardly get from the front door to the bathroom—and I've got the biggest proposal of my career to finish by Friday.*

COACH: *How important is it to get settled at home? This is the most productive time you've had in your business since you started.*

Client: *I know, but if I don't help out with moving in, I could be living solo soon, if you know what I mean. My wife did nearly all the packing last month while I was traveling.*

COACH: *How can you deal with the situation at home—and still maintain your momentum with the new business?*

Client: *I could clone myself.*

COACH: *I can see this is a real dilemma. You've got values to honor in more than one important area of your life. Let's look at some options. Would that be useful?*

Client: *Yeah. Good. Frankly, I was starting to feel trapped—like there was no way out.*

Here the coach is listening at Level II—following the client's lead, actively listening and checking.

Level III—Global Listening

When you listen at Level III, you listen as though you and the client were at the center of the universe, receiving information from everywhere at once. It's as though you were surrounded by a force field that contains you, the client, and an environment of information. Level III includes everything you can observe with your senses: what you see, hear, smell, and feel—the tactile as well as the emotional sensations. Level III includes the action, the inaction, and the interaction.

If Level II is hardwired, then Level III is like a radio field. The radio waves are entirely invisible, yet we trust they exist because we hear music coming from the radio. In Level III listening, we are hearing the radio waves. They cross our antennae and become information we can use. But it takes a special receiver to pick up Level III, and most people need practice because they don't often make use of Level III awareness the way a coach does. For many people, this is a new realm of listening.

One of the benefits of learning to listen at Level III is greater access to your intuition. Through your intuition, you receive information that is not directly observable, and you use that information just as you'd use words coming from the client's mouth. At Level III, intuition is simply more information. As a coach, you take in the information and respond. Then you notice the impact. How did your response land? What did you notice about that?

Level III awareness is sometimes described as environmental listening. You notice the temperature, the energy level, the lightness or darkness, both literally and figuratively. Is the client's energy sparking or flat? Is she cool, lightly present, or tightly controlled? You will know by listening at Level III. You'll learn to trust your senses about that, and you can always just ask: "I get the sense that you're in an awkward place. Are you? What's that about?" Performers develop a strong sense of Level III listening. Stand-up comedians, musicians, actors, training presenters—all have the ability to instantly read a room and monitor how it changes in response to what they do. This is a great example of noticing one's impact. Anyone who is successful at influencing people is skilled at listening at Level III. These people have the ability to read their impact and adjust their behavior accordingly.

To listen at Level III, you must be very open and softly focused, sensitive to subtle stimuli, ready to receive information from all the senses—in your own sphere, in the world around you, in the world around your client. The environment itself is giving you information you can use in your coaching even when you can't instantly articulate what it is you are sensing. Sometimes this environment is shouting; sometimes it is whispering.

Level III Dialogue

Client: *The new house is a mess. I've got boxes everywhere. I can hardly get from the front door to the bathroom—and I've got the biggest proposal of my career to finish by Friday.*

COACH: *How important is it to get settled at home? This is the most productive time you've had in your business since you started.*

Client: *I know, but if I don't help out with moving in I could be living solo soon, if you know what I mean. My wife did nearly all the packing last month while I was traveling.*

COACH: *It sounds like this is a more important issue than just some boxes to unpack. I get the sense that you're packed as tight as some of those boxes.*

Client: *Is it that obvious?*

COACH: *You just don't sound like the Steve I'm used to talking to. You sound trapped.*

Client: *That's what it feels like—and with no way out. Cornered. In my relationship and in my work.*

COACH: *What do you want to do about that?*

Client: *What I've been trying to do is step around it, or over it, and that doesn't seem to be working. I guess it's time to sit down and work it out—unpack it all, so to speak.*

In this case, the coach is tuned in at Level III: the nuances of the space between coach and client, beyond the words, including all the energy and emotion that were spoken and unspoken. Note that in the dialogue samples, we crafted the conversation to illustrate the distinctions between the three levels. In real coaching conversations, of course, coaches switch constantly between Levels II and III—and when they slip into that Level I place, they recover as quickly as possible.

The Coach Is Listening

Everything in coaching hinges on listening—especially listening with the client's agenda in mind: Is the client on track with his vision? Is she living her values? Where is he today? The coach is listening for signs of life, the choices clients are making, and how those choices move them toward balance or away from it. The coach is listening, too, for resistance and turbulence in the process. Listening is the entry point for all of the coaching. In one sense, all the other contexts depend on listening at Levels II and III. Listening, then, is the gateway through which all the coaching passes.

As coaches listen, they make choices that change the direction and focus of coaching. That's what we mean by the "impact" of listening. One of the ways this impact shows up is in the spontaneous choice of which coaching skill to use next.

COACHING SKILLS

The following coaching skills are generally associated with the context of listening. Of course, effective listening is a prerequisite for the use of all the coaching skills. For this section, we selected the skills that seem particularly appropriate responses to a listening situation. These skills are also highlighted in the coaching samples on the CD. You can hear them being applied in an actual coaching conversation.

Articulating

This skill is also known by a longer name: "Articulating what's going on." With your listening skills at Level II and Level III fully engaged, you have a heightened sense of awareness. You have a picture of what is going on with the client at this moment. When you combine that sense of what is happening right now with what you know about this client, you have a tremendous amount of information. Articulation is the ability to succinctly describe what is going on. Clients often can't see for themselves what they are doing or saying. Or perhaps they can see the details but not the bigger picture. With this skill, you share your observations as clearly as possible, but without judgment. You tell clients what you see them doing. Sometimes, articulation takes the form of the hard truth, and it can confront: "I see you're continuing to schedule evening and weekend time away from your family. You've said in the past that your family is a high priority, and this overtime work seems inconsistent with that commitment. What's up?" Not sidestepping the mess in the road is part of the coaching alliance. And articulating—as in pointing out the mess—is part of the coach's job. Cleaning up the mess is the client's job.

Articulating is a skill that helps clients connect the dots so they can see the picture they are creating by their action or, sometimes, lack of action. As the coach, you have a responsibility to articulate what you see but at the same time, as with all of the coaching skills, not feel attached to being right about it. This ability to boldly say what you see without needing to be right, allowing plenty of room for counteroffers and different interpretations, is key to the co-active nature of the skill. As long as coaches can let go of the pressure or the need to be right, there is tremendous freedom to speak what appears to be true—and it is a great gift to clients to hear this expressed.

Sample Dialogue

Client: *. . . so that's why I came up with this alternative plan. I think it's a reasonable alternative. I think I can make the deadlines they've set.*

COACH: *Can I tell you what it sounds like over on this side of the line?*

Client: *Sure. You see a hole in there somewhere?*

COACH: *Actually, no. I'm sure the plan is sound. What I see, though, is an old pattern of accommodating other people's demands, almost no matter how unreasonable, at personal cost to you. It's one of the things you said you wanted to change. This looks like backpedaling.*

Clarifying

Many of us have a tendency to operate from vague or incomplete thoughts and unresolved feelings. We may leap to conclusions or draw conclusions based on sketchy information. Clients may ramble or get caught up in their own stories. They may be drifting in a fog, trying to paddle their way out. They get stuck in fuzzy thinking and outdated ways of looking at their world. They may be reading old maps. Coaches serve as a resource to help clients create greater clarity.

The skill of clarifying is a combination of listening, asking, and reframing. Sometimes it's simply testing different perspectives: "Here's what I'm hearing . . ." "Is that right?" "It sounds like you're looking for . . ." Clarifying brings the image into sharp focus, adds detail, holds it up for inspection, so the client can say, "Yes! That's it!" It's a way to move past the fog and get back on course.

Sample Dialogue

Client: . . . *unless he decides to go to New York. In that case, I'll stay here, at least for a while.*

COACH: *It sounds like there are two separate decisions for you to make, maybe three, and they're more dependent on what he does than on what you want. Help me out here.*

Client: *It sounds like I'm waiting for him to make his move before I make my decision.*

COACH: *And it sounds like you need to decide (a) whether you want that job at all, and (b) whether it's worth uprooting your life to have it, and then maybe (c) whether the relationship is sustainable. Or something like that.*

Client: *Sustainable under what conditions, really. Okay. I've got some work to do here.*

Meta-View

Get in the imaginary helicopter with the client, take it up to about 5,000 feet, and look down on the client's life. This is the coaching skill of meta-view. It is especially useful when the client is in a rut and can only see six inches of dirt on each side. Meta-view presents the big picture and opens up room for perspective. The coach might ask: "What do you see from up here? What's the truth you can see from this vantage point that you couldn't see down there?" The meta-view reconnects clients to their vision of themselves and a fulfilling life. When they're struggling at the foot of the mountain, looking up at the daunting work to be done, meta-view allows them to float above it and get a fresh perspective.

Another way to look at the meta-view is to see it as an elevated platform—a high place where coaches can stand to survey the client's life with all its circumstances and issues. The coach can see more than the client can from this vantage point. In fact, that is the coach's job: to maintain clarity of perspective and hold the big picture. This platform allows the coach to speak from outside the details of the immediate conversation. If the client is struggling with a co-worker, for example, the coach might say: "This story reminds me of the conversation you had with your ex-boss and the situation with your sister. Is there a pattern here?" Another example might be the client who appears to be making a great effort but never gets anywhere. In this case, the coach might say: "There seems to be a lot of struggle. What are you getting out of your suffering?" In this last example, the meta-view is from a higher level that captures the underlying theme. Meta-view presents a panoramic view of the journey.

Meta-view is a useful way to provide context, especially when the situation makes it easy to be drawn into the details of a problem. For example, a client comes to the coaching session worried about the reaction she expects over the upcoming firing of a staff member. The coach asks her to look at the situation from the meta-view—from the point of view of building a work culture—rather than focusing on hurt feelings or upsets. What are the costs to the organization of not firing that person? How will the firing affect communication and trust among co-workers in the long run?

Metaphor

The skill of metaphor enables you to draw on imagery and experience to help the client comprehend faster and more easily. The question "Are you drifting in a fog?" creates a picture, an experience, that engages the client at a very different level than "Are you confused?" which addresses the client's intellect. Clients can step into a picture of drifting in a fog. They know what it looks like and feels like. It's a whole experience. Metaphor provides rich imagery for exploration, and if the metaphor doesn't land in a way that bursts into insight, coaches can always try something else.

Acknowledging

The coaching skill of acknowledgment strengthens the client's foundation. The client can stand straighter after a true acknowledgment. This skill addresses who the client is. Praise and compliments, in contrast, highlight what people do: "Good job on that report, Janet." Or they highlight the opinion of the person giving the praise or the impact on the person giving the compliment: "Your presentation was thoughtful and inspiring to me." Acknowledgment recognizes the inner character of the person to whom it is addressed. More than what that person did, or what it means to the sender, acknowledgment highlights who the sender sees: "Janet, you really showed your commitment to learning." "You took a big risk." "I can see your love of beauty in it." Acknowledgment often highlights a value that clients honored in taking the action. The client values fun: "You made it really fun for yourself. Congratulations. I know you had to take a risk to do that." Or the client values honesty: "Great job. You took a stand for honesty and authenticity. It wasn't easy."

Acknowledgment is almost a context of coaching. At some level, coaches are always supporting who clients must be in order to make the changes they want. The client had to be courageous, or had to be a person willing to stand up to the fear, or had to be tenacious for the sake of a relationship.

The skill of acknowledgment helps the coach celebrate the client's internal strengths. Acknowledgment helps clients see what they sometimes dismiss in themselves out of a distorted sense of humility or simply don't see at all. By acknowledging that strength, you, as the coach, give clients more access to it. Clients will know when the acknowledgment is honest and true. They will be more resourceful in the future because they recognize the truth you illuminated. Acknowledgment might take this form: "Look at what you were able to tell your boss.

Think about how far you've come in the past four months. Your ability to be clear and ask for what you want is so much stronger today. You've really shown you can stand up to the fear and speak your own truth." Acknowledgment goes right to the heart of where the client is growing and getting stronger (and, often, feeling the need for validation). When you acknowledge this, you empower clients to keep growing.

There are actually two parts to every acknowledgment in co-active coaching. The first part we've already covered: delivering the acknowledgment. The second part is noticing the impact on the client. This is a way for the coach to make sure that the acknowledgment was truly on target. Notice the client's reaction. By listening at Level III, you will know if you found the right description of who the client had to be in that situation. The acknowledgment will definitely land in a way you can hear, sense, and see. It is enormously moving—and rare—for clients to be seen and known in this way. That's the power of acknowledgment.

Sample Dialogue

Client: *Maybe I should have kept my mouth shut. It just gets me into trouble.*

COACH: *What you did was take a stand for treating people right, all people, all the time. And you spoke up even though you knew it would come at a cost. That's who you are.*

Client: *Thanks. I may not get invited back, but at least I'll be able to sleep at night with a clear conscience.*

1. Listening at Levels I and II

The goal of this exercise is to listen completely at Level I—that is, focused entirely on your own thoughts and opinions. To do this exercise, ask a friend or colleague to take a half hour or so to play the Level I and Level II listening games with you.

Level I

Describe Level I listening to your partner and ask that person to describe a trip he or she took, including stories about things that went well and things that didn't go so well. As your partner tells the story of the trip, your job is to listen to the words and interpret the story entirely in terms of your own experience. Make frequent comments in which you offer your opinion. Think about how you would have done the trip differently or how you might improve on your partner's story. What's going on in you while this other person is talking? What does this story remind you of in your own life?

After fifteen minutes or so (if you last that long), tell each other what it was like to listen at Level I and what it was like to be listened to at Level I.

Level II

Work with the same partner—and the same story—for about fifteen minutes. But this time, without describing Level II, be curious. Ask questions, clarify, and articulate what you see. Be alert for your partner's values as they are expressed in the story. Stay completely focused on your partner by listening and responding at Level II.

Tell each other what it was like to listen at Level II and what it was like to be listened to at Level II. How was the experience different from the Level I listening?

2. Listening at Level III

Take a field trip or two to venues where the Level III activity is likely to be noticeable, such as a library, a hotel lobby, the waiting area in an emergency room, an airport bar. Pay attention to your awareness at Level III. Notice how people are feeling: angry, frustrated, joyful, bored, at peace, anxious? What else do you notice about the environment? What is the buzz in the room? Notice where the energy is in the room and how it shifts as people arrive or depart. Write down your impressions. Then try listening at Level III with your eyes closed. How is it different? What do you note that you didn't notice with your eyes open? Compare a church sanctuary to a fast-food restaurant. What are the differences as you listen at Level III?

Variation: Have a friend enter the room clearly annoyed and angry. Notice how the room reacts at Level III. Or have two friends enter the room and start a loud, rude conversation. Notice how the Level III energy changes.

3. Meta-View

A meta-view is the big picture. It is part theme, part positioning statement, and part vision. Here are some examples of meta-views:

- Launching a new life
- Being in transition
- Struggling with change
- Drifting at sea
- High-speed action machine
- Peaceful unfolding

What is the meta-view for your own life today?

Write down the names of ten close friends or relatives. What is the meta-view for each of them at this time?

4. Metaphor

Create a metaphor for each of the following client situations:

- Stuck between two appealing choices
- About to enter an exciting new period with a lot of unknowns
- After a long period of inaction, everything happening at once
- Chaotic work environment
- Two new romantic relationships
- Money losses because of mismanagement
- Going from too little exercise to overdoing it
- Making great progress building the business until the interruption
- Success
- Sadness
- Series of windfalls
- Exhaustion
- Denial

5. Acknowledging

List five friends. Write an acknowledgment of who they are or who they have been in order to get to where they are today. Write an acknowledgment for yourself.

4

Intuition

Maybe you've had an experience like this: You're driving in the country on back roads that aren't marked very well. You come to an intersection of two roads and instinctively turn to the right, trusting your sense of direction. Or this may have happened: You're having dinner with a friend. Everything seems normal. The conversation has its usual flow. And then suddenly you ask, "What's wrong? Is there something you need to tell me?" To you, something just seemed out of tune. It may have been a gut feeling. Maybe you've made an unexpected phone call to someone or spontaneously mailed a card to a friend. You weren't sure quite why you did it then—and later you found out that the timing was important for some reason. Some people have great hunches about investments. Others get a feeling about the answer to a question even when it doesn't seem to make much sense. They'd rather trust their instincts about some things because the feeling is so much stronger than the data.

These are all examples of intuition at work, of gathering nonempirical information—usually in response to a question, spoken or unspoken. *Which way to turn? What's going on with her? Which investment to choose? Which job is better suited to me? Why did the client just withdraw in our conversation?* Intuition comes up with a response.

Speaking from your intuition is extraordinarily valuable in coaching. It is right up there with the ability to listen deeply and deftly. Yet, even though we can define it in words, the experience of intuition is sometimes hard to explain—which also makes it difficult for some people to accept. For many people, the trouble starts with the difficulty of verifying intuition. Sometimes there's no observable evidence for the conclusion. In some cases, the conclusions people derive from their intuition are actually contrary to observable evidence. People who operate from their intuition will say things like "I know because my intuition is usually right about these things."

Those who have trouble believing in intuition frequently treat it as guessing or being lucky. They just don't understand, trust, or believe in intuition. Facts that can be measured, recorded, verified—that's what people frequently say they want when they're making decisions. It's certainly the scientific research model and the method advocated by a majority of people. People are sometimes shy about admitting they have used their intuition. Even those with intuition in abundance are often reluctant to use it, or admit they have used it, and so this ability atrophies in all of us. That's too bad, because it's a powerful asset in coaching.

THE KNOWN VS. THE UNKNOWN UNIVERSE

Most of us have come to believe that the known universe is within hand's reach. It is within our field of vision, our range of hearing, susceptible to our five senses. A thing is known when others corroborate it and come up with the same data. Intuition, however, is not directly observable—although sometimes its effects are. Like the wind in the trees, it may not be visible, but we can see and hear its effects. That's why it is sometimes called the "sixth sense." It is a sensitivity that goes beyond the physical world.

Suppose someone says, "It's going to rain today." You ask, "How do you know?" The answers might be:

I heard the National Weather Service report on the radio.

There was a red sky this morning.

The barometer on the wall has been dropping fast all morning.

The wind is from the east and clouds are building in the west.

I feel it in my bones.

I just know.

Of course, some people really do feel approaching rain in their bones. The point is that there are many ways of knowing. One of those ways is scientifically verifiable evidence, but there is also "just knowing." When you look at this list of possible answers, you might want to ask: *Which source is right?* A different question would be: *Which one do I trust?* Many people would say there's a direct relationship between what they can observe and their confidence in knowing. For these people, their trust is in the concrete experience. They would also say that intuition is way down on the trust scale—maybe even 0 percent for reliability.

But instead of insisting that there is only one form of knowing, let's suppose there are two. Conventional, observable knowing is one form; intuition is the second. Together these two dimensions give depth and perspective to any issue.

BUT IS IT RIGHT?

Part of the difficulty of describing intuition as a way of knowing starts with the definition of knowing. One way of looking at intuition says that it is neither right nor wrong—it's more like a nudge we receive. For example, answer these questions: *What day of the week is tomorrow? What is tomorrow's date? What season will it be tomorrow? What will the weather be like during this particular season in this particular year? What's your theme during this season of your life in this particular year?* Notice that the answer to each question is found in a different place. One of the places is your memory, another place is your logical mind, another place is your history. And perhaps another place is your intuition. What if intuition were a place—not a place we are used to visiting, perhaps, but simply a place that we go to, like memory, that provides us with an answer. We take the nudge and give it expression.

In order to express our intuition in words, we make an interpretation. It's our *interpretation* of the intuitive nudge that can be off target. The intuitive impulse itself was neither right nor wrong. Imagine this scenario: Your client is in the midst of a report about the action she took last week. It's a great report, with one success after another. She's followed through on everything just as she said she would. But your intuition tells you she's holding something back. So despite the overwhelming evidence of accomplishment, you say: "My intuition tells me there's something you're not saying about last week. Is that true?" Your intuition gave you a nudge. Your interpretation is that the client is holding back, so that's what you say. It doesn't matter whether you are right or wrong about your interpretation. If the client is holding back—great, you opened a door to talk about that. If the client says she isn't holding anything back—great, you reinforce the success story. The thing about intuition and coaching is that intuition always forwards the action and deepens the learning, even when it lands with a clang instead of a melodious ping.

Intuition often shows up in unexpected ways in the coaching conversation. Sometimes it's a hunch. Or it might appear as a visual image or an unexplained shift in emotion or energy. The important thing to remember in coaching is to be open to intuition—trusting it, aware of it, and completely unattached to the interpretation. In the end, intuition is valuable when it moves the client to action or deeper learning. It is irrelevant, really, whether your intuition was "correct."

Sample Dialogues

Example A: Something Overlooked

Client: *It's like I've run out of options, and I'm worn out. Doing the same things over and over, talking to the same people, showing the same old résumé. Even when the faces and names change, it's all a repeat performance.*

COACH: *My intuition tells me there's something else—something that's been overlooked. Like it's right there in front of you but you don't see it. What could that be?*

Client: *I don't know. I feel like I've been going down this road for so long that I'm in a rut.*

COACH: *The road's a good image; let's work with that. Imagine there's a fence running along this road, and there's a gate in the fence. What's the gate?*

Client: *It's the road not taken.*

COACH: *And where does that road lead? If you were going to make something up, what would that be?*

Client: *Actually, it reminds me of my grandparents' home in Connecticut. My grandfather is the only person in our family who worked for himself. I thought he was about the smartest man alive to be able to do that. I really admired his independence.*

COACH: *What does the gate mean to you in your own life?*

Client: *That gate's always been there—and I've always walked past, because I thought I wanted security. This could be the time for me to take a serious look at what it would be like to create my own sense of security, working for myself.*

Example B: Drawing on Client Interest

Client: . . . *by the end of the third quarter. Which means I will need to just about double my output—comparing last year to this year. I really want to hit the mark, I really do, but I just don't see how it's possible.*

COACH: *How would the marathon runner do it?*

Client: *Where did that come from?*

COACH: *Intuition, I guess. You once told me you were a marathon runner. Isn't that right?*

Client: *Not since I took this job, with these hours, but yeah, in the past.*

COACH: *So, looking at the task ahead as if it were a long-distance race, what do you know you need to do?*

Client: *That's easy. Build in rest days for starters. Okay—this is fun. Like drawing up a training plan.*

INTUITIVE INTELLIGENCE

Another way to think of intuition is to regard it as a kind of intelligence, like musical intelligence or visual intelligence. All of us who are not blind or color-blind can identify colors. We start in preschool, and many of us add to our color vocabulary over the years, becoming more adept at recognizing colors. Artists learn to identify and name many shades of colors. In their minds, they can picture the subtle differences between hundreds of shades. Intuition is like that. It is an intelligence everyone has been given in some measure, and we can develop it just as artists and musicians develop their talents.

One of the interesting things about intuition is its elusive quality. Looking too intently for it makes it more difficult to find. If you are working too hard to find your intuition, your attention is on you and your efforts. By shifting your attention to the question or the other person and opening the channel, you can more easily find the answer. The key seems to be to take a soft focus, be open. Your intuition is there, giving you messages or clues, just below the surface. This is the paradox of intuition: an open hand will hold it; it will slip through a fist.

OBSERVATION AND INTERPRETATION

We have said that intuition starts with a nudge, a feeling. It could also be an observation, although it might not be clear that you have observed something specific. Calling it simply an "observation" makes it neutral. You can say "I have a feeling," or "I have an observation," or "I have an intuition," and no one can dispute it. It is your feeling, observation, or intuition. What happens next is often an interpretation of the feeling, intuition, or observation. We need to put some words around this very subjective nudge. It is natural to give the intuition a meaning, and it is this interpretation of the intuition that can be off base.

For example, in listening to your client, you sense something that is unsaid. It's as if you can hear a note that is out of tune. You might say: "Something doesn't sound quite right here. Help me out if I'm getting this wrong, but it feels like you're holding something back, something important. What's your sense of this?"

In this example, you are communicating an observation: the feeling that something doesn't sound quite right. And you are also communicating an interpretation: something is being held back. If you jump right to your interpretation, it will too often come out as a conclusion, an accusation, or a judgment. The client's job is to take the information you provide from your intuition and apply it to his or her situation. What fits? What doesn't fit? In the end, it is the client who comes up with the conclusion.

The lesson here is that if you're going to use your intuition effectively, you can't be attached to your interpretation. In fact, this desire to be right about their interpretations is often the reason people hold back their intuition. They're afraid of being wrong or appearing foolish.

The best approach is to be prepared. When you express your intuition, clients may disagree. Even so, they will learn as much as if your intuition were somehow "correct." What was correct was the intuition to say something. What was correct was whatever the client learned. What's more, clients count on your intuition. When you hold back, you withhold a crucial source of information and sensing. The key lesson: do not be attached to your intuition, no matter how certain you feel. Being attached to being right is something you do for your sake. Coaching is for the sake of the client.

FINDING YOUR OWN ACCESS POINT

We develop our access to intuition in the same way we develop talents or muscles. Intuitive fitness is just as possible as physical fitness. Fortunately, coaching is an intuition fitness center. In practical terms, how do we find access to our intuition, especially if we're not accustomed to looking for it? It can be somewhat elusive. Compared to the triceps muscle, which is in pretty much the same place for all of us, our intuition is found in a different place for each of us.

Many people find their intuition in the body—in their chest or stomach. It's no wonder people talk of intuition as a "gut response" or a feeling "in my gut." Some feel a burning on the forehead or a tingling in the fingers. For others, intuition is not felt in the body at all. It may be above you, or it might be a bubble that surrounds you. Take some time to find out where you sense your intuition. Stop, pay attention, and listen to your body or your experience at that point in order to determine where the communication is coming from.

You may "see" your intuition in a visual way or feel it kinesthetically. Some people find that they're better able to access their intuition by standing up. For others, the connection is definitely verbal. Whatever your access point, eventually you'll need to verbalize the nudge from your intuition. You make sense out of the sensation by giving words to it. Let's be absolutely clear about this: Your responsibility as a coach is to speak what your intuition gives you. Clients get to decide what is useful about your intuitive nudge.

The Intuitive On/Off Switch

Speaking boldly from your intuition may be somewhat new for you. Until your intuition becomes a familiar and easy tool to use, you may want a way to be reminded of it while you coach. You might post a note over your phone or wear your wristwatch on the opposite wrist. You could try standing up if you usually sit down. Bottom line: Intuition is a powerful asset in your coaching, well worth the practice. And the good news is that your intuition is always on tap. You don't have to generate it any more than you have to generate the electricity to run the lights in your home. You simply have to remember to turn it on.

Blurting It Out

Even after the nudge of intuition, there is often a natural tendency to hold back, to analyze it, to check and see if it is right or if this is the right time to say something. Unfortunately, by the time you've performed a set of validation tests on your intuition, the client has moved on to an entirely different phase of the conversation. Your moment is lost. Intuition is like a small flash of light that is already beginning to fade as soon as it appears. The most powerful moment is the first. Holding back out of fear and timidity, hesitating, will allow it to pass by. That's a shame, because blurting out your intuition can often create a dramatic shortcut in the coaching conversation, boring through many layers.

As coaches, we sometimes think we need to track the logical unfolding of a conversation, hooking together question and response and question and response in a neat sequence. This is an excellent way to build new learning and discovery with clients, but it is not the only way. Being willing to risk a jump with your intuition, taking the chance you'll end up with either a beautiful dive or a horrendous belly flop, gives you another way to go directly to something you can feel in the conversation that you may not be able to fully articulate or logically diagram in the moment. This willingness to fail at it, bow in good humor, and press on gives you license to use your intuition with more freedom.

Getting the Intuitive Hit

Sometimes intuition comes in the form of words, but it could just as easily be in shapes or sounds, as a feeling or a body sensation. Your intuition might communicate to you through a sense of heaviness, an ache, a mood. Sometimes the intuitive hint arises from the conversation itself. Sometimes it is out there in the environment. A scene outside your office window might inspire an intuitive remark. The scene creates an image . . . which your intuition signals to you . . . and you share with your client . . . and then you see what the impact is. For example, your client is describing a sense of confusion resulting from major changes at work. She wants to sort out what is important, and she's wondering what the right course of action is. You look out the window and notice it is a crisp fall day, one of the first. It's a strong impression, and you mention it: "I'm noticing it's a beautiful fall day. The leaves are changing color; the air is cooler today. What does that bring up for you?" It might suggest a sense of the changing seasons in her life and give her the means for sorting out the changes before her. Or it could remind her of chores that need to be done to get ready for winter. The source of the intuition is irrelevant. What is relevant is what happens to the client.

Phrasing It

This is a crib sheet for expressing intuition. You can use any of the following phrases to open your intuitive expression, and, of course, this is not a definitive list. In fact, it's good practice to simply begin with one of these phrases, having no idea of what will come out of your mouth, trusting that your intuition will fill in the blanks as you go along:

I have a sense . . .

May I tell you about a gut feeling I have?

I have a hunch that . . .

Can I check something out with you?

I wonder if . . .

See how this fits for you.

And perhaps the best one of all is also the simplest and most direct:

My intuition tells me . . .

Intuition is not magic, although sometimes it might feel like that, especially when we're delighted with the results. Intuition is like listening. It is a powerful talent that can be used to help clients move into action or deepen their learning.

COACHING SKILLS

The following coaching skills are associated with intuition, although they are not exclusive to that context. We chose these skills for this section because they naturally come from a place of intuition or help give intuition an opening for expression. We listed metaphor under the listening context, but it could just as easily be included here, since metaphor is often drawn from intuition.

Intruding

Because most coaching sessions are brief, it may be necessary to intrude on the client's report or storytelling in order to get to the heart of the matter. As coach, you use your Level III awareness to decide when it's time to do that. Rather than wait for a socially polite break in the conversation, you interrupt and redirect the conversation or ask a question. Often your intuition urges you to intrude.

Note that it isn't necessary to be rude, although your interruption may be perceived by some as rude, especially in parts of the world where such behavior is considered a faux pas. Remember, too, that clients usually know when they're droning on and on. If you don't redirect this type of rambling, clients begin to think of the coaching session as a place to tell stories, and before long they're dissatisfied and ready to abandon the coaching relationship. Clients do not want to use up all their time in a coaching session with "and then I . . ." or "and she said . . ." Some clients will also keep talking until you say something. In their desire to be good clients or to be thorough, they keep pressing on, hoping you will step in and save them or get the conversation back on track.

In general, it's best if you prepare your clients for these types of intrusions at the beginning of your coaching relationship. Explain that you'll sometimes interrupt the conversation in a way that may surprise them. Let them know that a coaching conversation is different from chitchatting with a friend over coffee. You may need to interrupt, and you ask that they not take it personally. Ask them to let you know if they feel offended so that the two of you can talk about it again if necessary. This should be all the permission you need, as a coach, to intrude whenever it seems appropriate.

Maybe you still feel reluctant to intrude, thinking that it's not your style. Here's the real point: You're not intruding on them; you're intruding on the story that gets in the way, that obscures and fogs the picture. Would you really rather be perceived as polite, or nice, than intrude to give your clients access to a fuller life? Remember that coaching is about the client, not the coach. Coaching is therefore not for the faint of heart.

Your job as coach is to work with whatever comes up and to leave your agenda and ego out of the conversation. However, there are times when you will need to take charge. Your experience and training in coaching give you the authority you need to serve the client. Holding back, being nice at this point, does not serve the client's best interests. There will be times when you'll have to jump in to clarify, make a strong request or pose a powerful challenge, or tell the hard truth. Since there is no hard-and-fast rule, this is a good place for trusting your intuition on when to intrude.

Coaches also sometimes fail to intrude because they believe they need more information, more background or context, before they can begin intervening with a coaching question. It's true that it is sometimes important to hear the story for its context. It may also be necessary so that clients feel heard, listened to; in this case, it is important for the sake of the relationship. But we assume you are already skilled at listening well to the story. What many coaches need is more practice intruding. The skill of intruding helps cut off unnecessary reporting— which can be a smoke screen put up by the client to avoid getting to the more challenging issues. Intruding accelerates the process of getting to the core: the action and the learning.

Sample Dialogues

Example A: Poor Use of the Skill

Client: *Mary's the one I told you about, the one who seems so contrary. If I say I think we should go east, she says no, we should head west. If I say the only way to meet the deadline is to hire outside help, she says no, it's up to us, it just means we need better teamwork. Teamwork! What could be more hypocritical? Over and over I've asked her to be a more involved member of the team. And it's always, "I don't have the time" or "This is your team to run." You know, just excuse after excuse. She's the one who's constantly undermining the team.*

COACH: *She's constantly undermining the team. It's got to be frustrating trying to work with someone like that.*

Client: *Well, yeah. Did I tell you her latest?*

COACH: *More of the same, I'm sure.*

Client: *Of course. It doesn't end . . . blah, blah, blah, blah, blah, blah, blah, blah.*

Example B: Good Use of the Skill

Client: *Mary's the one I told you about, the one who seems so contrary. If I say I think we should go east, she says no, we should head west. If I say the only way to meet the deadline is to hire outside help, she says no, it's up to us . . .*

COACH: *Sounds like an endless battle of wills.*

Client: *I'll say.*

COACH: *What will change the game?*

Client: *Excuse me? I'm not sure what you mean.*

COACH: *What will it take to break the cycle? What are the strengths you bring to this situation?*

Client: *Well, that's interesting . . . Compassion comes to mind. It's a huge value of mine.*

COACH: *How will being compassionate help break up this battle?*

Blurting

We've touched on the importance of blurting. Odd as it may sound, blurting is actually a skill worth developing. Most of us spend so much time trying to analyze and figure things out that we miss the opportunity to jump into action.

In coaching, it actually serves the client to go right into the messiness without sorting it out first. It's better to dive in and be willing to look a little clumsy. This often builds more trust than if you are always the polished, professional authority, always in control. Being clumsy or messy, and therefore more human, is also more authentic. And if you don't have to look good, your clients don't have to look good either. For example, as coach, you might say, "I'm not sure what the right words are here, but it's something like . . ." or "Let me just talk out loud for a minute. I'm not sure exactly what I want to say here."

CLIENTS AND THEIR INTUITION

It's worth noting that watching the coach work with intuition allows clients to experiment and take risks with their own intuition. In fact, learning the coaching principles, contexts, and skills can be a great benefit to clients. Clients who become proficient at listening at Levels II and III, for example, have a chance to be much more effective in their relationships at work and at home. Learning to clarify, or to keep the meta-view, in their personal lives will be a tremendous advantage, too.

In teaching clients to work with intuition, begin by asking them to simply spend some time noticing their intuition and playing with it. For clients who are not accustomed to accessing their intuition, you might ask them to just experiment, play with intuition, and urge them to free themselves from any attachment to doing it "right." Prepare them for the appearance of their internal skeptic—in addition to the external skeptics they are likely to encounter.

1. Intuition

Intuition is the sixth sense that helps us respond to a question. Sometimes the question is explicit and posed; sometimes it's part of the background of the conversation. In coaching, there is always a question in the air about the client's life.

To practice your intuition, meet with a friend or a colleague in a quiet place where the two of you can be undisturbed for a while. Have the person write down a series of open-ended questions about his or her life. Ask the other person to choose one question from the list and repeat the question out loud, reading it more than once, with a brief space of quiet between each repetition of the question. The two of you will then concentrate on the question for three to five minutes, with no conversation. Your goal is to increase your concentration on the question and open yourself to whatever your intuition offers. At the end of the time period, tell the person everything that occurred: the random thoughts, the feelings, anything you noticed in terms of visual images, sounds, smells, and touch, along with whatever else you may have noticed or anything that distracted you. Some of what you report from your intuition is sure to connect for the other person. As soon as that intuitive hit happens, ask what the connection is and explore that area for greater awareness.

You can double the intrigue in this exercise by having the person write the questions on slips of paper and then fold the slips so the questions can't be read. Pick a piece of paper from the pile, keeping the question hidden. Then you both spend three to five minutes concentrating on the question you picked even though you haven't read it. Again, report whatever comes up from your intuition. Then read the question and ask the person for comments. Where were the connections? Where does this lead?

2. Intruding

Sit down with a friend and let that person know that, in order to practice the skill of intruding, you are going to interrupt as he or she talks. Have your friend tell a story from a significant period of his or her life. It could be a learning experience, from school. It could be a story about meeting his or her best friend. Ask your friend to pick a story that can be stretched, since it's important that the story go on and on. As your friend is telling you the story, your job is to interrupt and change the course of the storytelling by using a coaching skill:

- Ask your friend to summarize: "What did that mean to you?"

- Interrupt with a provocative question (not a question for more information), such as: "What did you learn from that?"

- Interrupt by articulating what is going on in the story at that moment.

- Interrupt with a request.

- Intrude by announcing your intention to interrupt: "I'm going to interrupt here."

- Language for interrupting might include: "Excuse me, you just . . ." or "Let me ask . . ."

5

Curiosity

As a context for coaching, curiosity may be the quality that starts the process and the energy that keeps it going. The most effective coaches seem to be naturally curious and to have developed their curiosity in a way that opens doors and windows for clients. Being genuinely curious and eager to play with whatever shows up is at the heart of a co-active coaching relationship.

A DIFFERENT WAY OF ASKING

Curiosity starts with a question. The interesting thing about a question is that it automatically causes us to start looking. For example, when you read the question *Is it cold outside today or hot?* chances are that you instantly started thinking about the weather in your town. We have this Pavlovian response to a question. It nearly always throws us in the direction of the question, looking for an answer. Simply posing the question shifts the focus of the conversation. Being curious has the same effect. Coaches naturally draw their clients' attention to those things they both become curious about—like what brings the client alive or what is in the way. And yet, being curious about these aspects of the client's life is not the same as gathering information. Curiosity is a different way of discovering.

Our experience in school trained us to gather information by asking specific questions that enable us to deduce answers. In that environment, we learned that questions have specific answers—in fact, right answers. Even essay questions have correct answers that are specific, concrete, and measurable. We learned that questions are used to narrow the possibilities. This is the deductive method. We learned to fill in the blanks, and we learned about being scored on our ability to get the right answers.

There is a big difference between conventional questions that elicit information and curious questions that evoke personal exploration. The following examples illustrate the differences between the two types of questions:

Information Gathering	*Curious*
What topics will you include in the report?	What will finishing the report give you?
How much exercise do you need each week?	What would "being fit" look like for you?
What training options are available?	What do you want to know that you don't know today?

And the deadliest questions of all in this style of information gathering are the questions that ask for a yes or a no. They simply erect a huge stop sign in the middle of the conversation. The road ends abruptly, and the coach has to start all over again. Curious questions, however, are open-ended. They take the client on a journey and are easily phrased to avoid sudden stops. Notice the differences in responses that could be elicited by the following types of questions:

Closed	*Open*
Is this an effective strategy for you?	What makes this an effective strategy for you?
Is there more to be learned here?	How can you double the learning in this experience?
It sounds like you're stuck between those two choices— is that true?	What's another choice you could make besides the two in front of you?

Another form of the closed question is the leading question. The leading question implies that there is a right answer, a conclusion, built into the question itself. But the leading question leaves little choice. It pretty much forces the learner to come up with the answer the teacher is looking for.

THE VALUE OF CURIOSITY

In coaching, the ideal is to ask truly curious questions with a curious frame of mind. The curious coach doesn't have all the answers. When you are curious, you are no longer in the role of expert. Instead, you are joining clients in a quest to find out what's there. You are exploring their world with them, not superimposing your world on theirs. It is like looking at their world through the wondering eyes of a child.

As a consultant, you gather information so that you can come up with appropriate recommendations. You have the expertise, and you are casting for information to determine where to go. You're like a general contractor who has been hired to come in and build something with the materials you bring to the site. In co-active coaching, in contrast, you are curious. You come in as a collaborator with building experience and expertise and build with the materials that are there. The information is inside the client. Your curiosity allows the client to explore and discover. It opens a wider range of possibility because it is more flexible. Curiosity invites the client to look for solutions. Co-active coaches assume the client knows the appropriate solutions and has the resources to come up with them.

By finding the solutions in themselves—rather than in you, the coach—clients become even more resourceful. The effect of finding the answers is also very energizing because important learning takes place. Curiosity generates the search, defines and directs it, but it is the exploring that creates learning. And it is the kind of learning that lasts, because it comes from within. With questions that imply a correct or a purely factual answer, we search our inner files for the response that fits: the right answer. With curiosity, we have the experience of exploring, uncovering, digging around, considering, reflecting. This is the learning that leads to sustainable change and growth.

Building the Relationship

Authentic curiosity is also a powerful builder of relationships—an aspect of curiosity that is very valuable in coaching. Imagine yourself at a dinner party seated next to a stranger who seems infinitely curious about you: your life, your work, your interests, what makes you tick, what ticks you off. This kind of curiosity is not only flattering but encouraging. It allows you to reveal a lot about yourself in an unchallenged way, and so you build a connection effortlessly. Now imagine the same dinner party and the same stranger asking questions, but this time the person is not simply curious. Instead, it's your prospective mother-in-law, and the questions seem to be part of an inquisition. The questions themselves might be exactly the same, but the context is vastly different. Curiosity builds relationships; interrogation builds defenses. In the coaching relationship, curiosity invites the client to search and reveal while permitting safe exploration.

Steering Through Curiosity

The coach's question proposes a direction for looking, and the client's attention is naturally drawn in that direction. With each new question, the coach encourages additional looking along a path—or shifts the path, allowing the curiosity to steer the looking. Intuition and curiosity are both guiding the coaching conversation. Being curious in coaching is two things: not being attached to a particular path or destination and yet always being intentional about seeking out meaning, uncovering values, discovering learning for the client. It is not aimless meandering.

This would be a good time to emphasize that we are talking about curiosity for the sake of the client's discovery and decision making, not the coach's discovery and problem solving. This is an important distinction and is sometimes marked by a very fine line. Yes, of course, it is important for coaches to gather information and background in order to understand the issue under discussion and the client's desires. But in practice, coaches usually need much less information than they think they do. This is especially true of background information. Coaches rarely need to know how things came to be, and they don't need detailed information in order to solve the problem. Clients need to know, and coaches can be most helpful by guiding the client's discovery and learning.

Developing the Talent

Like listening and intuition, curiosity is a talent. Some people are endowed with a stronger sense of curiosity than others. As with listening and intuition, curiosity can be developed through practice.

The first step is awareness—simply paying attention to being curious. We are so accustomed to feeling we have to know the answer before we ask the question that we sometimes find it nearly impossible to ask without knowing. In coaching, however, you have to learn to stop asking questions as the expert—with the intention of sorting, analyzing, and categorizing the information for later use—and simply ask out of curiosity.

Clients know when the coach is asking a question with a "correct" answer in mind. They sense that they have two choices: either resist giving that answer or try to discern the answer the coach is looking for. When the question is asked out of curiosity, they will sense this, too. They will know they are being asked to find their own answers from within.

One technique for developing your curiosity is to use the phrase "I'm curious . . ." before asking a question. Notice how it changes the nature of the looking. Notice how it shifts the process of looking to the client but at the same time lowers the risk that usually accompanies coming up with the answer. Clients seem more willing to say, "I don't know," and then answer anyway. With curiosity, there is both playfulness and an unconditional sense that the answer that emerges is always the right answer because it's the client's. This doesn't mean it can't be challenged, however. It's a right answer because it's the client's, not the coach's, but it is also open to further coaching. When you ask the client, "How are you doing with making sales calls?" and the client says, "I'm satisfied with making four calls a day," you can still ask: "Your initial plan was for eight calls a day. What changed?"

Another application of curiosity is to notice the energy shifts in the client's responses using your Level III listening awareness. If your sensing radar picks up hesitation, be curious about that. If you pick up anger or resistance, ask about that. Be curious about a change in pace in the client's conversation—or a more energetic spirit, more jokes, more laughter. Use these clues as signals to pursue your curiosity and turn on your intuition.

How Curiosity Fits in Coaching

At some level, curiosity is one of those tools that are common to all helping professions. Curiosity is especially important in coaching because it taps into deeper sources of information. Asking questions for data will yield analysis, reasons, rationale, explanation. Asking questions out of curiosity will yield deeper—often more authentic—information about feelings and motivation. The information revealed through curiosity is likely to be less censored, less carefully crafted, messier. It will be more real.

The coach demonstrates curiosity in the very first meeting. Almost nothing is more engaging for prospective clients than a coach's genuine curiosity about them, their values, what they find important, what does and doesn't work for them. Curiosity is always present in the ongoing coaching sessions, too, of course. It is the means of uncovering new answers and new areas to explore, knowing that clients know the answers. Coaches don't need to know. Their job is to be curious.

Sample Dialogue

COACH: *I know you keep saying you want to exercise and lose weight—you just brought it up again—but week after week I notice you don't do anything about it. I'm curious. What's stopping you?*

Client: *Clearly, time is a big issue. You know what my schedule's been the last few months.*

COACH: *I know you're busy, but let's take a step back and really look at this. Maybe it's not that important?*

Client: *You mean I could just decide today that I don't care and I'd never have to go to the gym again?*

COACH: *That possibility certainly lit you up. What's that about?*

Client: *I hate going to the gym. I hate the smell. I hate all the comparison . . .*

COACH: *What is important to you?*

Client: *My health is important. My dad was overweight and out of shape. He was only sixty-eight when he died.*

COACH: *Imagine you are healthy and fit. What does that feel like?*

Client: *It feels great.*

COACH: *And what works for you?*

Client: *What would really work for me—at least it did once before—is having a workout buddy, somebody to exercise with.*

COACH: *How can you make that happen?*

Client: *I'll bet I could find somebody at work who would be interested in exercising during the lunch hour. I could put a notice on the bulletin board.*

COACHING SKILLS

The two skills in this section are ideal examples of the context created by curiosity. Both skills involve provocative, open-ended questions that send clients into the realm of discovery. The skills reinforce the core of curiosity. This is not about gathering more information; it is about inviting clients to look—not only with their minds, but with their hearts, souls, and intuition—into places that are familiar but that they may see with new eyes and into places they may not have looked at before.

Powerful Questions

A particular kind of curiosity takes the form of what we call powerful questions. Asking rather than telling is at the foundation of co-active coaching, and the powerful question is a cornerstone. You can see why when you understand what makes questions powerful to begin with. When a person asks you a question, especially a personal question, it sends you in a particular direction to find an answer.

Let's say a coach asks: "When you work on an important project, what do you consistently do that can jeopardize its successful completion?" The question invites the client to look in a particular direction. Or let's say someone asks: "What is a rationale for protecting the rain forests of the world?" Some people might recall seeing a map of rain forest locations. Others may think of images of rain forests or remember the experience of visiting one. Some people may consider the question from an environmental viewpoint or recall articles they have read about the issue. It's likely that this simple question will take everyone somewhere.

Think of questions as points of a compass. Asking a powerful question is like sending the client not to a specific destination but in a direction filled with possible discoveries and mysteries. Powerful questions invite introspection, present additional solutions, and lead to greater creativity and insight. They invite clients to look inside (*What do you really want?*) or into the future (*Look ahead six months. Standing there, what decisions would you make today?*). A powerful question is expansive and opens up further vistas for the client.

Powerful questions tend to stop people in their tracks, so there is often a sudden hush. Be sure to allow time for the client to reflect and then respond. There is a temptation to fill the momentary silence as if it were a void, or to assume that the client didn't understand the question. In fact, that silent moment may be full of thoughtful discovery. Just listen and wait. Clients are accustomed to reporting what they know, what they have thought about already; they are not as accustomed to having people ask them really strong, provocative questions that send them into uncharted territory. One way to tell that you are asking powerful questions is the thoughtful consideration clients give to answering. It is possible, in fact, to conduct an entire coaching session with powerful questions. (The Coach's Toolkit contains an extensive sample of powerful questions that will give you a sense of the form.) You can download the questions from the CD and keep them handy for practice. The coaching dialogues featured on the CD also provide numerous examples of powerful questions in action.

Sample Dialogue

Client: *I'm just not very happy at work.*

COACH: *What does that mean—"not very happy"?*

Client: *I'm bored and I don't feel like the work I do makes much of a difference.*

> **COACH:** *Let's start with "bored." That's what you don't want. What is it you do want?*
>
> **Client:** *I want to wake up in the morning excited about the day. I want to be more creative. I miss that energy and the collaboration.*
>
> **COACH:** *What else?*
>
> **Client:** *I want to feel like my talents are being used and that my work means something—that I'm making a contribution.*
>
> **COACH:** *How can you create that in your work now?*
>
> **Client:** *I'm not sure. I guess I never thought of it as possible.*
>
> **COACH:** *Give it a go. What's possible?*

Using Powerful Questions. Powerful questions fit anywhere and everywhere in coaching—from the original discovery session to the last completion session between coach and client. To use powerful questions powerfully, the coach must be willing to intrude, a skill we discussed earlier. In some situations, you can't wait for an opening and need to wedge your way in. For example: Your client is just getting into the groove of complaining—once again—about how impossible her work situation is and how helpless she is to change anything. You instantly recognize this groove as a rut, so when she pauses to take a breath, you ask, "What are you tolerating?" or "What is the payoff for you in all of this?" or "What's another way this could be?" To ask powerful questions, the coach must be very curious and very courageous on the client's behalf. The coach needs to assume the client has the wherewithal to handle even tough, direct questions.

Powerful Questions vs. Dumb Questions. Sometimes the most powerful questions are the ones that sound the dumbest, or, if you prefer, simple and profound. They slide in under the radar. Clients are well trained to handle the complex attack—they are practiced at offering explanations and rationalizations. The dumb question lands like a bomb in all of that. Imagine this situation: Your client has a tightly constructed set of reasons as to why the situation is so complex, with lots of explanations about the factors that limit his success and the difficulty of getting cooperation from this person and that person, and . . . In the middle of this, you ask: "What do you really want?" Boom. You could have tested the rationale or looked for ways of expanding perspectives or chipped away at the surface in some other way. But the simplest question, the dumb question, gets to the core.

Here are some other "dumb" questions:

- *What does what you want look (or feel) like?*
- *What's next?*
- *What about that is important to you?*
- *What else?*
- *What did you learn?*
- *What will you do and when will you do it?*
- *Who do you need to be?*

There are times when you may think the question is too dumb to ask. Go ahead and ask it and surprise yourself. Even if you get the answer you expect, remember that the reason for asking is not so you can hear the answer but so the client can hear the answer and learn from it. The reason for asking the dumb question is to let clients hear the answer: the truth, the new discovery, or the lie they keep telling themselves. It's like underlining. Asking the questions reinforces the learning before clients move on.

Not-So-Powerful Questions and Exceptions. The simpler and more direct, the better, when it comes to making questions powerful. A compound or complex question forces clients to sort out the essence of the question before they can respond, and they may get lost trying to figure it out. The powerful question is powerful because it cuts through to the heart of the issue. Short is good.

The closed-ended question creates a narrow tunnel that usually dead-ends abruptly with a yes or a no or with data. There's not enough depth for further exploration, which is why we recommend avoiding closed-ended questions.

Consider this question: "Is adventure important to you?" The answer could be "yes," "no," "very," or "sometimes." Compare it to this question: "Where do you want more adventure in your life?" This example also illustrates the exception with yes/no questions. Sometimes the coach is asking for clarification. In the first question, the coach is asking if adventure is a value. Sometimes there is a need to make sure the coach and the client are on the same page.

The "why" question is another example of a question that is often not particularly powerful because it invites the client to look for explanations or analyses. For example: "Why did you decide to move to Delaware?" "Why" questions often unintentionally put clients on the defensive. They feel a need to explain or justify a decision or point of view. A more powerful question based on the same situation might be "What are you moving toward?" or "What values motivated this move to Delaware?"

We point out these tendencies not so you will make it a rule to never ask a "yes/no" or "why" question but so you will pay attention to the impact of the questions you ask. For example, the following "yes/no" and "why" questions could be powerful: "It's time to stop analyzing and act, isn't it?" and "Why would you say yes to him and break your promise to yourself?" Given the right context and a tone that matches that context, a "yes/no" or "why" question can have a dramatic effect on clients, calling them to their own commitment.

Homework Inquiry

A homework inquiry is another special kind of question. In its phrasing, it can be identical to a powerful question. The difference is that the homework inquiry is often posed at the end of the coaching session and is meant to give clients time for continued reflection and exploration. For example: Your client is struggling with money issues—and with working more and consequently having less family time—but she is hounded by a lifelong determination to be rich someday. So you present this question as the homework inquiry for the week: "What is it to be rich?"

A homework inquiry may also be completely unrelated to that session's material or issues in the client's life at the moment. Because it appears to be coming out of the blue, this kind of inquiry can produce unexpected and profound results. For example, at the end of the session, you ask the client: "What is your prevalent mood?" The following week, after discussing what the client describes as her prevalent mood, you pose the inquiry: "How is this mood habitual and how does it serve you?"

The homework inquiry is a question asked for the purpose of provoking introspection and reflection. As with any powerful question, there is no right answer. It is not a question that has a resolution. The homework inquiry is set apart by its quality of investigation from many angles and the length of time the client takes to ponder it. Because there is a natural tendency to think that all questions should have their own right answers, you may need to remind the client that the goal of the inquiry is to be curious. In time, the inquiry leads to deeper understanding, new ways of looking at the issue, and more possibilities for action.

Here are some examples of homework inquiries:

- *What is a rich, full life?*
- *What is present when you're at your best?*
- *What are you resisting?*
- *What are you unwilling to change?*
- *What will make this easy?*

To help clients stick with the question, coaches may attach action to the inquiry. For example, you might ask clients to post the homework question in strategic places so they keep noticing it throughout the week. It's there in the daily calendar, stuck to the dashboard, posted above the computer, taped to the bathroom mirror, or printed on a card carried in a wallet. The key is to look at the homework inquiry in a new way each time and to keep engaging it at different times every day for fresh perspectives. Other action steps might be to process the question by writing in a journal, drawing pictures, talking to a friend, going for a walk. You can build accountability into the inquiry by asking clients to fax, phone, or e-mail their responses to you before the next session.

The homework inquiry is a potent tool in coaching because it takes the coaching out of the session and integrates it into the client's life. (For examples, see the Coach's Toolkit.)

Sample Dialogue

At the end of last week's coaching session, the coach left the client with an inquiry to ponder—a question that could have many different answers at different levels. The inquiry was: "Where do you abandon yourself?"

> **Client:** *Well, at first I didn't see anything. And then I started realizing my helplessness around my calendar—how I never seem to have enough time because other people are filling up my calendar with appointments.*

> **COACH:** *"Abandon yourself" in the sense of giving away your time to other people. What's it like when you give away your time?*

> **Client:** *I noticed I had this habit of saying "I can't do anything because my calendar is full"—until I finally realized that it's my calendar. I get to choose what I put in my calendar.*

> **COACH:** *Where else do you abandon yourself?*

> **Client:** *I also noticed it in my relationship. When my partner gets upset with me, I withdraw, disappear, or cave in. I'm getting better at taking a stand, but it's an old pattern.*

> **COACH:** *What else did you discover with the question?*

> **Client:** *Well, I just kept looking at it. I also noticed where other people give away their power.*

COACH: *Where was that?*

Client: *At a meeting last week. We had the divisional VP in to review forecasts, and some of the people were acting like nervous schoolkids in front of the principal. They just completely lost their self-confidence and authority. It was fascinating.*

COACH: *Was that true for you, too?*

Client: *More than I'd like to admit. I thought I was more beyond that than I guess I am.*

COACH: *Is there more?*

Client: *No, I think that covers it. Thanks.*

COACH: *So here's your homework inquiry for next week: Where do you take an uncompromising stand?*

Client: *Okay. I'll chew on that one.*

THE POWER OF BEING CURIOUS

As a coach, your curiosity leads you to know your clients from the inside out. You learn, you are curious about what you learn, and so you keep asking. Clients in turn keep responding to your curiosity by going inside, too—looking for their own answers, trying to understand their world and the way they operate, what stirs them and what stops them. In time, you get to know their interior workings until, ultimately, you become their voice, asking the questions they themselves would ask. You, as the coach, are in a better position to ask these questions because you are not distracted by self-sabotaging talk, or history, or the opinions of colleagues and the feelings of loved one, or anything else. The inquiries become more intriguing; the powerful questions become more potent. And in the process, clients adopt some of the strengths of the coaching—as if they're building internal capabilities. Clients learn what it's like to be curious and less judgmental about themselves.

1. Curiosity

Spend a half hour in a coffee shop being curious about everyone in the place. Without actually talking to anyone at first, release your curiosity and pose the following questions to yourself: *I wonder where they are out of balance in their lives. I wonder what they value. I wonder what they are missing in their lives, what makes them laugh, where they have constructed self-imposed limits. What do they like about the day? What are their life dreams? What empowers them? What do they like about the people they're sitting with?* At the end of the half hour, find someone you can spend a little more time with and actually ask that person the curious questions. As you ask the questions, be aware of what is happening with the other person. How does this person respond to you when you are curious? Then look at your own role in the conversation. What do you notice at Level I? At Level II? At Level III? Afterward, be curious about your own curiosity. What did you learn about being curious? What was easy? What was hard? What made it easy or hard? How could you be more curious? What would that give you?

2. Powerful Questions

One of the simplest ways to experience the power of powerful questions is also one of the most challenging. In this exercise, the goal is to have a ten-minute conversation with another person in which you are allowed to ask only powerful questions: no making statements, no summarizing, no offering advice or telling stories of your own, no drawing conclusions. Your role is to ask powerful questions and nothing more. (You may want to review the list of powerful questions in the Coach's Toolkit.) Afterward, ask the person for feedback. What was it like when all you did was ask questions? Then tell the person what it was like for you to be confined to questions. What worked for you about that? What made it difficult?

3. Homework Inquiry

A homework inquiry is an open-ended, powerful question that helps clients explore an important area of their lives for a period of time, usually a week or more. To do this exercise, start by reviewing the homework inquiries in the Coach's Toolkit. Then go back to the list of ten friends or acquaintances for whom you wrote meta-view statements. Using the meta-view and what you know about the person, write a homework inquiry for each one.

6

Forward
and Deepen

The most visible outcome of coaching is also the primary reason clients want coaching in the first place: action. Clients want change; they want to see results. They want to move *forward*. It's also true that "action" will look very different for different clients. For some clients, it will mean achieving specific goals or performing at a higher level. For others, action will mean integrating new practices or firmly establishing habits. For still others, it will be paying attention to the more subjective quality of their lives. In whatever way clients define "action," it will be a focus in their coaching.

In co-active coaching, we would say that a second, complementary, and just as important outcome is learning. What clients learn along the way helps them make continuously better choices and, ultimately, makes them more competent and more resourceful in the areas on which they concentrate in coaching. In fact, it's this cycle of action and learning over time that leads to sustained and effective change. Clients take action and learn, which leads to more action based on what they learned, and the cycle continues. Coaching is ideal for this process because the relationship is ongoing and is designed to focus on this interrelated pair. All of the coaching skills are used to forward the action and deepen the client's learning.

From the client's perspective, the emphasis in the previous sentence would be on the words "action" and "learning." The coach, however, would focus on "forward" and "deepen." Action and learning are what the client experiences. To forward and deepen is the job of the coach.

Within the container of the coaching relationship, coach and client work together on the client's behalf. Clients bring an agenda for change. They bring desire and a host of qualities that include willingness to dive in, commitment to their lives, and dedication to their own purpose. They bring the courage to take risks for the sake of change. In the best coaching relationships, clients bring 100 percent of themselves and these qualities. In the same way that coaches are curious for the sake of their clients, coaches also bring an ability and a commitment to forward action and deepen learning, for their clients' sake. We would say that in the best coaching relationships, coaches bring their own 100 percent in four areas: authenticity, connection, aliveness, and courage.

AUTHENTICITY

In rock climbing, the device that secures a rope is called an anchor. These ingenious devices are wedged into cracks and openings in the rock wall and can be removed later. They are temporary fixtures, but they are designed to hold a climber's weight, even if the climber falls. A coach is like that anchor. This anchor-coach makes it possible for clients to take the risks they need to take in order to climb on in their lives. It's important that clients be able to depend on that anchor, know that it is real and solid, that it is reliable and will hold.

In human terms, that means you, as the coach, must be yourself, authentically, so that clients can feel the honesty and integrity of who you are. You will be their model of what risk taking looks like, what it means to be real and honest. When you are authentically yourself, and not playing the role of "professional coach," you create more relationship and more trust, and clients will swing out more in their own lives. There are times when clients really need to lean into the coaching relationship; at that point, they want to lean into a solid wall, one that is true all the way through, not a flimsy facade.

Authenticity shows up in lots of ways. Personal style is one in particular. Personal style is simply your natural way of being with people, and if humor or eccentricity is an authentic part of your personal style, you need to bring that into your coaching. Coaches sometimes think they have to be serious all the time. This is serious business, after all, they think. Obviously it is important to take serious situations seriously and to behave professionally, but even so, there is plenty of room for lively engagement. Humor can lighten a situation at just the right time, making it possible for clients to move forward.

CONNECTION

Imagine there is an instrument that can measure the strength of the connection between coach and client. This invisible connection exists, like the radio waves used by mobile phones, and there are times when the emissions are strong and the communication is remarkably close, and times when the display on the phone would read "no signal" even though both people are talking.

Part of the coach's job is to establish, monitor, and maintain the strongest possible connection signal with clients. This signal strength is especially important when clients are moving into new or uncharted territory in their work or their lives. In our model, we call this a Level II awareness, or connection, and coaches monitor by listening at Level III and adjusting as necessary to maintain the connection.

There will be times in the coaching when the coach takes a risk with the client: to challenge or to tell the hard truth. If the connection is strong, there will be trust and relationship and a greater opportunity for success.

ALIVENESS

The doing of coaching is made up of all the skills and methodology. And then there is the being of coaching: the environment in which the coaching takes place. By "environment," we do not mean the physical environment, although that can play an important part in coaching. We are referring instead to a feeling in the atmosphere between coach and client: it feels very alive.

As a coach, your senses are alert, and you can feel that the client is alert as well. The emotional atmosphere might be almost anything: sad, serene, excited, angry. Alive does not necessarily mean enthusiastic, although that is one of the possible qualities. If you put the environment on a continuum, you might have words like "dead," "dull," "remote," "indifferent" on one end and "alive" on the other. Note that there are times when "alive" will be very dramatic and times when it will be very quiet. Like a really great piece of music, the quiet can sometimes be incredibly alive because it is in contrast with the dramatic movement. Coaches sometimes think that a coaching conversation should be smooth and polished, even smart. Of course it can be, but not at the expense of being alive. We have all been in conversations that were very alive even when the subject was uncomfortable. In order for clients to leave their comfort zones, there will be times when the coaching will be alive and darned uncomfortable.

COURAGE

Speaking of uncomfortable, how far are you willing to go for the sake of your client's agenda? How courageous are you willing to be on his or her behalf? Your willingness to be courageous will be a model, a mirror for your clients. When you are courageous on their behalf, you demonstrate that you are as committed to their success as they are, on some days even more committed. At those times when clients want to give in, you may need to courageously call them out of their fear or sense of defeat. This does not mean nagging, judging, or shaming them. It means speaking fiercely to the courageous part of your clients while ignoring the part that is self-sabotaging. You do this not for the sake of your ego but for the sake of the client's life and possibility. This is a commitment to be fearless—to care more about the client's agenda than about being liked or winning approval. It may mean taking big risks: risking the client's disapproval or anger, maybe even risking being fired. Fierce courage is a commitment to go to the edge with clients.

TAKING CHARGE

Your job as coach is to forward and deepen. You do that by the choices you make as a coach: you choose to use this skill or that one; you choose a direction to take, toward the client's fulfillment or balance or process. Clients choose the agenda for their focus, but you choose the tools and manage the time and structure of the coaching session.

Clients are responsible for their action and learning, and almost all of that action and learning takes place between, not during, coaching sessions. In the best coaching interactions, there is a dance between coach and client that has pace, range, ups and downs, ins and outs, and an overall flow that might look smooth or disconnected. But the coach takes the initiative in choosing the session's direction.

In the co-active coaching model, we emphasize that clients have the answers and coaches are unattached; we emphasize that clients are in charge of the agenda. We do want to be crystal clear, however, that the coach is primarily responsible for forwarding and deepening. That's what it means to take charge of the coaching. Clients expect and depend on the coach to do this. You will still dance with the answers that clients give and be willing to take the coaching in new directions that will move them forward and deeper. Taking charge is not about being stubborn. Ultimately, the coach takes charge for the sake of the client's movement.

ACCOUNTABILITY

One of the defining qualities of coaching is that it creates accountability: a measuring tool for action and a means of reporting on learning. It is important to be clear here, at the outset, that "accountability" is simply this: clients give an account of their action and learning. There is no judgment, blame, or scolding. Clients give an account of what they committed to: What were the results? What worked, and what didn't work? What would they do differently next time?

Accountability helps keep clients on track as they plan and commit to action and as they learn from the action they take, or don't take, in some cases. Accountability gives structure to the ongoing coaching. As coaches, we hold clients accountable—not to see them perform or even to measure how well they perform, but to empower them in making the changes they want to make. Along the way, we celebrate their achievements and dig into the obstacles they encounter. Accountability is the fundamental structure that keeps the conversation going.

It is very important that coach and client have a mutual understanding of what the client will be accountable for, regardless of whether the action plan is very specific or very subjective. The basic questions to ask for clarifying commitments are simple and clear:

- What will you do?
- When will you do it? (Or on what schedule, if it is a practice or an ongoing action.)
- How will I know (if there is to be a specific report)? (Or ask how the client will track his or her progress and report back to you.)

Even when accountability focuses on qualitative goals, there can still be specific accountability. For example: One of your clients wants to focus on his value of creativity and another wants to be a more decisive manager. The accountability might take the form of a homework inquiry for daily journaling: "What does creativity add to my life?" or "What are the qualities of a decisive manager?" The accountability might be in the form of an end-of-the-day report to self: "Today I was creative when . . ." or "Today I was more decisive when . . ." or "Today I failed to be decisive when . . ." These same end-of-the-day reports might be sent to the coach by e-mail along with notes about what the clients are discovering.

CELEBRATING FAILURE

That may seem like an odd pairing of words, "celebrating" and "failure" side by side. And yet it may be one of the most important concepts in coaching. Fear of failing is the number one killer of grand plans and good ideas. More than a lack of knowledge or skill, more than the lack of a clear strategy or action plan, the biggest obstacle in the way of progress for clients is the paralysis caused by the fear of failing.

Most of us learn early in life that failure is bad, even shameful. We learn to hide our failures, make excuses for them, or ignore them. Worse than that, we begin to stop taking risks; we become more cautious in order to avoid even the possibility of failing. We start to limit our choices to only those actions that have a high probability of success. And so our choices become limited, and our field of play becomes smaller. It doesn't have to be that way.

Failure is one of the fastest ways of learning—ask any toddler. Small children do not stay up late at night reading the "how to walk" manual, learning the mechanics. They flop, fall, crawl, stand up, and flop and crawl some more. There are bumps along with steps and statistically more failure than success, but it never seems to dampen their enthusiasm. In order to take the risks that will enable them to walk and run in their lives, clients must be willing to flop, fall, and get back up and learn from the experience. Learning is the key here. Failing at any action, even failing to take action, is a rich learning opportunity. It is this learning opportunity that we celebrate and explore with clients.

Action will lead to learning, but along the way, clients may need to go through the land of failure. Here is an essential distinction that will help you pave the road through that territory: there is a difference between failing at something and being a failure. People are naturally creative, resourceful, and whole. They are not failures, even if they fail sometimes.

In fact, in order to make significant changes in their lives, clients often have to go to the edge of their ability or capacity. Sometimes they go too far and fail; sometimes they don't go far enough and fail by missing the opportunity. Whether a person fails or succeeds, one of the underlying goals is always to look at the learning that results from the experience. That's why we believe that failing is valuable. It is something to honor in clients because it requires courage and commitment to take the risk and to fail. Clients will often learn more from what doesn't work than from what does work. And that is why we can enthusiastically put the words "celebrating" and "failure" side by side.

At the same time, we recognize that celebrating failure doesn't mean ignoring the disappointment that often accompanies it. Clients may need a little time to absorb the bump before they can dig into the learning that is available there. Celebrating in this sense means having a reverence for, an appreciation of, the client's experience. We have a high regard for failing because so few people are willing to put themselves in that position. It's worth celebrating when it happens.

CALLING FORTH

Coaches want to be helpful. They also want to be effective and successful and maybe even respected for their work, but at the core, they have a deep desire to help others. It's no wonder coaches jump at the chance to help clients solve problems. That's the obvious way to be helpful: find the problem and solve it, make it disappear.

Unfortunately, with this orientation, coaches may become so focused on understanding the problem or the issue that they shift their attention from the client to the problem. In the long run, it is more helpful for coaches to help clients make choices. This puts the emphasis back on the person instead of the issue. As coaches, we should remember that we are not merely solving problems; we are helping clients become more resourceful and more capable in their work and in their lives. Our job is to look for and call forth this inner strength and capacity from our clients. We work with clients to forward their action and deepen their learning for the sake of this bigger, more gratifying life. That's what it really means to be helpful.

If we are to call forth our clients, we will need to call ourselves forth, too. There will be times when it is easier or more comfortable to hold back, to play it safe, to coast, to settle for less from our clients. When we do that, we betray an unspoken trust. Those are the times when we as coaches need to find the courage to speak up, to insist or challenge or even demand, on behalf of our clients, that they live up to the capabilities we see in them. We need to be ready to call forth the best in people, and sometimes that means we start with ourselves.

COACHING SKILLS

Each of the following skills is designed to forward the action and deepen the learning. The skills range in effect from tame and collaborative to powerful and assertive; all are designed to help clients address the issues they face. The skillful coach will know when it is time to encourage the creative breadth of brainstorming and when it is time to light the dynamite of challenging.

Goal Setting

Without a specific goal, there can be endless drifting, a floating on the winds of this good idea and then that one. Goal setting gives clients a specific direction and an action plan for making something real. Naturally the goals may shift over time as clients progress with their agendas, but moving in the first place starts with setting their sights on a goal or outcome.

Goal setting falls into two main categories: first, goals to reach at a specific time in the future and, second, ongoing goals. A goal for a specific time in the future might be "six completed projects by December 31" or "one completed project each month for the next six months." An example of an ongoing goal would be "working on new projects three hours a day, Monday through Thursday."

Part of your role as coach will be to help clients create goals from their plans and intentions. Splitting the goal into manageable pieces is the first breakthrough for some clients. Whereas once all they could see was the continent they had to cross, afterward they see many short excursions.

Helping clients with the basics of goal setting can make a big difference in their success. The best goals are specific. They are measurable, or there is some way to track or monitor results. They are action oriented, even if the intention behind the action is qualitative. For example, the goal "think about moving to Alaska" will be strengthened by action. The client could buy a book about Alaska. Find a poster that features Alaska. Write in her journal about her memories of visiting Alaska. Talk to someone who lives there. And when there is a schedule involved, clients are much more likely to take action.

Goal setting may seem so fundamental and obvious to you as a coach that you may take it for granted. But even though it is fundamental, its importance and value should not be underestimated. As a coach, you need to have a clear understanding with clients about how you and they will handle goal setting, looking for the ways that work best for each client.

Sample Dialogue

Coaching provides a powerful structure for helping clients get into action, stay in action, and learn from their action. Sometimes the action they crave is inaction.

> **COACH:** *I got your e-mail. You took Wednesday afternoon off, just like you planned. That's great.*

> **Client:** *It was weird.*

> **COACH:** *The whole afternoon?*

> **Client:** *Yeah. I almost called in for my messages, but I didn't.*

> **COACH:** *What did you learn?*

> **Client:** *That the world doesn't collapse if I'm gone for four hours.*

> **COACH:** *Useful to know. What else?*

> **Client:** *That I hired competent people—people I can trust.*

COACH: *Anything else?*

Client: *Micromanaging good people annoys them. And it takes up time I could be using to move the company into new areas. I've got to let go of control in some areas. I also learned I need downtime to recuperate. I'll burn out like a flash fire if I keep this up.*

COACH: *So what's the next step?*

Client: *Raise the bar?*

COACH: *Right. Now that you've had a taste, what's the stretch?*

Client: *I actually know what it is. I want to start planning a vacation for July. Maybe even for two weeks.*

COACH: *Sort of takes your breath away, doesn't it? In order to make that happen, what will you do by next week?*

Client: *I'm planning to visit a travel agent in our building this afternoon to pick up brochures on Bali and British Columbia.*

Brainstorming

There are times when even good intentions and strong desire can be stalled by a simple shortage of ideas for action. Yes, of course, clients have the answers, as we have said, but sometimes it may be necessary to prime the pump. That's where the skill of brainstorming comes in. Brainstorming is a creative collaboration between client and coach with the sole purpose of generating ideas, possibilities, options. The client will sort through the pile of ideas that are generated and pick the ones that have the most appeal.

There are a couple of ground rules that will make brainstorming work effectively. The first is that there are no bad ideas. Don't worry too much about practicality at the brainstorming stage. In fact, as coach, part of your role is to suggest out-of-the-box ideas and outrageous possibilities. Clients tend to propose ideas they have had or minor variations on those ideas. You make the process more creative and fun by stretching the net of possibilities. The second ground rule is that coaches should not be attached to their own good ideas and, above all, should not use brainstorming as camouflage for pitching their own solutions.

Brainstorming is generative, so look for ways to build on ideas, not just take turns adding one more idea to the pile. This can often make a commonplace suggestion into a more creative or personal one for clients. For example, if your client suggests a half-day strategy meeting with key players, you might volley back with the idea of an off-site re-treat and strategy meeting.

Sample Dialogue

> **Client:** *I'm a little stuck here. I haven't been on an actual date in fifteen years. I'd like to find a way to meet people, but I don't even know where to start. What do people do?*
>
> **COACH:** *What would you like to do?*
>
> **Client:** *I don't know. Have you got any ideas?*
>
> **COACH:** *Want to do a little brainstorming?*
>
> **Client:** *Sure. I'm desperate.*
>
> **COACH:** *Okay. You go first.*
>
> **Client:** *I used to go to bars when I was in college. I don't think I want to do that anymore.*
>
> **COACH:** *So maybe you won't choose it—but it is an option. At this point, there are no bad ideas, just possibilities. Okay, the theme is social situations. What do you like to do for recreation? Skiing? Rollerblading?*
>
> **Client:** *Hiking. Day hikes. Almost anything in nature.*
>
> **COACH:** *Great. You could join a hiking club, or you could start one for singles. What's another option?*

Client: *One of those computer dating services, I suppose.*

COACH: *How about volunteer work? You place a high value on community service. What would be an area where you might volunteer your time?*

Client: *The school where my kids go. I would like to be more involved with them.*

COACH: *What other values would you like to tap into as you create opportunities to meet people? You mentioned nature . . . and we talked about community service . . .*

Client: *When you said "nature," it made me think of gardening. I'm sure there are ideas there.*

Requesting

Over and over, we've emphasized that this is the client's agenda, that the client is resourceful, that the client knows the answers. Still, it will be appropriate at times for you, the coach, to request certain actions. Based on your training, your experience, and your knowledge of your clients, you'll have a sense—usually based on actions clients are already considering—of what direction they might take for maximum learning. You simply put the action into the form of a request so that the action is clear and the client accountable.

For example: You and your client are working on family finances and ways of creating order. You might say to your client: "This week, my request is that you create a detailed monthly budget for personal and household expenses. Will you do that?" Note that the language of a request takes a somewhat specific form: there is the request itself stated in a way that is specific and measurable (the client can actually be accountable for something) and there is the question at the end that asks for commitment. This is more powerful than simply asking a client to work on finances this week. The language draws a line in the sand and puts the client on notice that this is important business. In time, using this format, clients learn that taking on a request is an act of personal commitment, not just acceptance of an assignment from their coach.

The key to making a successful request is to not be attached to it. The moment you become attached to the brilliance of your own idea and start thinking it's the right way for the client to get results, it's your agenda, not the client's. With a request, there are always three viable responses: yes, no, or a counteroffer. The client can agree to your request, turn down your request, or negotiate for something else. If your idea is turned down, feel free to defend it a little. You might explain why you think it works and the value it would have. Maybe the client didn't understand completely the first time. You might even probe to make sure that the no was not simply a fear reaction.

If the client turns down your request, look for the counteroffer. You might ask, "What will you do?" As far as you, the coach, are concerned, the whole point is some form of action or learning—and as long as that happens, it doesn't matter who comes up with the action plan.

Sample Dialogue

Client: *I suppose I'm like everyone else with a ten-year reunion. I'd love to lose about ten pounds.*

COACH: *How's your workout program going?*

Client: *I get to the club about once a week. I know it's not enough.*

COACH: *What kind of exercise do you enjoy the most?*

Client: *Swimming. I love the water.*

COACH: *Great. My request is that you swim a minimum of thirty minutes four times a week. Will you do that?*

Client: *You know what? I'd rather do forty minutes three times a week. That saves me one trip to the club, and it's the same amount of time.*

COACH: *How do you want to be accountable?*

Client: *I'll make it a weekly check-in statistic—right when we start.*

COACH: *Anything else you want to add?*

Client: *Go for a walk or bike ride with my wife or son on Sundays.*

Challenging

A challenge asks clients to extend themselves beyond their self-imposed limits—way out to the edge of improbability. If the challenge is powerful enough, it should cause clients to sit up straight and exclaim, "No way." If that's the response, you know you're in the right territory. Your idea of their potential is much bigger than the picture they hold of themselves. Clients often respond with a dual reaction: exasperation when confronted with the enormity of your challenge but also a sense of being emboldened because someone believes in them that much. Most clients will flatly turn down your challenge but then make a counteroffer—at a level higher than anything they would have considered on their own initiative.

As coach, you say to your client: "I challenge you to say no twenty times a day this week—make it thirty." Your client says: "No way. That's impossible. I'd be fired and divorced in a week. I'll do ten a day, but that's my limit." So instead of not being able to say no at work or at home, your client will be practicing this essential skill ten times a day. Such is the power of the challenge.

Sample Dialogue

Client: *It's like a dark cloud that's been hanging over me for the last six months!*

COACH: *The way you've talked about it, it feels like much more than a cloud. You've been in this dark mood for weeks. You said you felt listless and you're not eating well . . . all because of this manuscript you have to finish.*

Client: *Research paper. Actually the research is done. All I need to do is write it up.*

COACH: *When will you get it done?*

Client: *At this rate, I don't know.*

COACH: *How many hours will it take? What's your best estimate?*

Client: *Hard to say. Maybe thirty hours—a little more, a little less.*

COACH: *I have a challenge for you. My challenge is that you finish the paper before we talk next week.*

Client: *Next week? That's crazy!*

COACH: *Could you do it in a week?*

Client: *Well, yeah. If that's all I did.*

COACH: *What will you do?*

Client: *I'll work on a rough draft.*

COACH: *Excellent. What would it be like to be able to say "I'm finished" in a week's time?*

Client: *I don't even have the words for it.*

PUTTING STRUCTURES TO WORK

We know that accountability in the coaching relationship is a structure. It's a means by which we create focus and discipline. In fact, a structure is any device that reminds clients to be in action. Setting an alarm to wake up is a structure. Turning your wristwatch over or wearing it on the other arm is a structure that reminds you to do something. There are millions of structures, an endless variety of creative ways for sharpening focus and discipline. They appeal to different senses: tactile, auditory, visual. Putting fifteen minutes a day for meditation in your day planner is a structure. The physical act of writing it down plus the visual reminder in the calendar create a structure for this important activity in your life.

Here are some other examples of structures:

- Create a special screen saver with a theme line or visual image
- Post notes around the office or home with affirmations or reminders
- Track daily or weekly progress toward major goals on a wall chart
- Cut out pictures of a dream home or vacation destination
- Play a particular piece of music while completing a project—a special theme song
- Listen to a meditation tape
- Wear a particular piece of clothing—magic armor—when making sales calls
- Light a candle or burn incense
- Put a special reminder in your pocket, something like a small stone or toy
- Change the lighting in the room by making it brighter or dimmer, or changing the color
- Create deadlines, such as inviting people to your house for a party so that you will finish painting a room or do some housecleaning
- Establish creative consequences or rewards

Structures are a way of sustaining the action and learning in the time between coaching sessions. Each client will be somewhat more responsive in different sense areas. Experiment with structures to find out what works, and keep playing with them. The key word here is "play." The reason for the structure is to provide discipline and focus in an area where it may be difficult for clients to stay on track. By making structures playful, you increase the chances that clients will follow through.

1. Requesting

Complaints are often uncommunicated requests. In a restaurant, if you've got a complaint about the draft blowing down on you from the overhead air conditioner, you can sit with your complaint or you can make a request. When an appropriate request is made, action often happens, and that takes care of the complaint. So here's the exercise: Make a list of twenty-five complaints in your life—things that just aren't going your way. They don't have to be reasonable. If you have a complaint about the weather, write it down. Acts of God are not off limits for complaints or requests. When you have your list of twenty-five complaints, compose a request that addresses each complaint. Target your request to a specific person whenever possible, someone who has the power and the ability to do something about your request. Then, for as many as possible on your list, actually follow through and make the request. And remember, there are always three legitimate responses to your request: yes, no, or a counteroffer.

2. Challenging

Go back once again to the meta-view list of ten friends or colleagues you made in Chapter 3. Your goal in this exercise is to write a challenge for each person, addressing each one's meta-view in a way that dramatically raises the bar. You are trying for action steps that will move these people forward and provide extraordinary learning. Make sure you come up with true challenges—that ask them to go further than you know they will go—so that they end up making significant counteroffers.

3. Structures

Here is a simple and somewhat typical situation: Your client is much too busy to keep his office clean, yet the chaos that results is seriously distracting him. It has reached the point of no return. Something must be done. Your job is to come up with fifteen structures that will help this person stay in action to get his office orderly and organized.

7

Self-Management

This is the picture we continue to hold as the ideal: you and your client, 100 percent connected. You, as coach, listening intently at Level II, following, tracking. And listening at Level III, aware, sensing, open to your intuition as you let the conversation flow through you and around you. It's as if you and the client are in a bubble, a safe chamber that isolates the two of you from the distractions of the outside world. That's the ideal. But sometimes, in the midst of this intense, engaged conversation, the phone rings. Or a metaphorical bell goes off in your mind: a thought, a feeling. Suddenly, that protective zone evaporates. You disengage, detoured to that other thought or feeling. You are disconnected from your client.

It happens. In any given conversation with a client, it may happen many times. Something in what your client says triggers a distracting thought or reaction in you or reminds you of an experience in your own life, a strong memory. These are very human reactions that will cause you to go away in your mind and feelings, even if it is only temporary.

It could be a completely unrelated thought: You suddenly remember you have forgotten to make dinner reservations at the restaurant after promising you would handle it. The coaching itself might create a distraction, such as a moment of special brilliance or a feeling that you're handling the coaching badly and the judgment that goes with it. Or you may be distracted by something that happens in the environment: dogs barking, sirens sounding, a storm outside. It might be something only you notice—the window is open and the rain is coming in, soaking a pile of important papers.

Naturally, you want to create an environment and conditions that minimize the chances of these sorts of distractions, but they will happen from time to time. The context of self-management is a combination of self-awareness and the skill of recovery. It is an awareness of yourself, an ability to notice where you are or where you have gone in relationship with your client, and it is about the ability to get back, to reconnect.

BUMPED OFF COURSE

Clients are human—which is another way of saying they are somewhat unpredictable. One of the most common situations involving self-management is when a coaching session takes surprising twists and turns or the client's coaching focus changes direction from session to session. This ability to engage with clients wherever they are when they show up for coaching is so essential to being an effective co-active coach that we have made it one of the four cornerstones: the ability to dance in the moment.

The context of self-management also involves knowing the boundary between simply going wherever the client leads and holding a particular focus with the client. Asking yourself, *Are we still on track here with the bigger agenda?* may take you away from the conversation momentarily, as if an observer in you is watching the conversation unfold. And yet there are times when that moment of objective distance, of Level I attention, is important to the coaching.

It gets trickier when you, as the coach, are distracted by the content of the coaching or even the agenda itself. You may find yourself suddenly up to your ears in technical details or the client's work jargon, or the agenda may create a distraction. You may even have reservations about a plan of action your client wants to take. In fact, you may not always agree with your clients' plans, and yet the self-management course is to honor their action as theirs: theirs to work with, to change as necessary, to fail at completely or succeed at gloriously, and to learn from, always. For the sake of your own integrity, you may decide to share your reservations but with the caveat that you are offering your own experience and opinion, not advice or judgment.

Thoughtful awareness regarding the content and direction of the coaching is one aspect of self-management, but self-management includes a whole range of reactions. After all, coaches are human, too, and sometimes the conversation, a subject or just a word, sparks a reaction on the coach's part. Your clients may say something disparaging about welfare mothers or divorced men or an ethnic group, or they may use language you find unacceptable. It's bound to happen that, out of all the material clients bring to you, something will trigger your own pet peeves, or your personal standards will bump up against a client's comments. You could become judgmental, ungrounded, even opinionated. This is known as being "hooked," as if a very large hook had been inserted in you and yanked. There you are, lost in your own thoughts and opinions, at Level I, and no longer focused on your client.

It can happen when you least expect it. For example, you have a client who has been practicing the skill of saying no: no to working long overtime hours without being compensated, no to unhealthful snacks that deplete his energy, no to co-workers who take up valuable time with chitchat, no to a particularly toxic relationship. Progress on this commitment has been inconsistent, but lately he seems to be moving forward. In today's coaching session, it all comes apart: he has agreed to work overtime this weekend, he has binged every afternoon on snacks, and he's decided to give that relationship one more chance. You would like to be calm, compassionate, and patient, but you have seen this backsliding one time too many—you can also clearly see this client's ability and the price he pays for caving in. It makes you crazy that he can't see it for himself. You can feel the steam building under your collar, your heart beating faster. You've really had it with this crap!

Whoa! Even if this anger comes from the best possible intentions and your caring for this client, in this minute, the steam, the frustration, the temper are in danger of taking you away, breaking the connection between coach and client.

The opposite can also happen. Say you've been working with a client for three months and nothing of consequence has happened. She is no closer to her goals today than on the day you two started your coaching relationship. She keeps droning on, repeating the same reasons why she can't take action. You've tried every technique and trick you can think of, but it is like pushing water up a straw. Today your own self-judgment is having a field day with your inadequate coaching. You have failed; you are in over your head; you don't have the skills; you have done nothing in three months to help this deserving soul who is counting on you. Now you don't even have the courage to admit it and assist her in getting the help she needs and deserves from another coach or a therapist. Meanwhile, as you are having this self-flagellating internal conversation, your client is floundering, maybe wondering where you have gone.

The signals are there to see. When you find yourself trapped in self-analysis—defending, judging, feeling annoyed—the alarm bells should be going off. When you find that you are hooked or caught up in a personal emotional reaction, you are no longer with your client; you are with your own Level I reactions, thoughts, and feelings. You are trapped in a cage, racing inside that little exercise wheel, going nowhere. You need to find your way back to your client and reconnect.

FORBIDDEN TERRITORY

Self-management is also about where you stop your coaching. It would be wonderful if all great coaching could happen within the coach's comfort zone. But there are places coaches don't want to go, where they are unsure of themselves or are afraid of the consequences.

Maybe, in coaching, you sometimes hold back from telling the hard truth because you don't want to make waves or upset clients—especially if they become upset with you. Maybe you hold back because you don't want to lose a client or you're afraid of repercussions in the organization. Coaches may hold back because they don't want to risk offending, but what they risk instead is a less resourceful life for their clients. Is it possible that a client will get upset and leave? Yes, it's possible. That's a price the coach must be ready to pay in every session. Repeat: in every session. The risks we sometimes don't want to take are the same risks clients don't want to take. They're the very things that keep clients from reaching important goals and living full lives. These are often among the reasons that clients come to coaching.

Take a hard look at the areas in your own life where you are uncomfortable and have held back in the past. Chances are that these are the same areas you are unwilling to probe in the coaching sessions, regardless of whether or not they are risky areas for your clients. For you, they are blind spots, created out of defensive habit. They are probably invisible to you most of the time. Maybe one day you'll work through what holds you back in your life, but you can't wait for that to happen before you explore those places with your clients. Maybe loneliness is unbearable for you, so when a client raises the issue of loneliness, you quickly shift the coaching in a different direction and find something else to talk about. Because of the emotional charge the issue has for you, you don't do the kind of exploration that would benefit your client. Or maybe the issue is telling the truth even when you know it will disappoint someone, or awkwardness around money or intimacy. Delving into these areas may be crucial to your clients' action and learning. Self-management is about recognizing that these are uncomfortable issues for you but exploring them anyway for the sake of your clients. You must be willing to coach outside your comfort zone.

SELF-JUDGMENT AND GOOD JUDGMENT

It is probably safe to say that, as a group, coaches place a high value on learning and growth, their own as well as those of their clients and the other people in their lives. Consequently, coaches often have a highly developed habit of self-analysis, which can sometimes manifest as crippling, unwarranted self-judgment.

Self-management is about recognizing the self-judgment going on inside your brain and knowing the difference between constructive analysis and self-destructive chatter. The key for you as a coach is the same key you give your clients. First, notice. Make sure you record it well in your mind. What was the criticism or observation, precisely? Be clear, be descriptive, be attentive to the experience. Then ask yourself a couple of questions: *What is the truth in that for me? What's in that for me to learn?* Something happened in there that hooked you or caused a reaction, and it's worth paying attention to.

Before you take on the worst possible interpretation of the experience, allow yourself some room to reflect. Obviously this reflection is something you will undertake outside the coaching session, on your own, with a colleague, or with your own coach. It's important to recognize that these disruptive experiences are part of learning and growing stronger as a coach and a person. The more adept you become at recognizing and working with your own self-judgment, the more you'll be able to help clients work with theirs.

Self-management is also about knowing when you really are in over your head. When that realization strikes, be gentle with yourself. In such a situation, the most constructive thing you can do for the client—and for yourself, by the way—is to refer him or her to another coach or another resource for help. People don't want to feel that they've failed. But in some cases, the best course of action—and the most professional—is to end the relationship for the client's sake. This client may be better off with a career counselor or a therapist or a more detached coach. If the alliance won't work, you can't hold it together on your own. So if you truly feel you cannot work with a client, the two of you are best served by moving on.

PRACTICES

Let's be honest. Despite your best intentions to always be present, you will disconnect from your client sometimes. It can happen for lots of reasons—some significant, some trivial. You happen to glance at your desk and notice a bill that's overdue . . . somebody is knocking on the door . . . something your client just said reminded you of a very sad conversation in your past. One of the most powerful things you can do at that moment is to admit it: "I'm sorry, I just went blank for a moment. Would you repeat what you just said? I missed that."

Admitting that you disappeared actually creates trust. You may think you hide your vanishing act from clients, but they often sense your disappearance even if they don't articulate it. More than that, you model the veracity that builds a strong relationship between you and your clients. Clients respect your honesty about what happened—that you didn't try to cover it up—and see your admission as a way of saying that you are really committed to them, not to pretending.

In order to be present and ready, many coaches have a ritual they use before the start of the day or before each appointment. It is a structure for orienting themselves to the coaching—preparing for clients in physical, emotional, mental, even spiritual ways. This kind of preparation is especially important when your personal life is getting the best of you. You are a human being as well as a coach. Periodically, things will happen that can cause you to focus your attention on yourself rather than on the client. On the day you get stuck in traffic on your way back to the office and are rushing, harried and anxious about being on time, you need to clear your feelings before speaking with your client so that you can concentrate fully on the client and not on your troubles.

Apart from the everyday annoyances that may knock you off balance before a coaching call, there is also the punch in the solar plexus. Maybe you just received bad news about a friend: the biopsy is back, and the lump is cancer. Or you just walked out on a devastating argument with your partner over an issue that won't go away. Clearing and grounding allow you to be fully present in coaching without burying your own feelings. It's not easy. Sometimes it's not even possible, and you need to tell clients that you have to reschedule their appointments. Yes, you need to be strong for your clients. Gritting your teeth and persevering when the going is tough is admirable—but only up to a point. Self-management is about knowing where that point is.

OPINIONS AND ADVICE

The urge to give good advice and to be helpful is so strong that it is sometimes nearly unmanageable. This is another case in which self-management is a judgment call, not a rule to follow.

We emphasize that clients are naturally creative, resourceful, and whole and that they do have the answers or know how to find them. Still, at times it may seem pointless to withhold your knowledge or experience when it is clearly relevant and could spare clients time, money, and effort. As long as you are conscientious about framing the conversation as your experience and encouraging clients to find their own best way while exploring a number of alternative pathways, your experience will be seen as one more potential course of action and not the "expert's" way. In short, don't make it a rule that you will never share an opinion or a bit of advice. Self-management is a context of discretion, always in the client's best interests.

This discretion also extends to sharing your personal story. Most of the time, it's best to keep your personal story to yourself. As a coach, you have a different relationship with your clients than you would have if you were their friend. Your relationship in a coaching session is different even from those that clients have with co-workers, colleagues, or managers. The attention in the coaching session and the coach's attention are both directed to clients and their lives and agendas. In almost all cases, it is inappropriate and a waste of the client's time for you to share your personal story. We say "in almost all cases" quite intentionally, because there may be times when a little of your story will be important in building trust and relationship with a client. The fact that you are human, not just an anonymous, impersonal resource, will contribute toward building a strong, co-active relationship.

The key word there is "relationship." We believe that strong relationship creates trust, safety, and openness, and it is this deeper relationship that allows clients to take the bigger risks they need to take in order to make the boldest, life-giving choices. But as you can see, it leaves room for interpretation and discretion. Ultimately, in the co-active model, the decision hangs on what will be best for the client in the long run.

We have described the context of self-management here primarily from the point of view of the impact on the coach, but a coach's developed sense of self-management benefits clients, too. As the coach models the attributes of self-management, clients see the impact; they learn to become more aware of what is happening in the moment, noticing when they have disconnected. They learn to speak up about what is true even if it might be awkward, and they learn to recover, to reconnect to the relationship. This benefit ripples out beyond their coaching sessions and into their lives, creating stronger relationship.

COACHING SKILLS

A number of coaching skills are generally associated with self-management. These skills underscore the dynamics in the relationship and help coach and client maintain their individual strengths.

Recovery

Clearly, the most obvious skill for this context is the skill of recovery: the ability to notice the disruption or disconnection and to reconnect. For the coach, the disconnect could simply be a case of confusion—losing the thread of the client's conversation—or it could be a much stronger emotional reaction to the subject at hand or something the client said. There are three parts to the skill: noticing, naming, and reconnecting.

Notice It. This awareness step is crucial. It is not necessary to know exactly what happened and completely unnecessary to know why or what caused it—at least in the moment. It is important to simply notice the gap, the shift, the disconnect.

Name It. Describe what just happened: "I got lost," or "I was distracted for a minute." This is optional, but encouraged, especially as you begin practicing the skill. In most cases, it is best to name it out loud so that your client is clued in to where you are. It is amazing how quickly the coaching can get back on track simply by realigning with the client.

Reconnect. Each person will have a different tactic for connecting, and each situation may require a different process. Fundamentally, it is the process of turning your attention back over to your client. Find the part of your client you believe in, want more of, can easily celebrate. Connect with the part of your client you admire and want to see excel.

Asking Permission

One of the most important techniques the coach uses to remind clients that they are in charge of the coaching direction is to ask permission: "May we work with this issue?" "Can I tell you what I see?" "Would you like some feedback on that?" When the coach asks permission, it demonstrates that clients have power in the relationship. It demonstrates, too, that the coach knows the limits of his or her power in the relationship. Asking permission is a sign of self-management on the coach's part and allows clients to take responsibility for managing the relationship and their work. Clients are honored when you ask permission; their boundaries are respected. This is especially important when the issue you'd like to work on is unusually intimate or may make clients uncomfortable: "May I tell you what I see about the way you've been handling this?"

Sample Dialogue

Client: *I guess I realized that the plan we worked out just wasn't going to work. I had to improvise on the spot . . . tap dance my way through it. It was like old times, making it up as I went along.*

COACH: *First of all, there's nothing sacred about the plans we work out. You still get to choose the best course of action for you. I trust that you know what's right and that you'll move forward and learn from whatever you decide to do. So what did you decide?*

Client: *That's basically what I did. I took action. Just a different course of action.*

COACH: *But before we move on, I'd like your permission to give you some feedback on the action you took. Would that be okay?*

Client: *I have a feeling I may not like all of what I hear. But yes, of course. If there's a chance to learn something valuable, I'm all ears.*

Bottom-Lining

There are times when a client's telling of his or her story begins to expand and take over the coaching session. Or times when the client starts wandering tangentially through story after story. Sometimes it's the client's style of conversing; many times it's a way of unconsciously avoiding difficult or direct conversation. Bottom-lining is the skill of getting to the point and asking the client to get to the point, too.

It is helpful if you cover this skill during your early work with clients so they are not caught unawares the first time you ask them to get to the bottom line. It's not that the particular story isn't interesting; in fact, it may be fascinating. But the story is the background, and in the coaching relationship, the background is secondary. With the limited time available for most coaching sessions, there simply isn't time for long-winded, detailed stories. You need to coach the essence, and asking clients to get to the bottom line helps them discover the heart of the matter.

Bottom-lining is also an important skill for the coach. As coach, you should not be talking much. Your conversation should be bottom-lined. Clients do the talking.

Sample Dialogue

Client: *I know I'm starting to sound like a broken record on this, but there just wasn't time this week. Really, I'm not spinning a story here. I'm out of town one or two days a week . . . I'm still carrying the one evening class . . . I need to spend some time with my family . . .*

COACH: *So what's the bottom line here, Tom?*

Client: *I'm committed to my health. I just can't live up to the time commitment to make it happen.*

COACH: *What will you commit to about your health?*

Client: *I'm still committed to eating right and working out. I just don't see how I'm going to fit it all into my schedule—especially now . . .*

COACH: *Bottom line, Tom. What will you commit to?*

Client: *I'll commit to eliminating snacks between meals and three days of exercise every week.*

Championing

We discussed acknowledgment earlier. Acknowledgment means recognizing who clients had to be in order to do what they have done. To champion clients is somewhat similar, but here the focus is on supporting clients rather than identifying traits. You champion clients by standing up for them when they question their abilities. It is not empty cheerleading. As the coach, you champion what you know is true; clients will know if you aren't sincere. When you're not sincere, you not only destroy the effect of the championing but put your own credibility at risk. But when you point out your clients' abilities, their strengths, their resourcefulness and let them know you believe in them, you give them access to a little more of themselves.

Perhaps it is a capacity they didn't realize they had or strengths they don't give themselves credit for. You champion when the road is steep and the client is weary. That's when you recharge the client's enthusiasm: "You are so committed to this. I know you can do it." Or "You've shown over and over how you can be caring and firm. You can do it again." Or "You have the creative gifts—in abundance. You can do this." Championing is an affirmation. It is your capacity to see their capacity. It is a form of future looking. You see them at the finish line, the top of the hill, goals accomplished.

Sample Dialogue

Client: *It's a great opportunity, but it's also a huge risk. I could be a hero, and I could be the world's biggest goat.*

COACH: *To mess with the Olympic slogan, I say, "Go for the goat!" What will it take to be a gold medal winner?*

Client: *You've got to be kidding.*

COACH: *Maybe I'm kidding to take some of the pressure off. Mary, I know you can do this. It's a perfect match with your heart's desire and the path you laid out for yourself. You've got the skills to do it—and the panache to pull it off. Of course it's risky. That's where the adrenaline comes from, and that's why it feels like you're on the edge. I just know you can do this.*

Client: *I know you do. And it gives me confidence when I don't have any of my own.*

Clearing

Clearing is that valuable skill of venting in order to become present and open to the coaching. We already mentioned clearing for the coach, which prepares the coach to be present for clients. Clearing is valuable for clients, too, and for the same reasons we discussed for coaches. Clients call when they've just been fired, when a best friend has gotten into a serious traffic accident, when they just got off the phone about a bank overdraft, when they lost the big account to the hated competition. Or alternatively, they call when they have just gotten back from vacation and their minds are still fogged with piña coladas or the euphoria of newfound love.

When clients are preoccupied, it interferes with their ability to have useful, in-depth coaching conversations. Often, the need for clearing is obvious. The client is clearly disturbed, annoyed, upset, agitated about something, and the something is big and present. However, the signals that tell the coach clearing is called for may also be muted—you don't always hear huge alarms going off. The client may seem slightly miffed, or perhaps you sense a minor disturbance in the energy field. Initially, clients may not even want to discuss it. But when you notice that their normal creative expression is blocked or constrained, you may need to push for clearing.

In this example, your client is annoyed about some injustice; there's a mood about her that just hangs in the air like an unpleasant odor. You might say: "You seem really blocked. Let's take a couple of minutes to get this out. Really complain, whine, feel sorry for yourself. Exaggerate." The best thing you can do at this point is to help the client clear. In fact, it is important that the coach recognize the volume of clearing necessary. Clients often feel awkward about just venting and want to quit before they're completely clear. So you must really push until the last gasp of bad air is out. Make it a game and keep pressing for more: "Turn up the volume. What else happened? And then what? How did that feel? What a jerk! Tell me more."

Sample Dialogue

COACH: *You seem distracted—it's like we're having to work too hard to stay on track this morning.*

Client: *I am distracted. I lost $2,500 yesterday in a stupid stock deal. I feel like an idiot.*

COACH: *It sounds like you need to clear that before we can move on.*

Client: *I think you're right.*

COACH: *Take a minute. Ventilate.*

Client: *I feel like a chump. Worse than that, I convinced two of my friends that this was the sweetest deal in a century, and they both lost money, too.*

COACH: *Ouch. What else? Let's turn up the volume.*

Client: *Okay. I'm mad at myself for getting sucked into an "easy money" scheme. I'm ashamed about looking like an easy mark . . .*

COACH: *Go for it. What else?*

Client: *I'm afraid my wife's going to shoot me. I let her and the kids down. How am I going to come up with another $2,500 for vacation this summer?*

COACH: *You feel like you let your family down . . . What else?*

Client: *I should have seen this one coming.*

COACH: *So you've got a judgment—"should have seen this coming." What else?*

Client: *It's a pretty empty feeling.*

COACH: *Deep sadness and regret.*

Client: *Exactly.*

COACH: *What's next?*

Client: *I think I need to get past the sour feeling.*

COACH: *How will you do that?*

Client: *This clearing is a good start. I think working out tonight will help. I can sweat off some of the anger and sadness.*

COACH: *Is this the issue you want to be working on today?*

Client: *No, actually, thanks for asking. Maybe next time. I've got something more important for today.*

Reframing

Clients frequently get stuck with a certain way of looking at a situation or an experience. Their perspective, moreover, has a message that is in some way disabling. Your ability to reframe the experience provides a fresh perspective and a sense of renewed possibility. Let's say your client had his hopes set on landing a major consulting contract and just found out it has been put on hold for at least six months. Naturally, he is focused on the disappointment. As his coach, you point out that it gives him the time he has been seeking to write a series of articles that can help him land new business. Thus you are able to recast this experience in terms of his ultimate goals. Using much the same data, you interpret the experience in a way that includes more of the client's life: the big picture.

Reframing is looking on the bright side of things, true enough, but it is more than just being perky for the client. Reframing offers more than cliché comfort—as in "There are plenty of fish in the sea" or "Tomorrow's another day." Reframing takes real pieces of the client's life and shifts the perspective to show an opportunity or a pathway that wasn't apparent minutes before. For example, your client is struggling with credit card debt and tells you that it's hard to make progress, especially when major appliances keep breaking down and needing repair. You point out that she has managed to change her buying habits and has regularly paid down her outstanding balance for several months. The reframing doesn't change the fact that it is a struggle. But it does show the client that she is resourceful and committed—and making progress. Reframing changes the theme from "credit cards have control of my life" to "I have control of my life."

Sample Dialogue

In this case, the client starts with a certain perspective: He has wasted six weeks developing a business plan that dead-ended. Still, he learned a lot that will help with new business plans and made several good contacts. In short, there is plenty that is positive in this experience. And that's where the coach is headed: to reinforce the action and learning that accompanied this effort.

Client: *Absolutely a dead end. Nada. Six weeks shot to hell.*

COACH: *You followed a path that looked very promising six weeks ago. I remember you were pretty excited.*

Client: *I was excited.*

COACH: *What did you learn in those six weeks?*

Client: *I learned how to write a business plan. Not that it did me much good.*

COACH: *What else did you learn?*

Client: *I learned how to present my business to people outside my field.*

COACH: *Nontechnical people?*

Client: *Yeah. Bankers and venture capitalists.*

COACH: *What else did you learn?*

Client: *I guess I learned that this is something I can do—even though I don't enjoy it as much as I enjoy the engineering.*

COACH: *In that case, what's your assessment of the last six weeks?*

Client: *I wish I could have had the same learning in half the time. And now that I've got the presentation formatted, and practiced, I might as well keep giving it to investors until somebody sees the opportunity and gives me the money.*

COACH: *Great. What do you want to do about that this week?*

Making Distinctions

Reframing is one way of helping clients see a situation from a fresh perspective. Another way is to help them pull apart collapsed beliefs by making clear distinctions for special cases in which two facts have been tangled into one limiting often disempowering belief. The belief appears to be a fact of life, and it's not.

For example, let's say a client believes—because she's the mom and the wife—that she needs to be the one who manages the housecleaning. She's stuck and frustrated because she believes she is responsible and she can't seem to manage it all. The separate facts are that she is the wife and that there is housework to do. As her coach, you have the objectivity to see the distinction. Here's another example: A manager believes that because she wants to treat employees fairly, it means treating everyone the same. She has equated fairness with treating everyone the same, and the high performers in the department are not happy. They believe they've earned recognition and reward. It's time to help this manager make the distinction. You might ask a question like "How can you maintain fairness and still reward the high achievers?" These are classic examples of collapsed beliefs that need to be separated so that clients can become more resourceful about selecting options.

Sample Dialogue

> **Client:** *I plan every week. I use a planner. I take the time on Sunday night to plan my week. None of it helps. By Tuesday, my week is in a shambles.*
>
> **COACH:** *What happens when you try to stick to your plan?*
>
> **Client:** *People make requests. They've got urgent things they need from me—things I didn't necessarily have in my plan—so wham, it's all out of kilter.*
>
> **COACH:** *What happens if you say no?*

Client: *Not in this organization. It doesn't work that way. If you're going to succeed around here, you have to move fast, be flexible, respond to the fire that's burning. That's what they mean by "teamwork" in this company.*

COACH: *Sounds like you end up paying a pretty high price for that. It also sounds like you've got a couple of things tangled together. What if we try to separate them?*

Client: *Like what? I'm not following you.*

COACH: *You seem to be saying: "When people make requests of me, I need to abandon my plan."*

Client: *I'd say that's true in this organization.*

COACH: *So . . . would you be willing to play along with me here? I'd like to find an alternative point of view, just to give you some additional perspective.*

Client: *Sure.*

COACH: *Here are the two facts: people make requests, and you have a plan. In the past, you've said yes to the requests automatically. What would be another way to deal with requests?*

Client: *I could postpone saying yes by telling people I have to check my calendar first.*

COACH: *Good. What would be another way?*

Client: *I suppose I could learn to say no sometimes.*

1. Self-Management

Where are you likely to get hooked in the midst of a coaching conversation? Where are you most likely to need self-management? List ten things your client might say that would pull you to Level I. For example: "I don't think you're listening to me." Next, list ten things you can do to return to the coaching conversation and stay detached.

Get to know your coaching self-judgments. Where do you automatically find fault with your coaching? The more aware you are of these judgments, the less likely you are to be hooked by them in the middle of a coaching call.

What topics are most uncomfortable for you? Which topics make you feel inadequate, inexperienced, or simply uncomfortable?

2. Championing

Pull out that list of ten friends or colleagues one more time. Call, write, or e-mail them as their champion. Let them know they can do the things they need to do. Be specific.

3. Clearing

Train a friend or a colleague in the skill of clearing so that he or she can clear you. Your partner's job is to encourage you to go deeper, to turn up the volume until you reach the bottom of whatever it is you are trying to clear. This person doesn't need to understand what's going on with you; the point is to prompt you to vent, like cheering an athlete to the finish line.

Then select an area of your life where you need clearing and process the clearing exercise with your partner. When it is over, talk with that person or make notes about what happened as you became clear. What happened to the "charge" when you allowed yourself to express it completely?

Co-Active Coaching Principles and Practices   **III**

The practice of coaching, as we have said, focuses on the client's agenda. In the co-active coaching model, we would say that at the foundation of all coaching is an agenda that reflects the client's desire for fulfillment, balance, and process—what we call the three core principles. In this section of the book, we describe each core principle, describe the practices associated with coaching those principles, and provide exercises and examples for coaches. Part Three concludes with an integrated overview of coaching practices and a vision of the contributions coaching can make to the lives of the people it touches.

8

Client Fulfillment

Think about your own life for a moment. What is your vision of a really fulfilling life? What would that be like? Whatever answer comes to mind, notice that the question takes you deeper than simply asking, "What do you want?" This greater depth is the reason that fulfillment is one of the three core principles in co-active coaching.

Let's be honest. Most people don't come to coaching with the desire for a more fulfilling life—at least not in those words. Usually, they have something much more specific and urgent at the forefront of their minds. And yet, underneath that agenda is a deeper yearning for something even more valuable. A fulfilling life is a life of meaning, purpose, satisfaction. We believe that this yearning is like the keel of a boat in the lives of your clients; it is the shape of their lives beneath the surface that keeps them on course. Without that keel, a boat will drift and shift directions on the vagaries of the wind. One of the most valuable things we do for clients is to help them get clear about that very personal shape of fulfillment. With that in place, they can take their lives in any direction they choose. And the tools of fulfillment coaching help clients find that shape.

It sounds simple enough. But in our experience, it takes tremendous courage and commitment on the part of the client to really choose and keep choosing a course of fulfillment. The world we live in is designed to squeeze people into boxes—often very comfortable boxes, but boxes nonetheless. Choosing to create a truly fulfilling life is almost certain to upset the status quo and create ripples in the pond. That's the nature of setting fulfilling goals and getting into action. It's important for coaches to understand the scale and impact of fulfillment as they begin their work with clients.

THE HUNGER FOR FULFILLMENT

Part of the difficulty in finding a fulfilling life starts with where clients are looking. They are looking for ways to *have* a fulfilling life. So they look at what they have . . . and what they don't have . . . and see a gap . . . and then look for things to fill the gap. Clients often come to coaching in search of something they need to have in their lives. That "something" can be the obvious: a higher-paying job, a vacation home, a successful business. The search can also focus on getting things that are less tangible: a wonderful marriage or a promotion. Unfortunately, *having* things is momentary, and the satisfaction is fleeting. You know that from your own life. Think of something you really wanted to have. Think about the moment of ecstasy when you acquired it and how quickly the glow began to fade: six months after the new car, or the new promotion, or the new relationship. As long as we continue to look for ways to have a fulfilling life, we are likely to be temporarily filled and constantly hungry.

To Be Fulfilled

Co-active coaching creates a different frame for fulfillment. It asks clients to look at what it would take to be fulfilled. And not just "some day in the future" when the goal is reached, but today, because fulfillment is available every day of our lives. That is the stand we take with co-active coaching. Of course, envisioning a future that is even more fulfilling is by itself a fulfilling exercise. Working toward goals that make the vision real is also fulfilling. The point is that fulfillment is an exercise of choice and not something that will happen someday.

Part of the confusion about fulfillment is in the language. We know what it means to be "full" and think fulfillment is a state we will eventually reach: filled, capped off, finished. Instead, fulfillment is a paradox in that we can be filled today and filled again tomorrow, maybe even in a different way, and then be filled again the next day and the day after that. It is disillusioning to try to capture fulfillment. "Having" fulfillment is like trying to bottle daylight.

This doesn't mean that your clients will stop wanting to have things in their lives. Clients will still want to have things: a successful business, more money, romantic relationships. But these things are the expressions of their fulfillment. They are not fulfillment itself.

Feeling Good Is Not a Sign

This is an important distinction. We often confuse being fulfilled with feeling good. The two conditions may coexist, but that is not necessary. In a state of fulfillment, there's often a sense of effortlessness—of harmony and congruence with the great laws of the universe. But fulfillment can also exist when life is difficult, challenging, or uncomfortable. Some people will say that the times when they felt most fulfilled were times when they had the least, when life was a struggle. They were doing what was important to them—things that claimed their passion and commitment. There, in the midst of scarcity, life was abundant. Perhaps the simplicity of the time gave them a clearer picture of what was truly valuable and fulfilling for them, but their sense of fulfillment was not about feeling good or being happy all the time. Living a life of purpose, mission, or service can be intense, sometimes heartbreaking and exhausting, and at the same time enormously fulfilling. The paradox of fulfillment is that it is possible both to have a sense of inner peace and to experience an outer struggle at the same time.

To Be Alive

In fact, describing fulfillment may be as simple as this: Fulfillment is about being fully alive. Fulfillment is the state of fully expressing who we are and doing what is right for us. Clients have a sense of that feeling. They describe it as wholeness, satisfaction, a sense of rightness and harmony. A word we use for this feeling is "resonance." Life is vibrating at a frequency at which everything we most value is in alignment. We feel it in the choices we make. The vibration in the moment may be very dramatic, thunderous, exciting, edgy. Or it may be still, serene, pastel, intimate. It might be a unique combination of all of those qualities—defying physics and our metaphors. But the client will feel the resonance. The pieces of their lives or careers come together in a very personal sense of wholeness and of feeling very alive. It may be experienced through doing meaningful work, feeling well used, contributing, giving and receiving, playing to win, being in the flow, creative, expressed. It is an experience of being complete.

Big "A," Little "a"

We are referring here to the first letter in the word "agenda." In co-active coaching, we see an agenda that is always on the table even if it is not always articulated. This is the Big-"A" agenda, and it is at the heart of the coaching: it is the client's full, resonant life. This is a life that is lived from the client's values. It is in dynamic action, balancing the client's priorities in life, and it is lived fully in each moment. Clients are completely in the process of living. There is an underlying question that coach and client are always tuned to, even if it is not always stated: What do you want your life to be? In this question, the emphasis is on the being state.

There is also an ongoing conversation about action and the doing of life; otherwise, coaching would be nothing more than very interesting conversation. Action is where clients make that fulfilling life real. This is the little-"a" agenda. Not little by comparison or less important, and certainly not to be minimized. This is simply a convenient way to talk about both aspects of fulfillment. Both are essential. The little-"a" agenda consists of goals, action, and accountability. With each coaching session, there is an issue to work on, plans to make, goals to define, and accountability to create action and learning. In fulfillment coaching, we look for the client's Big-"A" agenda with questions such as *What is your vision? Who are you becoming? What is present when life is most alive for you?*

In this model, the little-"a" agenda leads to fulfilling the Big-"A" agenda. That is crucial. Part of the coach's job is to hold this meta-view for clients, probing to make sure that the action being contemplated is aligned with the client's resonant, fully alive life—and not motivated by circumstances, fear, or a corrupted sense of duty.

FULFILLMENT AND VALUES

Imagine you could do what brings you the greatest joy or deepest satisfaction: be with the people you love, use your natural talents, exploit your gifts to their fullest. That would indeed be fulfilling. It is a picture of a person living according to what he or she values most.

The link between values and fulfillment is so obvious that it may be overlooked. Helping clients discover and clarify their values is a way to create a map that will guide them along the decision paths of their lives. When you clarify values with your clients, you learn more about what makes them tick: what's important and what's not. Clients discover what is truly essential to them in their lives. This helps them take a stand and make choices based on what is fulfilling to them.

Honoring our values is inherently fulfilling even when it is hard. If authenticity is a very high value for your clients, they may find there are times when they must suffer discomfort in order to live according to that value. The discomfort will pass, and a sense of integrity or congruency with their values will remain. When that value is not honored, however, the client feels internal tension or dissonance. Because human beings are flexible and resilient, it is possible to absorb a tremendous amount of discord and keep going, but there is a very high price to pay—a sense of selling out on oneself—and the result is a life of toleration or betrayal rather than fulfillment.

Values, Not Morals or Principles

Values are not morals. There is no sense of morally right or wrong behavior here. Values are not about moral character or ethical behavior, though living in a highly ethical way may be a value. Values are not principles either, like self-government or standards of behavior. Values are the qualities of a life lived fully from the inside out. There is nothing inherently virtuous in your client's values. What is to be admired is not the value itself but your client's ability to live that value fully in his or her life. When we honor our values, we feel an internal "rightness." It's as if each value produces its own special tone. When we live our values, the various tones create a unique harmony. When we are not living our values, there is dissonance. The discord can get so extreme, so jarring, that it can become literally unhealthy.

Because our language is imprecise, it's often easier to cluster values than to try to invest all the meaning in a single word. Thus, we might separate a series of value attributes with slash marks to indicate a grouping of value words that communicates a composite sense. For example, freedom/risk taking/adventure is different from freedom/independence/choice. In practice, the words are not as important as the client's ability to feel the impact of that value. All of these values or value clusters will be unique to each person. Just as our physical features give us our unique appearance, the articulation, prioritization, and clarity of our values determine our individual identity. It's not even important that you, as coach, understand exactly what clients mean by the words they choose. It is enough that clients are clear about what the words represent, so when they find they're off track, the wording of their values can help set them back on course. In fact, the client's own unique metaphor or expression very often is better than the common vocabulary at capturing the sense of the value. Clients may have values like these:

- Coyote/wild dancer/mischief maker
- Luminous/chenille/lavender
- Standing ovation/going for it/buzzer beater

Values are intangible. They are not something we do or have. Money, for example, is not a value, although money as a resource could lead to honoring values such as fun, creativity, achievement, peace of mind, service to others. Travel is not a value. Gardening is not a value. But both are examples of cherished activities that honor certain values, including adventure, learning, nature, spirituality. And yet, although values are intangible, they are not invisible to others. You can walk into a room of strangers and get a sense of what people value by what they wear, how they stand in the room, how and with whom they interact, and the topics of their conversations. You can sense the values in the room: power, friendship, intimacy, connection, independence, fun, and more.

As coach, you will be able to help clients clarify their values as you hear about their lives, their action, the things they choose and don't choose. You will see them when they honor their values and when they don't, and you and your client will learn something either way. This is one of the reasons why you will return to the values clarification process from time to time.

The Value of Values Clarification

The most effective way to clarify values is to extract them from the client's life experience. Ask clients to describe the values they see in their own lives, perhaps clustered together, using their own words. Almost any life situation can be used to mine for values, but those that have a strong impact, either positive or negative, are especially productive. This way, values rise naturally out of the client's life instead of being selected off a checklist. When clients are presented with a list, they are often tempted to go shopping for values: "This would be nice to have . . . people would admire this." Because people tend to judge their values, they often list values they think they should have, like spirituality or integrity, and exclude the ones that society says are not so admirable, such as personal power and recognition.

Values are either present in or absent from the choices clients make every day, which means that any given daily activity can be linked to a value honored or a value betrayed. As coach, you might ask: "Where is this value showing up?" "What values do you sometimes neglect?" "Which are the values you will not compromise?" Once you have worked with a client to develop a personal list of values, another fruitful exercise asks the client to prioritize the values, ranking the top ten from the most important on down. The outcome of the exercise, a prioritized list, is not as important as the process itself. Clearly, the client is free to change the order of items on that list anytime. The prioritizing exercise forces clients to see and feel each value and, by putting the values in order, to feel the importance of each one. Some coaches set the stage by making it a kind of game: "If you can take only ten values with you into a strange and possibly dangerous territory, which are the ones you absolutely must have?" So it's not about which value is most important. It's about what clients learn about their values by having to give up something they care about.

The next step is to ask clients how they are honoring these values on a scale of 1 to 10, with 1 meaning the value is not at all present in their lives, and 10 meaning it is honored completely all the time. There are almost certain to be values that are ranked at 4, 5, or 6 in some important aspect of the client's life—most likely a place where there is upset, anger, or resentment because the important value is getting squashed. It's a great opportunity for coaching: "What's that about?" "What would it take to live that value in those circumstances?" "What is the price you pay for not honoring that value?" "What's stopping you?"

COACHING FULFILLMENT

As you can see, fulfillment is intensely personal; it is also constantly evolving. What was fulfilling at age twenty-five may have lost its fascination by thirty-five; the empire-building passion of thirty-five may give way to a search for inner peace by forty-five. It is important to help the client develop a clear picture of a fulfilling life as it is today. To that end, there are a number of practical ways to help people clarify their

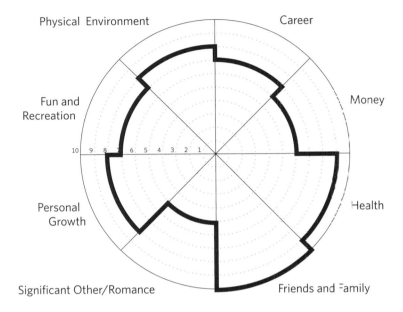

Physical Environment · Career · Money · Health · Friends and Family · Significant Other/Romance · Personal Growth · Fun and Recreation

10 9 8 7 6 5 4 3 2 1

FIGURE 4 **Wheel of Life: Fulfillment**

personal definitions of fulfillment, and you can continue to use these tools in an ongoing relationship to refine that vision. (For more information about specific tools, see the Coach's Toolkit.)

Level of Satisfaction

For a big-picture snapshot of where the client is in terms of fulfillment on any given day, the Wheel of Life (see Figure 4) is a very effective device. As you and the client look at each area in the wheel, discuss the state of the client's fulfillment, on a scale of 1 to 10. Ask how fulfilled he or she is in the area of money, or relationships, or health and wellness, for example. Or what a fulfilled life would be like in the area of career. Notice that you are not asking what the client needs to have in order to be fulfilled in his or her career. The question is "What would it take to be fulfilled?" Then keep probing in that direction. Whatever comes up, follow it with: "What else?" or "Tell me more." The idea is to uncover deeper and deeper levels of meaning and, from time to time, to clarify what you hear and play it back to your clients so they can hear what they're saying. For example: "I heard you say you'd like a sense of security when it comes to money—a sense that there will be enough in an emergency. It sounds like security might be a value. Is that right?"

Using the Wheel of Life, clients will see for themselves the parts of their lives where they are unfulfilled. With your help, clients will go through a process that allows them to define what fulfillment means to them. For example: "In health and wellness, you say your sense of fulfillment is 6. What would it take to raise that 6 to 10? What will you do to make it fulfilling?"

Values and Decision Making

In coaching, values help determine the "rightness" of choices. They also illuminate unfortunate choices. Clients can look back over decisions they've made and see where their values were honored or were ignored. For you as coach, knowing the client's values is a tremendous advantage. You can quickly see how certain courses of action will be blessed with a sense of flow and ease because the activities are congruent with the client's values. By knowing when the client's values are not being honored, you can also see the potential iceberg in front of the *Titanic*.

A values conversation can be very useful at any decision point. As clients choose various action steps, their values become a litmus test for action: "Will this action move you closer to honoring your values or further away?" "If you make this decision, what values will you be living?" When the client is considering an important life decision, ask how this course of action will honor the top ten values and to what extent. A decision based on the client's top values will always be a more fulfilling decision. It may not be the easiest or the most enjoyable. It may require sacrifice and even have uncomfortable consequences. But on balance, over time, it will be the most fulfilling.

We have seen the opposite too often. Again and again, clients have made decisions based on their bank balance, or their fear of creating discomfort, or their worry about others' displeasure. They decide based on what is easiest at the moment or will make the least waves. Such decisions never work out for the clients' fulfillment because they have sold out on themselves and their values. (See the Coach's Toolkit for more on values clarification.)

Fulfillment and Future Self

It can be daunting, standing at the foot of the mountain with your whole life in front of you. But if you could get a glimpse of the future— a sense of where you would be, say, twenty years from now—it might make you more confident about the future and even give you some information about how to get there. Short of providing a time machine, the only way to do that is to have clients create an image of their future selves and use this future self as a personal mentor and guide.

This future self is the one who no longer cares about the opinions or judgments of others. The future self—it could be called a "higher self"—totally knows his or her own strengths, the obstacles in the road ahead, the heart of the decision. Even when clients think they don't have the answers, almost inevitably their future selves do. The future self can look back with detachment and compassion and let the client know what the right decision is. The future self represents a powerful image of a life of fulfillment and accomplishment. Although it's composed of what the client knows today, it is created without today's restraints. Since it is created out of the client's imagination, it is not limited to what is considered realistic in the client's version of the world.

Clients may access their future selves in a variety of ways. The coach may invoke a client's future self whenever the coaching focuses on questions of fulfillment, especially when the client is unsure about the path ahead or feels locked into a path that is unfulfilling. One way to experiment with possibilities is to have the client imagine how a future self might solve the problem or work through the situation. (You'll find an effective visualization exercise in the Coach's Toolkit.)

Fulfillment and Life Purpose

A life purpose statement is another way of capturing the essence of what it means to be fully alive—living life intentionally, making choices that increase the value of life to one's self and to others. There are many ways to elicit the client's life purpose, and there is more than one way to describe this definition of what our lives are about. Some call it a "mission statement" or a "vision statement." It gets to the heart of what a person's true life legacy will be—the difference this life will make for the planet. It answers these questions: *What will I leave behind? What difference will I make in the lives of those I touch?* The life purpose is a path, not a destination. And along the way, clients will encounter plenty of voices, internal and external, telling them to go in other directions. Sometimes they will listen, especially when they are unsure of their purpose. Finding and claiming a life purpose gives clients a powerful sense of direction for their lives. The truth they find in the life purpose statement can make them virtually unstoppable.

Defining one's life purpose is a process that usually takes time. It can involve personal reflection, reading, keeping a journal, or interviewing others. Finding the one statement that rings true requires peeling back the layers until the client reaches the statement that addresses the central questions of his or her life: *What is the hunger I am here to feed? Where is the pain I can ease? What is the teaching I am called to do? Where is the building I have the tools to accomplish?*

Life purpose is about clients using their talents as well as the unique learning of their lives, their experience, and their wisdom. A fulfilled life is one they are able to live with purpose—intentionally, not by accident. (A number of exercises in the Coach's Toolkit are designed to help clients clarify a life purpose statement.)

The life purpose statement has value in coaching because it focuses attention on a fully alive, fully expressed, fulfilling life. The coaching that goes into creating the life purpose statement is rich with self-discovery, value clarification, and vision. Clients are challenged to use all the talents they have been given. It is also a fruitful place for acknowledgment when clients make the sometimes difficult decision to follow their purpose instead of taking the easier way. Living a life of purpose, a life based on one's values, is a rare accomplishment indeed.

Dissonance

When you are honoring your values regularly and consistently, you might say you have a formula for living happily ever after. In that case, why don't we honor our values all the time? There are a hundred variations on the answer to that very good question. A common theme is that our fear is stronger than our desire for fulfillment. That fear, which leads to self-sabotage, comes in a variety of guises.

If a client is not making choices based on his or her values, then the effect will be some form of dissonance. It can be frustration, boredom, indifference, anger, resignation, or persistent justification for a course of action that looks very much like self-betrayal or martyrdom. As a coach, you will be able to sense it in the air. It may have the acrid smell of fear, or it may be masked in the fragrance of flowery rationalizations. As you use your Level III awareness to listen between the words, you will feel the dissonance. It may be a disturbance in the force—something is not quite right.

Clients may believe that this voice is trying to protect them from danger, loss of relationship, a catastrophe of some kind. The voice is there to keep clients from taking unsafe risks, but it is often overcautious at a time that calls for risks, for the sake of change and a more fulfilling life. This is the voice of an internal saboteur. The same voice may recite an old litany of judgment, rules, and limiting beliefs. It says things like "You aren't working hard enough," "You should be further along in your career," "You don't do well on tests"—you're not smart enough, attractive enough, wealthy enough, experienced enough, old enough . . . you're not enough. Or it could be the opposite: You're too old, bald, frumpy, young, aggressive, introverted, extroverted . . . you're too much.

Most of the time, this voice operates quietly in the background, influencing choices and lobbying for its preferred course of action or inaction. Be aware that whenever people take the initiative to change their lives, an alarm sounds and the Saboteur will awaken. Expect it. You can even forewarn your clients. Throughout the book, we give suggestions for working with this self-sabotaging voice.

A clear example of this sabotaging voice is presented in the first coaching sample on the CD. Listen especially for the tone that is created and how that tone shifts when the coach moves to metaphor and values.

FULFILLMENT AND THE COACH'S ROLE

Fulfillment sounds so good—like a really great meal—satisfying, tasty, and ultimately filling. And yet the path to fulfillment can be difficult, unfamiliar, and scary for clients. Choosing to live our lives based on our values is not what society has taught us to do. It is not the easy, well-trodden way. Most of us settle for what we can have. We make choices based on what others want, what would be easiest, what would cause the least discomfort. We tolerate. We compromise. We give up. It's no easy task to get on the track for fulfillment, or to stay on track after that path has been chosen. This is why we emphasize that choosing a fulfilling life is a radical act.

The coach's role is to challenge clients to pursue their fulfillment, in spite of the circumstances, in spite of the voices all around them offering bad advice and contrary agendas, and in spite of the client's own inner Saboteur. Even when clients don't want to go there, your job as coach is to be out front, encouraging, pointing the way to a life fully lived, a life that is valued and without regret. If you falter or forget, remember that this Big-"A" agenda is, at the core, the most life-giving choice clients can make. Whatever results clients achieve on their goals and plans, this is the true satisfaction for them and the coaches who serve them: that at the end of the day, there is more life in each day.

9

Client
Balance

In the co-active model, balance is one of the three core principles because it is fundamental to the quality of life. At least, if you ask clients, that's what they say. Over and over again, clients tell us that they want more balance in their lives. This issue of balance exists on two levels: the underlying quality of life and the day-to-day experience.

In the big picture, fulfillment is about living a life that is valued and alive, and balance is about living a life that is in action and flowing. When it comes to balance, what clients want is the ability to juggle the precious priorities of their lives so that the mix and movement are satisfying. They want less struggle, more ease of motion. They want more tools to manage their activities and relationships so that these relationships and activities line up and move forward more harmoniously, and the elements of their lives are more in tune. Clients want to be more empowered and less at the mercy of circumstances and other people's expectations and demands. They don't necessarily want all the pieces of their lives to have the same weight or even to stay the same over time. Balance is not about evening out everything.

Balance also should not be confused with reaching some ultimate equilibrium. There is no static point in life; life is inherently dynamic. We are constantly balancing. Balance is not about slowing down, although slowing down may be just the recipe some days. Balance is not about simplifying, although sorting out the pieces, saying yes to some things and no to others, may be the ideal way to create the most fulfilling flow. In short, what most clients want is, not to go faster or slower or to have less or more, but to have a smoother ride supported on the rails of a fulfilling life vision. How they get that smoother ride is the objective of balance coaching. Note that some clients *want* the exhilaration of a bumpy ride, at least from time to time, and balance coaching can help them make that choice, too.

DAY TO DAY

That said, clients are not likely to come to coaching with "a more balanced life" at the top of their list. That's not where their attention is. They're focused on the issues that are hitting them on the chin that day or that week: the boring job, the stalled project, the dreaded family reunion, the credit card debt, the new relationship. They have their attention on the action of their lives, especially in those areas where they are not getting the results they want. After all, that's why they are working with a coach—so they can get the desired results.

They may see themselves as blocked, at a crossroads or a dead end, even out of options. They are often resigned, defeated. They may feel powerless, lost, or trapped in a repeating cycle. To you, as coach, the emotions are palpable. You may be tempted to break the problems down into bite-size bits and brainstorm solutions, anything to get rid of the strong feelings. Instead, balance coaching starts with the way clients look at the situation—the need for different action is not the starting point. The client's point of view is often the main contributing factor to the blocked, stuck, or stalled feeling.

Balance coaching is designed to restore flow, to get clients into action on today's issues in a way that brings them back into alignment and back in control of their own lives. Balance coaching begins by looking at the boxes in which clients find themselves, because the limitations of those boxes are impeding their progress. In doing so, clients restore flow to those immediate areas and, in the process, learn important lessons about creating more flow in their lives. They learn to be more adept at seeing the boxes that hold them in, and the experience of breaking out of those boxes serves them in other areas. This is how balance coaching works with the Big-"A" agenda. Being more fully alive means having the power to choose; balance coaching helps clients make life-giving choices.

CIRCUMSTANCES VS. POSSIBILITIES

There are always reasons why clients are not getting the results they want. Just listen and they will tell you. The reasons almost always sound realistic and convincing. Then begin listening underneath, and you will hear a particular tone or flavor that accompanies the reasons and rationalizations. You will hear about difficult situations and uncontrollable circumstances. You will hear about rigid timelines and expectations, people who are inflexible or unwilling. It may or may not sound like complaining, and it might sound quite normal and understandable.

In fulfillment, you tune your ear to hear the aliveness of values being lived, honored, and celebrated, but you could hear the opposite: deadness, anger, crankiness. In balance, you will hear a life in flow filled with possibilities and alternative courses of action, freedom, and creativity, or you will hear the harshness of unchangeable circumstances and unyielding boxes. We write these distinctions between fulfillment and balance as if they were sharply different colors on a color wheel, yet we don't mean to imply that the distinctions will be so clear in a coaching session. It should be pretty clear whether you are picking up red or blue, yellow or green, but the shades of emotion may not obviously communicate fulfillment or balance. As you will see, knowing for sure is not crucial to the coaching. By moving in one direction, you will uncover more, get more feedback from the client, dance with it, and then continue in the same direction or switch to another. In balance, we listen for the hard edge of unavoidable circumstances and a boxed-in perspective on the issues.

A FORMULA FOR BALANCE COACHING

The formula for moving from stuck to possibility and from possibility to action has five steps: (1) perspectives, (2) choice, (3) planning, (4) commitment, and (5) action.

Step 1: Perspectives

The first step in balance coaching is to identify the client's perspective and then expand the perspectives that are available. It is much harder work to get clients into action from a stalled or dead-end perspective compared to a perspective that has zoom and flow in it.

As humans, we tend to limit what is possible by what we believe is true, and if a client sees a situation as hopeless, it will be very difficult to create the conditions for change. After all, the client has already been gathering evidence that confirms this view and can tell you with complete authority that the situation really is a dead end. The perspective may be firm, and is often well developed, but it is a box. Clients are likely to reveal a habitual way of thinking about certain situations. They tend to apply the same rigid thinking to specific situations, layer by layer until, over time, these ways of thinking appear to be true, immutable, obvious. Case closed.

When we take a perspective on an issue, we have an opinion, a belief, assumptions and expectations. We make predictions based on the assumptions that belong to that perspective. We believe we can predict the outcome because "that's how things always go" or "that's just the way it is." A perspective is a very powerful filter that allows us to see only certain things. If something is not part of the perspective, it is invalid or simply invisible or may be dismissed out of hand. Stereotypes are perspectives of a sort, a habitual way of looking at people that limits possibility: everyone in a particular box is the same, and the expectations and assumptions fit all of the people in that box.

The client's perspective excludes the possibility of flow, yet it is only one way of looking at the situation. That's why balance coaching starts with seeing the limiting perspective and then naming it. Once we can name it, we can work with clients to develop alternative perspectives that are more resourceful and creative and will provide more action possibilities.

You can generate more perspectives by simply asking clients: "What is another way of looking at this that would work for you?" You can also brainstorm metaphors or images that provide creative material for additional perspectives. For example: "How would a five-year-old see this?" or "What is the 'good news' perspective?" Or choose one of the client's values or a future self: "How would this look to your future self of ten years from now?"

Geography. Imagine placing an object in the middle of a room—a sculpture of some kind, for instance. Now imagine walking around that object, looking at it from a variety of angles. Each perspective would give you a little more information about the object. Working with perspectives has that effect. But it is much more than just a visual difference as we shift from perspective to perspective. What we discover is that each perspective is a world of its own, with a different landscape, a different climate, and different rules for expected behavior. What might be normal in one perspective/world is not normal in another. When we explore the conditions within a perspective with clients, we are looking at the geography of that world. There is a native language in that perspective. There will be cultural rules and well-formed roles. There will also be a posture to that perspective, sometimes quite literally, because people embody the perspective they are in and portray it physically, in their bodies.

Consider this perspective: "A walk in the woods is a glorious embrace of the natural world." There is a tone in the language. You can practically smell the fragrance and hear the natural sounds of that perspective. And if you allowed your body to represent that perspective, your posture would incorporate its inherent attitude and beliefs. Now notice how dramatically all of that changes with a different perspective. Consider this: "A walk in the woods is a dangerous, messy, bug-ridden, slimy waste of time." See how the tone changes. Body posture changes to reflect the different inherent beliefs and expectations. Even the smell is different.

These are simply two perspectives on a walk in the woods. Neither is right or wrong, although those who are advocating for one or the other have no doubt been very busy collecting evidence to support their point of view and are prepared to insist very persuasively that their perspective is the right one, the one that is true.

The Topic Is . . . The example of a walk in the woods also points up the importance of having a clear topic with the perspective. You need a specific, identifiable topic for consideration, like the sculpture you imagined placing in the middle of a room. The topic could be a situation, a decision that must be made, an event, or a category of events. It could be a contemplated action or an opportunity. It could be a relationship with another person or a relationship between the client and something specific such as a debt, cancer, or technology. Note that it is easier to work with perspectives when the topic is more specific, even if it is a relationship. The topic itself is neither positive nor negative. The client's reaction to the topic reveals a perspective. And it is the perspective that brings emotion or judgment.

Step 2: Choice

Playing with perspectives involves exploring the rich territory in each land of the geographic map. You might have clients stand in different parts of the room and embody the different perspectives, trying on each one like a costume, getting a feel for the atmosphere and language. Eventually, clients will need to choose a perspective—one of the perspectives you have been playing with, a combination of perspectives, or even an entirely new perspective that came out of the exploration.

In our formula, "choice" is more than deciding on a certain perspective. To be aware of choice is to be aware of the power of choosing. It is crucial that clients feel they are absolutely, unequivocally in charge of their choices. How clients choose will also be a revealing part of the process for clients and coach. Does the client choose quickly? Impulsively? Is there a great deal of analysis or a complex system for comparing and analyzing? This information will be valuable background for you as you learn how your clients typically handle the decision-making process.

Step 3: Planning

In our approach to balance coaching, we take a rather broad view of this step. Consistent with the principle of balance, we begin by expanding the range of possibilities so that choice comes from a place that is alive.

With that in mind, the first step in planning is to open up possibilities by creating a variety and range of action options. This is an intentionally expansive phase in planning that emphasizes creativity. The skill of brainstorming is one way of generating ideas and options, but no matter what form the creative process takes, the coach's job is to encourage clients to push the edge of possibilities, to travel beyond familiar alternatives. In this expansion mode, the intention is to redefine what "possible" means, outside the old boundaries and past what is normally considered "realistic." The idea of what is "realistic" is too often a holdover from the boxed-in perspective.

Given the rich world of possible actions, the next phase in the planning process is to narrow the list. This is the next choice point in balance coaching and an opportunity to make sure, again, that the course of action being considered will lead to more flow. One of the things to watch for is a condition we playfully call "OOPS": Overly Optimistic Planning Syndrome. Yes, we encourage creating an abundance of possibilities, and we help clients build a motivational fire that powers their move into action. But we do this to expand the range, not to cause burnout in our clients, so checking in and consciously choosing are important parts of planning. There is, in fact, a point of balance between what is possible and what will result in flow. It is not a perfect formula; that's why we add learning to the action as clients move forward.

Ultimately, it is our goal to make sure that there is movement in the issues clients bring to the coaching session. Narrowing the action list is the step that moves the conversation into reality. In coaching, it is not enough to have really good, even profound or wildly creative talk about clients' issues or lives. It is essential that clients be in action and that something is made real in the world that they can see and take note of. (The Coach's Toolkit includes a section on tools that will help in this phase of planning, specific structures for identifying what will happen and when and will give clients a variety of ways to turn optional possibilities into accountable action.)

Step 4: Commitment

One of the core questions for coaches is: *What is it that sustains change over time?* We know that clients are often willing to choose a new direction; this is the way they move beyond the dead end or stop their aimless wandering. But once they are on the road, what will sustain them? The energy of commitment is one answer.

Beyond Choice. Planning can be just another cerebral activity. There's a lot of thinking about different ways of making things happen, allocating resources, and calculating. The plan is external, however. As a coach, you want the plan to live inside, in the client's muscle and bone, not only in the brain, where a minor distraction could easily displace it. So before you invite clients to take action, make sure they've really made a commitment to their plans.

People gain a mysterious strength and resolve when they make a commitment. Commitment goes beyond making a choice. We make a choice between lasagna and linguine; we make a commitment to other people, to life, to a course of action. Commitment implies there is no turning back. This is the point where you draw a line and ask the client to cross into new territory: "Will you commit to that plan and take action? Will you do that?" Up to this point, clients may simply have been playing along. Chances are that they will experience a shift once they realize that they are committing to a different way of operating in their world. And so you ask: "Will you commit to this plan?" This question raises the stakes. We're no longer talking about losing ten pounds or paying down the credit card balance this month; we're talking about taking control of their lives. In fact, this act of commitment is so powerful that the coach sometimes asks clients to actually draw a line—real or imaginary—on the floor in front of them, take a deep breath, and, when they're ready to commit to the plan, step across the line. But only when they're truly ready to commit.

Yes and No. These words, "yes" and "no," are two of the simplest words in any language. Depending on the context of the question, however, they can also be two of the most difficult words to say out loud for the whole world to hear. As clients are preparing to commit to action, they must choose between saying yes to their plans and saying no to something else.

In the context of commitment, those words have a deeper ring; they reverberate into your clients' lives. That yes to a simple action is a yes to some deeper commitment, a promise, even a new or deeper way of being in their lives. Saying no to a simple action is much more than taking that one thing off the list. It often means saying no to old beliefs or old expectations, no to self-betrayal, no to habitual ways of reacting to the demands of others. As coach, listen for the depth of the yeses and noes from your clients. You may even ask them to take part in this yes-or-no exercise for a period of time as a way to get clearer about the root choices they are making. For example: "In your life these days, what are you saying yes to? What are you saying no to?" or "In your relationship with your spouse, what are you saying yes to or no to?"

Step 5: Action

The action of coaching does not take place in the coaching session. From the coach's point of view, this is something of a relief. It eliminates the pressure to be brilliant or perfect or transformative. The real action of coaching takes place in the client's life, in the action he or she takes—or doesn't take—between coaching sessions. That is where the power is. Without action, the balance coaching is incomplete, just an enjoyable conversation about point of view. Action steps in the client's life keep the client moving and motivated.

At the next session, you will check in on progress, explore what worked and what didn't, and go over what the client learned from both. You will uncover what this person wants to take into his or her life from here, as he or she balances circumstances and possibilities and makes life-giving choices in action.

Sample Dialogue

> **COACH:** *(after listening to the client's unenthusiastic report on a particular project at work): I'm guessing you thought you would be much more excited about the project than you are.*
>
> **Client:** *That's an understatement. I thought this was going to be the creative crème de la crème.*
>
> **COACH:** *And it's not.*
>
> **Client:** *Nope. Definitely not crème de la anything. Oatmeal, I'd say. Day-old oatmeal.*
>
> **COACH:** *Sounds like you're up to your hips in this day-old oatmeal.*
>
> **Client:** *Yeah, I'm not going anywhere fast. With half the people pulled off the project for other things—and a project manager who is not at all invested in making this a priority—it's discouraging.*
>
> **COACH:** *So there you are in the oatmeal perspective, looking at the project. What's the air like in that perspective?*
>
> **Client:** *Air? Stale. Old. Rank.*
>
> **COACH:** *Hard to get very motivated from this place.*
>
> **Client:** *I'll say.*
>
> **COACH:** *Want to try looking at it in a different way?*

Client: *Sure. Anything's got to be an improvement on this one.*

COACH: *So, what would a different perspective be?*

Client: *Well, it could be summer vacation. You know, school's out, no more teachers, no more books.*

COACH: *Good. What's the theme in this perspective?*

Client: *Freedom. I can do anything I want.*

COACH: *Okay. Just so we can keep track of these as we go along, let's draw a circle and divide it into eight wedges—like pie slices. Put "oatmeal" in one of those wedges, then select one of the other wedges and put "school's out" in that one. Got it?*

Client: *Yes.*

COACH: *What would be another perspective?*

Client: *I'm not sure.*

COACH: *How about a perspective from your future self?*

Client: *Okay—this may sound a little odd—but "workshop."*

COACH: *Workshop? What does that mean to you?*

Client: *I have a workshop at home where I do some simple wood-work projects. It's a hobby. It relaxes me. I like working with my hands.*

COACH: *Sounds like you have a clear sense of this perspective.*

Client: *Oh yeah. I can practically smell the wood.*

COACH: *What's another way you could look at this situation at work?*

(The client finds a couple more perspectives, including one he labels "library." Coach and client explore the characteristics of the different perspectives.)

COACH: *Looking at my notes, I see that we've talked about six, seven if you include the original oatmeal perspective. Which is the one you will choose?*

Client: *The library.*

COACH: *And what is there about the library perspective that appeals to you?*

Client: *Well, I wish this project was up and running full speed with this really hot, creative team together. We talked about that, but it's not going to happen in the short term. What would be interesting, though, is to really go in and study the subject. I've got the time. I like the library as a metaphor because it's a quiet place. It's set aside for study, and there's lots of material to explore. No one's going to bother me there.*

COACH: *Great. So now that you're standing in the library looking at the project, what are some of the options? What might you be doing with your time?*

Client: *There's some online research I'd like to do . . . two books I've been meaning to order . . . I just haven't done it. And there's a guy in Ireland I'd like to talk to. He's involved in a similar project—we chatted by e-mail a few months back . . . There's also a conference coming up in a couple of months—I suppose I could see if the company would fund my trip . . .*

COACH: *Lots of options. What would be the stretch for you?*

Client: *Writing an article on the subject would be a stretch.*

COACH: *And what would you be saying yes to?*

Client: *I'd be saying yes to taking control of my time. I'd be saying yes to capitalizing on the opportunity. I'd be saying yes to making this downtime a real benefit to me in my career—being willing to be a colleague of sorts, with some of the people I admire—earning my professional credentials, so to speak.*

COACH: *And what would you be saying no to?*

Client: *Well, the obvious. No to whining and complaining that I don't get to play the way I expected. But more than that, I'd be saying no to that weary sense of helplessness.*

COACH: *How committed are you to writing this article?*

Client: *Very. This should be really interesting—and it leads to all sorts of other possibilities.*

COACH: *Good. What would lock in this sense of commitment for you?*

Client: *Committing to some kind of action step.*

COACH: *I was just about to ask, what do you want to be accountable for between now and the next time we meet?*

Client: *An outline. I would need to do some of the research I talked about—at least a quick look at some things—and I know what that would be. But I could have a draft of an outline.*

COACH: *All right, then. Here's my request: Send me a copy of the outline by e-mail on the day before our next meeting. Will you do that?*

Client: *Let me put that in my calendar. Okay, I'll do it.*

FINDING THE BALANCE

The purpose of the balance formula, and balance coaching, for that matter, is to move clients into action. Like a slalom skier speeding down the mountain, turning crisply at every chute, we live our lives in action, and being on the edge is an exhilarating way to experience life in motion. If the image of the skier and the mountain is a little too breathtaking for your taste, the same themes apply to the ice skater and the dancer. Grace and performance make the balance point of leaning into what is possible while still maintaining control.

And yet, we are not assisting our clients with just any action. It's not a service to clients to simply add more action to their lives. Fulfillment coaching will help identify action that is consistent with the client's values. Balance coaching will help clients find the flow, the way to balance priorities, expectations, and perspectives on the issues they bring to their coaching sessions. Our use of the word "flow" isn't meant to imply glassy smoothness. You may want to substitute the word "ride" for flow because our goal is to help clients create the ride of their life. The action clients undertake by working from the principle of balance is action that fits the big-picture ride that brings them a life of choice.

10

Client
Process

Clients usually come to coaching to do things differently or to do different things. They want to set goals, come up with plans, get into action, and use the accountability of coaching to stay on track. Clients want to be in motion, not standing still, so naturally a great deal of the coach's focus is on moving forward, envisioning the golden future, and helping clients create the path that will take them there. There is a leaning-forward, feet-moving, arms-pumping quality to the coaching. And yet, in co-active coaching, we believe there is more to life than tasks accomplished. Our focus is on the client's life experience, not just a list of action items completed. In fact, we believe clients actually want to enjoy the journey, to savor and appreciate each moment of their lives as best they can.

In general, fulfillment and balance focus on moving forward. Coach and client are aware of what is happening externally in the client's life, and they can see the results. Coaching that emphasizes moving forward is focused, directed, intentional. It is about generating, creating. Action orientation often has a fierce determination to make something happen—clients are looking ahead, and there is momentum.

Process coaching focuses on the internal experience, on what is happening in the moment. The goal of process coaching is to enhance the ability of clients to be aware of the moment and to name it. In process coaching, there is a quality of expanding into the present, being curious about it, slowing down to explore and appreciate it. Sometimes the most important change happens at the internal level and may even be necessary before external change can take place. Being in the moment immerses the client in the flow of life, the here and now. The feeling is expansive, like going up a mountain to a higher place or down into the valley to a deeper place.

The combination of going somewhere and going more deeply into the experience is the full spectrum of life. Being present in life expands awareness, leads to richer highs and robust lows that are the measure of a true life fully experienced. This is the process-coaching version of the client's Big-"A" agenda: a fully expressed and fully experienced life lived in the moment.

THE LOOK OF PROCESS

Process coaching focuses on where clients are now. Imagine life as a river, flowing through time. In one place, the river is steady, serene. Then it hits the rapids. Then a waterfall. There are eddies and whirlpools, backwater, and swamps. The river of life narrows and suddenly speeds up. Process is about being fully aware and alive wherever you are on the river today: whether you are floating easily on your back, enjoying the sky and sun, or tumbling through the chaos of white water. Clients have their plans and dreams, and sometimes they won't like where they are on the river. And yet, when you're in the rapids, the only thing to do is be in the rapids. You can wish it weren't so, but that's where you are. While you are busy making plans for the future, you are also in the present. You are in the process of your life. In this moment. Right now.

THE COACH AND PROCESS

Imagine the river on a bright afternoon. The sun reflecting off the water in glittering sparkles can be practically blinding. As with the river, it's easy to be distracted by the activity on the surface of life. Action can be dazzling. But when you look at the river through a polarizing filter, you tune out the distracting sparkles and see the flow of the water. That's the coach's job—to notice the currents below the surface. In process coaching, you are tuning your ear to hear any turbulence or resistance. It is a sign that something is likely to be obstructing the flow of the river. You can hear it by listening attentively at Level III, and as a coach, you become curious. Very often it is something the client is not conscious of or is avoiding.

PROCESS COACHING

Ultimately, our goal as coaches is to assist our clients in creating the work and lives they want. In a sense, we are always focused on moving forward to an envisioned future. However, the shortest distance between here and there is not always a straight line. Sometimes it is a curved line, as the U-shaped process pathway shows (see Figure 5). Sometimes the way forward involves going down into the experience first. Or, as we will see a little later, it may mean going up into the experience first, by simply turning the U-shaped curve upside down.

The flow in process coaching has the following five key steps: (1) the coach hears the turbulence and names it, (2) the coach explores it, (3) the client experiences it, (4) a shift happens, and the client integrates it, and (5) movement happens.

Step 1: The Coach Hears the Turbulence and Names It

Listening at Level III, you as coach hear what we have called "turbulence." It might be an emotion, or you may sense that something important is being ignored or bypassed, as if there were an unnamed elephant in the room. Process coaching draws on the coach's ability to

1. Coach hears the turbulence and names it

2. Coach explores it

3. Client experiences it

5. Movement happens

4. A shift happens

FIGURE 5 **The Process Pathway**

be aware of these fluctuations and to access his or her intuition. By monitoring the currents in the flow of conversation, you are often able to pick up on nuances or subtle shifts of which the client might be unaware. At other times, the condition might be very obvious, at least to you. For example, a client could be describing a change in departmental policies at work, and underneath the words, there is barely controlled outrage, a fire-breathing dragon. At this point, you become curious. Clearly, something very important is going on just below the surface. It can happen the opposite way, too: You expect your client to be euphoric about a recent success, but the client's voice and tone are dead flat. That's another good reason to become curious.

When the coach hears it, he or she speaks or names it—and invites the client to look there, too. In relation to the examples we gave, this means that you, the coach, share your observation, without judgment or attachment. It can be as simple as saying: "It sounds to me like there's something important here that is not being said." Or you could be more specific, especially in ongoing coach-client relationships, such as: "That's not the outcome you hoped for. It sounds like you're really disappointed."

We invite clients to look below the surface, below the facts and data. Why would we do this? The most powerful, most effective coaching we can do always works with what is most important for the client. When you point below the surface to the energy or emotion, you give the client an opportunity to learn more about what is obviously important. Clients are not always prepared to look below the surface; they often keep their emotional responses under tight control. By inviting your clients to explore the energy or emotion around the subject, you give them the opportunity to become aware and conscious of the impact these issues really have on their lives.

Step 2: The Coach Explores It

Once you have heard and named the turbulence, the next step is to explore the territory—but first you must ask the client for permission. This is important. With some clients, especially in an ongoing coaching relationship, you will find you have great latitude to take them into whatever territory you, as an experienced coach, feel would be most beneficial for them. These clients have granted permission broadly and empowered you to take the lead in deciding where the coaching conversation needs to go. With other clients, especially those relatively new to coaching or to you as a coach, asking permission creates a container of safety and encourages them to look deeper than the surface details of the presenting issue.

The goal of process coaching, as we have said, is to focus on what is true in the moment. One of the most effective access points for exploring the moment is the client's immediate physical experience: breathing . . . tension . . . a furrowed brow . . . tightness in the throat or a rapid heart beat. The body is remarkably expressive and a rich source of information about the client's internal experience.

Metaphor or imagery is another effective access point for exploring the moment. Sometimes the feelings are easier to describe in pictures than in words: *The feeling is a small tight ball . . . The feeling is a helium-filled Mylar balloon . . . It feels like walking through waist-deep mud . . . It feels like flying around and around and around in a little circle.*

Step 3: The Client Experiences It

The key here is that the client actually experience the sensation or emotion. It is important for the client to be able to name it and identify it, even if only in a few words, but just talking about it will not usually be enough to shift the feeling. As coach, you can tell the difference between a conversation about disappointment and a client who is reliving the experience of disappointment. An intellectual understanding of what caused the disappointment is a good start, but there is much deeper learning available.

Step 4: A Shift Happens, and the Client Integrates It

We have drawn the graphic of process coaching as a very tidy U-shaped curve, but a coaching session that followed that ideal path would be a near miracle. Most of the time, if you were to graph the movement, you would see that the coaching goes deeper, resurfaces slightly, plateaus perhaps, goes deeper again, and so on. There is no perfect template for process coaching because the coach is constantly dancing in the moment with each new response. And yet, listening at Level III, there is almost always a point in time when, as coach, you can hear the client rising up the far side of the U-shaped curve.

Step 5: Movement Happens

In this step, there is a sense that movement has occurred, that we have entered a new phase or even new territory. The atmosphere changes. Clients will have new images—about being more buoyant or seeing more light or more color. They may report a sensation of warmth or more flow. In terms of physical sensations, they may say they are more relaxed, more at peace or more energized, less stuck or resistant, and so on. In most cases, this new sensation can be linked to a new understanding or awareness in the client. The outcome of process coaching is a shift in the internal experience combined with new or renewed learning.

GOING UP INTO IT

The steps we've just described apply equally to those situations in which clients seem reluctant to go "up" into an experience. Clients can be so driven to move on to the next stage or the next project or challenge that they want to skip the celebration of their accomplishments—and miss the chance to discover more about themselves and the keys to their success.

Some clients have been told too often and for too long that they need to be humble or should not draw attention to themselves, and so they avoid what they consider self-praise and miss out on acknowledgment and learning. Some clients are simply afraid of being too happy, or they consider the more joyful emotions unnecessary or a sign that they are not taking the issue seriously. As a coach, part of your job is to listen for the kind of avoidance that keeps your clients from experiencing the whole range of musical notes available to them. When clients cut themselves off from the highs and lows, it's like cutting out musical tones. They end up with only a few notes to play, which makes for a very limited and monotonous life song.

FEELINGS AS INFORMATION, NOT SYMPTOMS

The presence of feelings or emotions is one of the inherent qualities of process coaching. When clients talk freely about issues that are deeply important to them, it should come as no surprise that the conversation takes place in an atmosphere of feeling. Coaches are sometimes alarmed and confused by this. They think that because the client is reacting with feeling, the coaching relationship has turned into therapy.

But emotions and therapy are not the same. Emotions are just emotions. When someone is passionate, even angry about a perceived injustice, it doesn't mean that she is mentally unstable; she is a human being having a human reaction. If a client is crying, it doesn't mean that he is ill. That's how people sometimes express strong feelings.

It's okay for coaches to allow emotion—sadness, pain, anger, loss—and actually to encourage it. Emotion is a legitimate form of expression, like words, music, and dance. Don't be a detective about it. Don't look at why the client is hurt or angry—which is the typical response. The cause itself is not important; accepting the feeling is important. Nor is it up to the coach to try to heal it or stop it—another typical response. Just explore it and acknowledge it: "That's a powerful feeling. There's some pain in there, I can tell."

Emotions are part of the normal functioning of a human being, not symptoms of disease. The whole, healthy, resourceful client has full access to his or her emotions. It's the hiding, denying, submerging that get clients in trouble. Our feelings give us a way of expressing ourselves. The process can be very cleansing, and if we don't permit our bodies to discharge and discover whatever we're holding inside, we don't grow. We can even get sick—physically and emotionally—by keeping things in. Process coaching is where emotions will show up because you're encouraging, even challenging, clients to visit the hard places and give in to the experience so they can include it in their lives. Unless you can explore those places, coaching lacks depth and breadth.

Even though process coaching can be powerful emotionally, there's still room for humor. Exploring forbidden territory with humor can give clients license to approach the dark areas on light feet or to feel curiosity about the depth of the murky water instead of fearing that they are about to drown.

Sample Dialogue

Client: *Looks like I'll have to dust off the old résumé again after all.*

COACH: *You finally heard about the job overseas?*

Client: *I heard. And it wasn't the answer I wanted to hear. So I'm cranking up the search machinery again.*

COACH: *You had a lot riding on getting that job. I remember how excited you were after the last interview. Sounds like you're kind of shrugging it off now—as if it wasn't that important. What's the truth there?*

Client: *I've got a decent job and little risk that anything will change there.*

COACH: *Up until today, that wasn't enough.*

Client: *I know. It's still not. The truth is, I am disappointed.*

COACH: *Not just a little, it sounds like.*

Client: *No. Really disappointed. I was really pumped for that interview. I don't see how it could have gone any better.*

COACH: *It's a huge letdown.*

Client: *I don't want to dwell on it.*

COACH: *I understand. Still, it looks as if your life wants to dwell on it.*

Client: *Boy, that's the truth. I can't remember being this un-happy—not about a job falling through. Maybe I had too much riding on getting the hell out of the country.*

COACH: *What does it look like to you? I'm sensing sadness. What's your experience?*

Client: *It's actually like getting punched in the stomach. I feel like it took my breath away. Like I can't even stand up straight.*

COACH: *What's the painful part?*

Client: *The loss, the waiting, the wasted energy.*

COACH: *Would it be all right if we explored that right now? I think it's important to go through this, not step over it.*

Client: *Sure. I want to get over it so I can get on with my life.*

COACH: *So what's it like there, right now? The place you got punched?*

Client: *It's dark . . . hollow . . . like a cavern.*

COACH: *Go into the cavern. Are you there?*

Client: *Yes.*

COACH: *What are you sensing?*

Client: *I'm sitting with my head in my hands.*

COACH: *What's the emotion?*

Client: *Sadness. I feel defeated. Utterly defeated.*

COACH: *Okay. What I want you to do now is turn up the volume on it, just a little at first. If it's at 5 right now, turn it up to 6.*

Client: *The sadness?*

COACH: *Yes. And the feeling of defeat. Go in there. I'll be right here.*

Client: *Okay. I'm turning up the volume. There's 6.*

COACH: *What do you notice?*

Client: *A sense of failure. Like a huge wave of failure. It's breaking over everything.*

COACH: *A wave of failure. Are you in a safe place?*

Client: *Yes.*

COACH: *When you're ready, try turning it up another notch to 7.*

Client: *Now I really feel the loss. Like a dream died. Like my last chance to build something important just vanished.*

COACH: *This is important for you.*

Client: *It's huge.*

COACH: *What do you notice now?*

Client: *That I can turn down the volume.*

COACH: *Do you want to do that now?*

Client: *I do.*

COACH: *What does it feel like now?*

Client: *The tension is gone from my shoulders.*

COACH: *Where are you? Are you still in the cavern?*

Client: *No. I'm sitting on a dock, looking out at the ocean.*

COACH: *What are you learning from this?*

Client: *A couple of things. One, I didn't realize just how important it was to me, to get that position, and how hard it is on me to not be chosen—especially when I really feel qualified. And two, I see that I do control my destiny and how I feel about it, just like I controlled the feeling of failure. I can choose to feel good about myself.*

COACH: *What's next?*

Client: *The résumé. I do want to work on that some. And I want to go back and do some research into possible overseas work opportunities.*

COACH: *Good. Sometime this week, create a plan with deadlines and send me a copy. Okay?*

Client: *Okay.*

COACH: *I also have a request—a homework inquiry—that you spend some time journaling about the question "What I have learned from failure." Will you do that?*

Client: *Are you kidding?*

COACH: *Actually, I'm not kidding. You know how to do whatever you need to do in the job search—write a résumé, do the interviews, whatever needs to be done. The hard thing for you is to live with the feeling of failure. The very prospect could derail you. If you could have more capacity to be with failure, what would it give you?*

Client: *Freedom. It would turn failure into learning instead of judgment about me. It's just . . . I don't have to be happy about doing this, do I?*

COACH: *You get to choose, as you said just a minute ago. It's just that this won't be the last time you'll face this sense of loss and failure. If you can be with it now—and develop some muscles to handle it—you'll be in better shape the next time you're in a situation like this.*

Client: *Like an emotional fitness program.*

COACH: *Something like that. And the universe has just provided a great gymnasium for you. Let's take advantage of it.*

PROCESS AND ACCOUNTABILITY

The co-active coaching model is very clear: the coach brings a context to the coaching relationship that includes deepened learning and action that moves the client forward in life. Accountability is just as important in process coaching as it is in fulfillment or balance coaching. Without accountability, coaching has not happened, even if coaching skills have been used. The action of coaching takes place in the client's life. With process coaching, the action is designed to support what the client discovers from the coaching session. For example, the session might uncover the client's fear of disappointing others when he says no to requests. In this case, the client is paying a heavy price to avoid the possibility of disappointing people in his life. The accountability might be to risk disappointing people by saying no five times in the coming week and noticing what happens. Or it could also be a habit or practice that is integrated into the client's life, such as recording, at the end of each day, the times when he said no.

TO BE WITH

A word or two is in order about the expression "be with," which is often used with process coaching. We might say, for example, that clients are "being with" disappointment, or the coach is "being with" clients and their disappointment. Think of it like visiting a friend in the hospital. Your goal is to be with your friend. There is really nothing for you to do except to be there. And it is more than just showing up. To be with is to be present and fully engaged, attentive, open, even interacting, but with no goal other than simply being together with that person in the experience. Being with is a powerful Level III environment—an experience shared at a deep level. When you are with clients at this level, they are free to share not only their thoughts and analyses but the honest emotions of their experiences as well.

On the CD, the second coaching sample demonstrates the coach's instinct to observe an underlying mood in her client and invite the client to be with the feeling. Together, coach and client discover an image that becomes a turning point in the coaching. It is a clear example of "the coach hears the turbulence and names it; the client experiences it and a shift happens"—all in the space of a few minutes.

CAN'T GO THERE

Process coaching often shows up when the river takes a turn into territory the client doesn't want to enter. As a coach, your curiosity is piqued. Where is it the client doesn't want to go? What is it the client doesn't want to deal with? You may hear any number of explanations: "I don't want any more chaos or judgment," "I don't want to worry

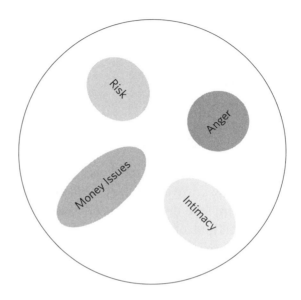

FIGURE 6 **Redirecting the Flow**

about money," "I can't be with the failure I created in my last job," "I
can't be with the happiness this person brings to my life."

Clients are uncomfortable, sometimes downright miserable, because their lives are taking them to places where they do not want to
go. Clients in this situation want to change course and avoid those
areas. What they get, over time, are lives filled with avoiding. They
don't realize what it costs them to cut out those parts of their lives. So
draw a large circle to represent the client's whole life (see Figure 6).
Now start marking off the pieces the client doesn't want to be with.
Color the pieces in and name them: this is the anger the client can't be
with. . . the disappointment . . . the risk taking. As each piece is colored
in, there is less life left for the client, and it becomes harder and harder
to navigate around all the "don't go there" zones.

Process coaching helps clients develop the capacity to be with conditions they have been denying or avoiding. Much of our work as

coaches is helping clients discover what is true, real, and important, so that they can choose well. We could also say that our job is to help clients stop avoiding, pretending, denying. From this empowered place, they will be able to make better decisions and be stronger in their relationships at work and at home.

WHERE DO YOU STOP?

Before we leave the subject of exploring the hard places, we should ask a pointed question: What areas in your life are hard for you to be with or explore? The answer is important because these are the places you'll be reluctant to go to with your clients. You might even stop in your coaching rather than get into these places. Let's say you have trouble dealing with money, or anger, or rejection. You may avoid these areas in your coaching. Yet these may be the places your clients need and are even willing to explore. If you are not conscious of your own off-limits areas, you'll shortchange your clients, because as soon as they start to go there, you'll steer them away. Coaches, therefore, must do their own rigorous process of self-discovery—ideally with their own coach. Begin to work on these areas so they can be included in your own life and become accessible in your work with coaching clients, too.

Integration, Application, and Vision

So far, we have spoken of the three core principles as distinct pathways of coaching. In separating them for the book, we may have left an impression that a coaching session follows one consistent principle, from first question to final accountability. In fact, in the course of a single coaching session, you, as coach, are likely to weave together elements of all three principles: fulfillment, balance, and process.

INTEGRATING THE PRINCIPLES

We might think of the three principles as three different sets of tools. When coach and clients are exploring values, future visions, or the self-sabotage that keeps clients from achieving their visions, the coach is pulling from the fulfillment toolkit. When the coach is helping clients look at an issue from a variety of different viewpoints or is considering plans or action options, the toolkit is balance based. The coach who is forming a container around the current moment and delving more deeply into it is in the general area of process. So how do you, as coach, decide which tool set to begin with? And how do you recognize that it is time to shift to a different principle? The short answer is that the coaching direction comes from listening at Levels II and III.

As we have said from the outset, in the co-active coaching model, the goals and focus areas for the coaching, and the issues for any given coaching session, come from the client. Clients set the agenda for the coaching relationship and each coaching session. That is their responsibility.

It is the coach's responsibility to determine what coaching approach to take. The client is actually counting on the coach to take charge of the coaching direction and flow. The coach is choosing a direction beginning with the client's very first statement in the session. In our listening model, we say that the coach is paying attention to the client, aware of the strength of the one-to-one connection, what we describe as listening at Level II. The coach is also paying attention to the client's shifting tone, the pace of speaking or breathing, the atmosphere that is created, even gauging the strength of the relationship itself: Is the client moving closer, drifting away, running away, defending? This is the coach listening at Level III. For the coach, the information about where to go next with the coaching is right there, in the moment, in the Level II and Level III listening. This is crucial for coaches working in this model. Coaches listen for an overall sense of strength or weakness and use that information to help form the next question or decide which skill to apply next.

This is definitely an art that requires attentive listening and then dancing with whatever shows up. It is not a technique to be learned, as in "When the client responds 'A,' then the coach asks 'B.'" It doesn't work that way. It also doesn't work for you, as coach, to have your attention on the tool set, thinking about which principle you are working in, which context of the model you are using, or what skill to pick from the glossary. This is awareness at Level I, and when you are at this level, you have disconnected from the client. It happens to the best coaches from time to time, and coaches then need to recover and re-connect to the client.

Notice we have specifically said reconnect to the *client* rather than reconnect to the *client's issue*. In coaching, our primary responsibility is to help clients determine their best course of action and support them in staying on track, helping them uncover the learning for themselves so that they become more resourceful over time rather than more depend-ent on us for answers. As coaches, we are always empowering our clients.

This urge to identify the "problem" as quickly as possible and find a solution in the blink of an eye is embedded in the culture. Yes, of course, there are times when it is crucial to solve problems quickly, but in coaching, we take a longer view of clients and their lives. In our model of coaching, coaches are holding the client's Big-"A" agenda—a resonant, fulfilling life, a life of choice and purpose and expression. We are helping clients look at the issues they bring to coaching within a larger context. For us as coaches, it is a professional hazard to be se-duced into wanting to understand all of the circumstances around a client's issue, as if our understanding would make us better equipped to help our clients. In almost every case, we overestimate what we need to know. After all, clients are the experts on their own lives and work situations; the coach is expert in helping them find the next course of action and reap the learning from the action they take.

We should note here that there is no superficial client issue, only superficial coaching. There is always something important underneath the situation presented, or it would not be worth the client's or the coach's time. Part of the coach's job is to look for whatever makes an issue important in a client's life. Every client situation has within it the potential to move the client closer to his or her version of fulfillment, balance, or better process in life. The issue that a client brings is a piece of a much larger puzzle. It should be treated with respect, not as a prob-lem to be solved so that it disappears but rather as an opportunity to move toward a larger goal. In the end, this is the real leverage of coach-ing: not an answer to a single issue, but a more empowered and re-sourceful client living a more alive and rewarding life.

Sample Coaching: Integrating the Three Principles

Client: *Picking up where we left off last time . . . I'm still playing with the possibility of buying the business I talked about.*

COACH: *You've been gathering data . . .*

Client: *. . . and I talked to the consultant again.*

COACH: *As you view this potential acquisition, where are you today? What's the big picture? [Vision: fulfillment]*

Client: *The big picture is, it's risky.*

COACH: *I notice "risky" hasn't stopped you before. In fact, risk taking is a big value of yours. What is there about this risk that's bothering you? [Values: fulfillment]*

Client: *It's complex.*

COACH: *Let's try to pull it apart a little. First of all, I trust you have a way to make sure the financial picture makes sense to you.*

Client: *I'm going to go over all of that with my partner and the CPA we've been working with, but basically, the analysis is handled. By this time next week, we'll know everything we need to know.*

COACH: *So there is some financial risk. Is that the risky part?*

Client: *Not really. I'm familiar with spreadsheets, and I can make a solid business decision based on the numbers.*

COACH: *So what is at risk here?*

Client: *You remember that theme we talked about, the theme for this year? My slowing down.*

COACH: *"Getting off the highway," I think, was the way you expressed it.*

Client: *Well, if I decide to buy this business, it won't be "getting off the highway"; it will be "moving into the fast lane."*

COACH: *Your voice just shifted there. What happened? [In the moment: process]*

Client: *I can feel the pressure building.*

COACH: *What's the feeling? [Being with: process]*

Client: *A sense of dread.*

COACH: *What sort of image comes to mind when you let yourself feel the dread?*

Client: *I get all hunched over at the shoulders, like I'm carrying a heavy weight.*

COACH: *That's what it feels like when you look at the decision through the lens of "moving into the fast lane." What if you could look at this acquisition through the lens of your theme, "getting off the highway"? What would that be like? [Perspectives: balance]*

Client: *That would be a stretch.*

COACH: *Want to try it?*

Client: *Sure.*

(Coach and client explore this and several other perspectives.)

COACH: *What are you taking away from the coaching today?*

Client: *Two things: one, that I can handle the financial analysis, and two, the financial analysis is only one part of the decision. What's really important is how this decision impacts my life. I see that I get addicted to the excitement of making a deal and can lose track of what's really important to me in the long run.*

COACH: *I have a homework inquiry for you to reflect on. Ready?*

Client: *Yes.*

COACH: *What is the payoff you most want from this potential acquisition? [Big-"A" agenda: fulfillment]*

Client: *That's good. I'll take that on.*

THE COACH'S COMMITMENT

Just how far you are willing to go for the sake of your clients' fulfilling life? And at what point do you settle into a state of comfort—especially with clients you enjoy working with—and find yourself supporting only a portion of their dream or holding a vision of their potential that is within reach, satisfactory but not great? It can happen, unconsciously, and it is a reminder that, as coaches, we need to be constantly vigilant, constantly holding a vision for our clients that on some days they are not able to hold for themselves.

Clients count on you to give them your 100 percent commitment. Be alert to those times when you begin to buy into their stories without question. Be willing to push back, to suggest a contrary point of view just for the sake of their exploration, so they are forced to be clear and rigorous in the stands they take. When your clients are presenting their descriptions of their world as if they were the truth and you find yourself nodding in agreement, pause long enough to question the underlying assumptions. For example, when clients say things like "I'm so busy, so committed, I don't have time to . . . ," become curious. It may be true that a client is too busy, but it may also be an excuse that allows this person to avoid a difficult choice that would work out best in the long run. You might wonder: "What is the client really committed to, after all?"

As coach, you are the model of courageous questioning. Part of your job is to be blunt, say the unpopular or even unreasonable thing, for the sake of clients reaching their potential, living their fulfilling life, however they define it. If living a fulfilling life is a radical act, as we have said, then there will be times when yours will be the voice of fierce courage. You need to be willing to ask the tough question or tell the hard truth, even if it means your clients will not like what they hear. There may be times when you must be willing to go too far and maybe even be fired. Sometimes the toughest question is for the coach: "What are you really committed to, after all?"

Sample Coaching: Courageous Questioning

COACH: *Is that your final decision?*

Client: *Yes. I'll be moving back to my hometown as soon as I can make the arrangements—maybe in a month.*

COACH: *I'm surprised.*

Client: *I know.*

COACH: *Look, Kathy, it's your life. You have to choose what you think is best, but as your coach and someone who really believes in you, I have to say I'm disappointed.*

Client: *You think I'm selling out again.*

COACH: *Don't you?*

Client: *I'm tired of fighting.*

COACH: *I understand. I've seen you battle. I've seen you face the rejection letters, work the part-time job, write late into the night. I've seen that struggle. Where did that determination come from?*

Client: *Maybe I was just fooling myself.*

COACH: *I'm going to push back here. You tell me if I go too far.*

Client: *It just seems so hopeless.*

COACH: *I don't remember "hope" on your list of values. I remember the dream. I remember the woman who came to this city filled with fire and determination, taking a stand for her life and believing in herself. You can't quit now.*

Client: *I was pretty wide-eyed.*

COACH: *I remember lots of doubt, too. Days when you were down. I don't believe the fire has gone out. I just don't believe it.*

Client: *The money's almost gone. My job is boring. I'm not having any fun. This is not the dream I signed up for.*

COACH: *I understand that, and I have a request: take a break from the writing, but don't take any action about moving. Will you do that?*

Client: *But if I'm not writing, what's the point? I'm just punching a clock.*

COACH: *You're tired. The dream is tired, too. Give it a rest. When we talk next week we can see how you're doing. Are you willing? You can say no and I'll let it go, but I'm truly asking on your behalf—on behalf of the person who believes she was born to write.*

Client: *Yes. Okay. For that person.*

WEARING MULTIPLE HATS

What happens when the coach really does have expertise that would be valuable to clients? It seems unfair, maybe even unprofessional, to hold back information or experience that could save clients from making costly mistakes or simply help them cut through a long and wandering learning process. The key in this situation is to be clear, on several different levels.

First, ask yourself, Is the information you have truly relevant to the client and the client's situation? What specifically will this client gain from your contribution? Second, be clear with yourself and your client that you are not wearing your coach's hat. You are wearing the hat of someone who has specific expertise or experience in the area under discussion. Third, make sure your client wants the information. Ask permission even if you are certain that the client will say yes. Asking permission before offering suggestions preserves the integrity of the coaching relationship. And be ready for clients to say that they'd rather find out on their own. Fourth, be clear that you are offering this without attachment. The moment you believe you have the right answer or the right way, you have begun to impose your agenda on the client's action. Be clear that you are offering this with no strings attached.

Another area in which to establish clarity is the design of your alliance with the client. In some cases, clients will choose a coach specifically because that coach has relevant experience. They hire a coach who they believe understands their world. When that is the case, it is important to talk to clients about your coaching role versus a consulting or mentoring role so that they know what to expect. Both client and coach should continue to revisit the design of the relationship as necessary as the coaching proceeds.

Distinctions for Coaching, Consulting, and Mentoring

As you can see, there is potential for confusion among these different roles, and that confusion is growing as the term "coaching" spreads around the world, especially in organizations. A growing number of consultants working with organizations have added coaching to their list of services without making the distinctions between coaching and consulting that we have made with the co-active coaching model. We are not saying that one is right and the other is wrong, only that the lack of distinction is likely to create more confusion for people who hire coaches and consultants.

Coaching and consulting can work together very effectively. There is an obvious role for consultants who bring specific skills, experience, and analytical processes to a situation. They are paid to understand the problem and present workable solutions. Coaching helps embed the necessary changes and supports the organization as it applies the solutions and makes the transition. Coaching is an ideal means of implementing changes and making sure they take root in organizations.

In addition to being clear about your role, it is just as important to be clear about the boundaries of coaching. If you are giving clients advice, you need to be clear that you have the authority and permission to give that advice. If you are providing professional services that require a license or certification, you need to be authorized. This is true of medical, legal, and financial advice and any other areas in which practice is restricted by law. If you have any doubt as to the propriety of offering advice, it is always best to ask the client to find a qualified source of information. Some coaches maintain a file of referral sources for situations like this.

Therapy and Coaching

Drawing the boundary between psychotherapy and coaching may sometimes be confusing for coaches. It is especially confusing when coaches assume that emotion is the realm of therapy and that they need to steer away whenever emotion appears in coaching. Actually, as we explained in Chapter 10, emotions are part of the human condition. They are as natural in coaching conversations as in any other human conversation, especially any meaningful human conversation. When clients talk openly about their goals and dreams, their hard-won victories or self-sabotaging defeats, there is always the possibility that they will tap into the underlying emotion.

Unfortunately, the boundary between counseling and coaching is not defined by a set of absolute rules and terms. Counseling and coaching often overlap, especially with some contemporary therapy modalities. What does seem clear is that, in general, therapists are trained to diagnose emotional problems and work with clients to heal the emotional wounds, while coaches are not trained to diagnose and do not focus on healing emotional wounds. Regardless of that distinction, it is also true that when clients in coaching make courageous choices in their lives, they often experience a sense of healing, of breaking old patterns and old bonds, of stepping out of a confining box and into a new strength. Coaching, however, does not focus on the emotional problem. Emotion may be present in the conversation, but it is not the work of the coaching. As long as coaches focus on the three principles and the contexts and skills of coaching, they are very likely to stay within bounds. (See Appendix C for the ethical standards for professional coaches published by the International Coach Federation.)

THE EXPANDING WORLD OF COACHING

In the past ten years, coaching has entered the mainstream of life and work around the world, on every continent and in nearly every walk of life. Where it once focused on two main categories, life coaching for individuals and executive coaching for corporate executives and managers, today it has evolved and spun off into hundreds of variations and hybrids.

You will find coaches working with individuals at every stage of life and in different life circumstances. For example, coaches now work with such diverse groups as teenagers considering college and career choices, college students exploring life and work, couples considering marriage, married couples who want better relationships, individuals who are changing jobs or careers or are relocating, workers preparing for retirement, and individuals facing life-altering or terminal illnesses. Coaches may specialize in working with certain groups, such as senior executives, biotech workers, artists and musicians, teachers, at-risk teens, or directors and volunteers at nonprofit organizations. Some coaches combine their work with other interest areas, including outdoor activities such as river rafting and rock climbing, financial planning, public speaking, time management, and fitness work.

One significant area of growth for coaching in recent years has been that of organization and relationship systems. Sometimes called "team coaching" in organizations, it works with multiple clients, from partner pairs to many individuals. This coaching focuses on the system and treats the system itself as a client. Coaches trained in relationship coaching are also working with romantic partners, business partners, and family-owned businesses. (For more on organization and relationship coaching, see Appendix B.)

FOR THE PROFESSIONAL COACH

The following suggestions for professional coaches range from considering the coaching form to options such as providing coaching as a complement to other work.

The Coaching Format

As we have noted throughout the book, there is no single, universal, or official format for coaching. Coaches and coaching formats come in every size, shape, and color. Factors to consider include the following: time frame, coaching medium, and length and frequency of sessions.

Time Frame. Some coaching relationships are open-ended and ongoing. They often start with an agreed-on minimum length, such as three months, but can continue for years. The coaching relationship becomes part of the client's support system as he or she continues to make important changes and faces new transitions and unexpected challenges.

Other coaching relationships are built on a fixed length, such as six months or a year. This is often the case for coaches working with clients in organizations or for consultants who include coaching as a means of implementing changes or programs.

Coaching Medium. There are many advantages to coaching by phone, including convenience, as client and coach can reach each other virtually anywhere on the planet. Both client and coach also develop an extraordinarily intimate sensitivity without the distractions of a visible presence and a physical environment. It may take a little getting used to for people who are accustomed to multitasking while they're on the phone, but the experience of coaches and clients has proved that coaching by phone really works.

At the same time, some clients and some coaches simply prefer meeting face-to-face. This is often simple enough to arrange inside organizations. And there is always the possibility of combining phone sessions and in-person sessions.

Coaches have experimented with a variety of other media as well, including e-mail, instant messaging, and teleconferencing when working with teams; Web-based conferencing is also finding its way into coaching. In one application, a coach working with hearing-impaired clients uses webcams to conduct long-distance coaching sessions in American Sign Language. E-mail and voice mail are also convenient ways of handling accountability and connection between coaching sessions.

Length and Frequency of Sessions. According to International Coach Federation surveys, the most common form for coaching is a thirty-minute phone session three or four times a month. However, the best answer to the questions "How long?" and "How often?" is "Whatever works best for coach and client."

This is a core example of designing an alliance that works for the relationship. That doesn't necessarily mean both coach and client need to compromise until they find common ground. It does mean that coaches need to be clear about what a fulfilling work life looks like and be willing to take a stand for it. So if, as a coach, you feel that you are most effective working with clients for forty-five minutes or an hour, you need to be clear with prospective clients about your work style. And if you have a strong preference on frequency of sessions, it's important to build that into the working policies for your practice. There are coaches who work with clients once a month or every week—even every day for a period of time if they are focusing on a deadline. Frequency is ultimately a combination of preference and negotiation. For many coaches, it takes a year or two of experimentation to find the pace that works best with their individual style.

Client Relationships

In this book, we emphasize coaching one-to-one with individual clients. Some coaches, however, prefer to work with couples, partnerships, families, work groups, or teams. Others do a combination of individual and team coaching. The key, in our experience, is to be very clear about your niche, your passion, your sense of mission. You will be most successful, and most inspired, when working with the people you care about most.

For coaches working with individuals or teams in organizations, there is another layer of consideration—the three-way dynamic created among the coach, the client, and the organization. (The elements of this triad are now more commonly known as the coach, the coachee [formerly "the client"], and the client [the organization or the person sponsoring the coachee and to whom the coachee reports].) For these cases, the coach needs to design a three-way alliance. Issues of confidentiality must be defined and roles clarified. Does the organization expect a report from the coach or the client? Who sets the goals and criteria for the coaching—client or organization? If coaching is to be effective, there must be sincere commitment on the part of the client, or the work may merely be a way of exerting pressure on compliance.

Special Considerations for Internal Coaches

We know from experience that the co-active coaching model works as effectively with coaches inside organizations as it does with external coaches. We have years of feedback from internal coaches in large and small companies, agencies, and nonprofit organizations around the world. We also know that there are certain differences that must be addressed in order for the coaching to be effective.

Here again, a three-way dynamic is at play among the internal coach, the client, and the organization or sponsor. The situation can be quite sensitive, and in our experience, the best approach is to establish clarity of roles and expectations in the early design of the coaching alliance involving all three parties. It is especially important for internal coaches to be clear about the boundaries for the coaching relationship. Some organizations insist that the coaching focus only on performance goals; in other organizations, coaches are empowered to help clients clarify and pursue the most fulfilling and motivating personal path, even if these individuals end up leaving the organization. There is tremendous power in an organization that is fueled by fully motivated employees, and many organizations are aware that unmotivated employees are a drain on momentum.

Coaching as a Complement to Other Work

Change that takes root happens over time and is most likely to be sustained with attention and support. Coaching is an ideal complement to program changes and a beneficial follow-up for activities or experiences designed to open up new insight or learning. A workshop, seminar, or off-site retreat can have extraordinary impact, but that impact may easily fade as individuals are separated from the experience over time. Coaching keeps the learning alive; in fact, it nourishes the seeds that were planted in that initial experience. Consultants and team leaders are turning to coaching more and more as a means of sustaining change. Experiential trainers, guides, and program leaders are incorporating ongoing coaching in order to continue the work that began in the initial adventure or experience.

Every system—human and natural—resists change. Inertia is a compelling power that tends toward keeping things as they are and exerts pressure to return to the way things have always been. There is also a complementary urge for change in every system, but in the human world, it seems to need a fair amount of encouragement and support. Coaching is an ideal mechanism for sustaining change.

So Many Options

We know we have barely scratched the surface of the wide range of possibilities for coaches. There are many books and other resources available for coaches who are looking at launching a practice. The key, we continue to emphasize, with new coaches especially, is to design your coaching offering so that it is fulfilling—so that it resonates with your values and provides balance in your own life. Make it a design that allows you to love and live in the moment. In other words, let your practice be what you preach.

COACHING SKILLS
FOR NON-COACHES

Coaching is more than a profession. It is also a communication medium with ground rules and expectations for conversation. This form of communication is also finding its way into business meetings, leadership courses, dialogue between teachers and children and within families. Coaching emphasizes open listening, mutual respect, clarity, and willingness to engage with even difficult and emotional conversations. Daniel Goleman, with his work on emotional intelligence, paved the way for broad acceptance of this world of open communication, especially the crucial importance of emotional intelligence as a necessary quality for effective leaders. Today, the skills we most associate with professional coaching are finding their way into all sorts of conversations.

IMAGINE A WORLD

Back in 1998, we wrote about a world we imagined; a world where coaching and coaching skills were a natural part of human relationship. That vision still holds today, but we have a growing sense that what we only imagined then is more and more a real part of the world we experience today.

Those of us who have trained coaches and coached clients know the extraordinary impact coaching can have on people's lives. We've felt it in our own lives as well. Now extrapolate from that handful of people in one person's coaching experience to a whole world where coaching is part of everyday life.

Imagine a world where the fundamental skills and approach of coaching were widely used—not just by coaches, but by everyone. What if the culture co-opted the principles of fulfillment, balance, and process and made them a basic expectation for everyone? What if the axioms we take for granted in coaching relationships found their way into everyday life? Imagine what that would be like.

In this world where fundamental coaching principles abound, people would be committed to fulfilling lives and work. They would be less likely to tolerate second-rate lives and more likely to decide they wouldn't settle for anything less than a full way of living that used their talents and skills completely. Children would learn that fulfillment is not something that will happen for some people someday when they are rich or famous, but is available in this moment, and every moment that follows, for those who are on a path of fulfillment.

Imagine a world where everyone had a compelling vision of his or her work: a sense of choice and purpose. Imagine a world of passionate, committed people determined to make a difference in the lives of others as they lived life fully themselves. This would be a world that received everybody's best effort, everybody's gift—instead of merely their compliance, their bodies sitting at desks, working at machines, or standing behind counters with 10 percent of their brains engaged. Although those people might be in the same jobs in our imagined world, they would have an entirely different frame of reference. The value of work would change because it would no longer be about what job you had but about the difference you made and the values you honored in the work you did.

Imagine a world where the axioms of coaching operated everywhere: in interpersonal relationships, work dynamics, international relations. Imagine the difference it would make if people designed the alliance before embarking on a business project or a relationship. What would it be like if people routinely told the truth to one another—even the hard truth—and insisted on nothing less than that without feeling the need to erect defenses? Imagine how our political system would change. Imagine a world where people were willing to truly listen, not only to the words, but to everything behind the words. What if we held out the biggest picture possible of what we and our children could be instead of pointing out everybody's limitations? What if we expected greatness instead of expecting failure or inadequacy but treated failure, when it happened, not as a disgrace but as a form of fast learning? What if we acknowledged people's strengths instead of picking at their flaws?

This would be a world of curiosity and wonder and listening in extraordinary new ways. It would be a world in which we gave our intuition permission to be expressed. We would hold one another to account for who we were and what we said we would do. In this world, we would be as committed to the truth about ourselves as we were to the truth we told others.

In this world, learning and growth would be valued over comfort and appearance. Imagine a world of compelling visions set loose to create and prosper, totally supported, totally encouraged, totally celebrated. Imagine.

The Coach's Toolkit

All forms, checklists, and exercises in the Coach's Toolkit are downloadable from the CD located in the back of the book.

Discovery Forms and Checklists for Use with Individual Clients

These sample forms represent a possible approach when working with individual clients, especially during the coaching discovery session. Please do not think that these are the "right" forms. They are supplied here to give you a sense of direction and to support you in creating forms that reflect your style and approach to coaching.

Individual Client Discovery Checklist
(Items to go over with the client)

1. Welcome the client.

2. Explain how the session will go today.

3. Explain about coaching.

4. Outline your background.

5. Discuss confidentiality and security.

6. Ask the client, "May I mention that you are a client?"

7. Design the alliance: "How do you want to be coached?"

8. Grant the coaching relationship power.

9. Explain balance and score the Wheel of Life.

10. Discuss values clarification and explain the Saboteur.

11. Fill out the Primary Focus form.

12. Review any other forms that will be used.

13. Write in the Completion Log any actions to be taken.

14. Set up the next three appointments in calendars.

15. Discuss how the calls will go, explain the homework inquiry, and remind the client about the ups and downs of the process.

16. Fill out the Coaching Agreement and Personal Information forms, noting the impact of vacations, late or missed calls, and other arrangements.

17. Receive money for the discovery session and the first month. Explain about the monthly billing process (written invoice or phone invoice).

18. Talk about the issue of commitment, discuss being human, and and explain that learning and change take time.

19. Other: _____

20. Thank the client and express your eagerness to begin work.

Co-Active Coaching (2nd ed.) © 2007 by Laura Whitworth, Karen Kimsey-House, Henry Kimsey-House, and Phillip Sandahl. Permission is hereby granted to reproduce this page for client use. Duplication for any other use, including resale, is a violation of copyright law.

Coaching Agreement

Client Name _____

This agreement, between coach _____ and the above-named client, will begin on _____ and will continue for a minimum of three months. The fee for the initial meeting is $_____, and the fee for the initial three months is $_____ per month, payable in advance each month.

The services to be provided by the coach to the client are coaching or tele-coaching, as designed jointly with the client. Coaching, which is not advice, therapy, or counseling, may address specific personal projects, business successes, or general conditions in the client's life or profession.

Upon completion of the three months, coaching will convert to a month-to-month basis. The client and coach agree to provide each other with fourteen-day notice in the event either wishes to cancel further services. It should be noted that the monthly fee is calculated based on an average of four weeks per month.

The coach promises the client that all information provided to the coach will be kept strictly confidential.

Throughout the working relationship, the coach will engage in direct and personal conversations. The client can count on the coach to be honest and straightforward in asking questions and making requests. The client understands that the power of the coaching relationship can be granted only by the client, and the client agrees to do just that: have the coaching relationship be powerful. If the client believes the coaching is not working as desired, the client will communicate that belief and take action to return the power to the coaching relationship.

Our signatures on this agreement indicate full understanding of and agreement with the information outlined above.

_____   _____   _____   _____
Client   Date   Coach   Date

Co-Active Coaching (2nd ed.) © 2007 by Laura Whitworth, Karen Kimsey-House, Henry Kimsey-House, and Phillip Sandahl. Permission is hereby granted to reproduce this page for client use. Duplication for any other use, including resale, is a violation of copyright law.

Personal Information Fact Sheet

(All personal information is confidential and will be treated appropriately.)

Contact Information

Full name _____

Name you prefer to be called _____

Address _____

Home telephone _____ Work telephone _____

Cellular phone _____

Pager and/or other telephone _____

Fax number _____ E-mail address _____

Web site _____

Employment Information

Occupation (what you do to earn a living) _____

Employer name _____

Personal Information

Date of birth _____

Marital status _____ Number of children _____

Significant other's name _____

Significant other's date of birth _____

Wedding/special anniversary date _____

Name(s) and age(s) of child(ren) _____

_____

Co-Active Coaching (2nd ed.) © 2007 by Laura Whitworth, Karen Kimsey-House, Henry Kimsey-House, and Phillip Sandahl. Permission is hereby granted to reproduce this page for client use. Duplication for any other use, including resale, is a violation of copyright law.

Wheel of Life Exercise

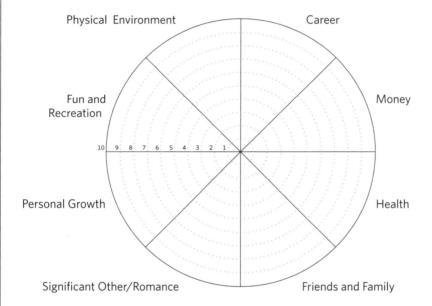

(**Note:** This wheel contains eight sections that, together, represent one way of describing a whole life. You, as coach, or your client may have other labels or categories or may wish to divide friends and family. The structure is up to you and your client. The exercise measures your client's level of satisfaction in these areas on the day he or she works through this exercise. It is not a picture of how it has been in the past or what the client wants it to be in the future. It is a snapshot taken in the moment. It is not a report card on how well the client has performed or what he or she has achieved. The emphasis is on the client's level of satisfaction in each area.)

Co-Active Coaching (2nd ed.) © 2007 by Laura Whitworth, Karen Kimsey-House, Henry Kimsey-House, and Phillip Sandahl. Permission is hereby granted to reproduce this page for client use. Duplication for any other use, including resale, is a violation of copyright law.

Wheel of Life Exercise cont'd

Directions: With the center of the wheel as 0 and the outer edge as an ideal 10, rank your level of satisfaction with each life area by drawing a straight or curved line to create a new outer edge (see example). The new perimeter of the circle represents your Wheel of Life. How bumpy would the ride be if this were a real wheel? Let's look at areas where you want to improve your level of satisfaction and begin to think about what you might do about it.

Example

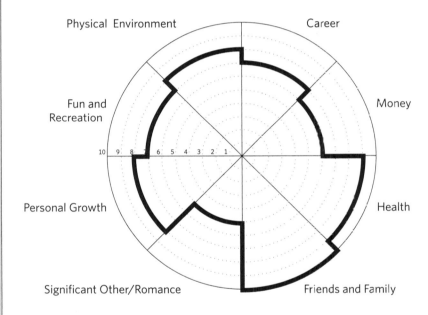

Co-Active Coaching (2nd ed.) © 2007 by Laura Whitworth, Karen Kimsey-House, Henry Kimsey-House, and Phillip Sandahl. Permission is hereby granted to reproduce this page for client use. Duplication for any other use, including resale, is a violation of copyright law.

Primary Focus

Identify five areas that you want held as your main focus during this coaching relationship. For each focus area, provide a simple heading and a description of a measurable result. For example:

BE MORE PRODUCTIVE.
I have a system to follow up on calls and letters, I'm on time, I get all tasks accomplished, I have realistic goals for new projects.

1. _____

_____

_____

2. _____

_____

_____

3. _____

_____

_____

4. _____

_____

_____

5. _____

_____

_____

Co-Active Coaching (2nd ed.) © 2007 by Laura Whitworth, Karen Kimsey-House, Henry Kimsey-House, and Phillip Sandahl. Permission is hereby granted to reproduce this page for client use. Duplication for any other use, including resale, is a violation of copyright law.

Individual Client Interview

As a coach, it's important for me to understand how you view the world in general and yourself in particular. Each person has a unique way of thinking and a unique way of interacting with those around him or her.

Answer each of these questions as clearly and thoughtfully as possible, expressing the best of who you are. These are "pondering" questions designed to stimulate your thinking in a particular way that will make our work together even more productive. I suggest that you take several days to compose your responses to these questions. Thank you.

1. What accomplishments do you think must occur during your lifetime so that you will consider your life to have been satisfying and well lived—a life of few or no regrets?

   _____

   _____

2. If there were a secret passion in your life, what would it be?

   _____

   _____

3. What do you consider your role to be in your local community? In your country? In the world?

   _____

   _____

4. If you could devote your life to serving others—and still have the money and lifestyle you need—would you do it? How would it look?

   _____

   _____

Co-Active Coaching (2nd ed.) © 2007 by Laura Whitworth, Karen Kimsey-House, Henry Kimsey-House, and Phillip Sandahl. Permission is hereby granted to reproduce this page for client use. Duplication for any other use, including resale, is a violation of copyright law.

Individual Client Interview cont'd

5. If you trusted me enough as your coach to tell me how to manage you most effectively, what tips would you give?

_____

_____

6. If you had a five-year goal and the continuing services of a coach to help you make it happen (and money were not an issue), what would that goal be? What difference would working with a coach make?

_____

_____

7. What's missing in your life? What would make your life more fulfilling?

_____

_____

8. Do you believe in God or in the concept of a higher power? If so, describe the most useful and empowering aspects of your relationship with God. If not, what reference point do you use?

_____

_____

Co-Active Coaching (2nd ed.) © 2007 by Laura Whitworth, Karen Kimsey-House, Henry Kimsey-House, and Phillip Sandahl. Permission is hereby granted to reproduce this page for client use. Duplication for any other use, including resale, is a violation of copyright law.

Strategic Planning Checklist

(Items to be evaluated for action and calendaring on a weekly basis)

1. What is important for me to do this week?

   _____

2. What career or business issues need to be planned for or acted on?

   _____

3. What can I do to increase my Values or Wheel of Life scores?

   _____

4. What family member/friend/colleague/employee shall I connect with this week?

   _____

5. What birthday or special occasion do I need to plan for?

   _____

6. _____
7. _____
8. _____
9. _____
10. _____
11. _____
12. _____
13. _____
14. _____
15. _____

Co-Active Coaching (2nd ed.) © 2007 by Laura Whitworth, Karen Kimsey-House, Henry Kimsey-House, and Phillip Sandahl. Permission is hereby granted to reproduce this page for client use. Duplication for any other use, including resale, is a violation of copyright law.

Completion Log
(To be used by the coach and/or client)

Item to Complete	Do By	Done
1. _____	_____	_____
2. _____	_____	_____
3. _____	_____	_____
4. _____	_____	_____
5. _____	_____	_____
6. _____	_____	_____
7. _____	_____	_____
8. _____	_____	_____
9. _____	_____	_____
10. _____	_____	_____
11. _____	_____	_____
12. _____	_____	_____
13. _____	_____	_____
14. _____	_____	_____
15. _____	_____	_____
16. _____	_____	_____
17. _____	_____	_____

Co-Active Coaching (2nd ed.) © 2007 by Laura Whitworth, Karen Kimsey-House, Henry Kimsey-House, and Phillip Sandahl. Permission is hereby granted to reproduce this page for client use. Duplication for any other use, including resale, is a violation of copyright law.

Coaching Preparation Form
(Note: Some clients fax or e-mail this information prior to the coaching session.)

Preparing for the coaching session will allow you to optimize your results and our time together. Before the session, you may wish to answer the following questions:

1. How am I, today, right now? How has my week been?

_____

2. What do I want to get out of the call today?

_____

3. What action did I take since our last session? What were my wins/challenges?

_____

4. What do I have to report? What do I want to be held accountable for?

_____

5. What issues do I want to deepen on our call today? What are the challenges, concerns, achievements, or areas of learning to be addressed?

_____

_____

6. Debrief last week's inquiry:

_____

_____

7. What else?

_____

_____

Co-Active Coaching (2nd ed.) © 2007 by Laura Whitworth, Karen Kimsey-House, Henry Kimsey-House, and Phillip Sandahl. Permission is hereby granted to reproduce this page for client use. Duplication for any other use, including resale, is a violation of copyright law.

Discovery Forms and Checklists for Use with Corporate Clients

Although we have used the term "corporate clients" here, these forms and checklists are appropriate for clients in any organization, including nonprofit and nongovernmental organizations as well as government institutions. Coaches who work with clients in organizations, especially at the management and executive levels, will want to do their own background work on the organization in order to understand the client's situation. The coach may be able to do this background discovery directly with the client or with the person who contracted for the coaching services. As part of the preparation for working with corporate clients, the executive coach should have answers to the following questions:

- How does the performance appraisal system work?

- Are there standard leadership and management competencies identified by the organization, and what is the evaluation process for employees like my client?

- Does the organization use a 360-degree tool (see the Assessments section of the Toolkit, p. 218) or process? May I have access to that information?

- What development processes are approved for use in the organization, and does my client participate in a development program?

The forms and suggestions in the following section are by no means exhaustive but will give you an overview of materials for coaches working with clients in organizations.

Corporate Client Discovery Checklist

1. Before the initial session, have a conversation with the client. Explain what to expect, what to bring (such as a calendar or performance reviews), how much time it will take, and anything else that would allow the client to get prepared and look forward to the session.

2. Be sure the environment and room setup for the first meeting are safe, quiet, and not distracting. No phones, beepers, or other machines are allowed to intrude.

3. Welcome the client and set the tone. Let the client know of your eagerness to work with him or her.

4. Explain how the session will proceed: the amount of time, whether you will be taking notes, whether the client will be taking notes, a sense of what will be covered (balance, values, goals, action plans, or other issue), what will result from this session, and anything else that will inform the client and put him or her at ease.

5. Discuss coaching and explain how it has developed as a profession. Cite examples of people (after obtaining their permission) who have used coaching and describe how it has benefited them. Tell the client about the kinds of tools you might be using, about the options for how often you will meet, whether by phone or in person, and so on. Give an overview of coaching, not the details. Indicate here that the coaching relationship is one of design and alliance.

6. Discuss your background.

7. Describe confidentiality and define exactly what it will mean. In most cases, the client is responsible for whatever report the organization requires; the coach maintains confidentiality with the client. In some cases, the coach, the client, and a person from the organization, such as the client's supervisor or the person hiring the coach, arrange to meet for the purpose of reporting results and evaluating next steps. It is important to have a clear understanding of the ground rules before the coaching begins. (Note: In order to clarify the three roles, it is becoming more common to refer to the three as coach, coachee [formerly "the client"], and client [the organization or representative of the organization that contracts for the coaching].)

Co-Active Coaching (2nd ed.) © 2007 by Laura Whitworth, Karen Kimsey-House, Henry Kimsey-House, and Phillip Sandahl. Permission is hereby granted to reproduce this page for client use. Duplication for any other use, including resale, is a violation of copyright law.

Corporate Client Discovery Checklist cont'd

8. Explain in detail how clients design the alliance to get them where they want to go. Then design the alliance, giving the client examples of how you might work with him or her. Include accountability, brainstorming, the amount of attention allotted to the client's personal life, skill development, 360-degree feedback (see the Assessments section of the Toolkit), and the like.

9. Explore values clarification and the Saboteur, and do some form of vision work.

10. Fill out the Primary Focus form with the client. It is useful to include some area of focus from his or her personal life or personal development. In this way, the client learns that the coaching is personal, not just about the job. This is where the client discusses what's really important. Plan to spend a good bit of time on this step.

11. Review other forms and tools you may find useful, such as planning calendars, information tracking forms, and personal inventory forms.

12. Design clear goals with due dates, and ensure that these items get posted in the client's calendar. Define accountability and illustrate how it works. Assure the client that he or she is the designer of action plans and that the coach is not a disciplinarian.

13. Discuss the anticipated high and the corresponding low (the loss of enthusiasm that often occurs four to eight weeks into the coaching). Explain that it is the client who grants the coaching relationship power, ask that he or she do so, and ask if you may remind him or her of this from time to time. Point to the expected emergence of the Saboteur.

14. Discuss how future coaching sessions will go. Set up future session times and establish ground rules for tardiness, missed sessions, vacations, and other interruptions.

15. Set up the nature of assignments and inquiries.

16. Close the session with optimism and a potent sense of the client's future.

Co-Active Coaching (2nd ed.) © 2007 by Laura Whitworth, Karen Kimsey-House, Henry Kimsey-House, and Phillip Sandahl. Permission is hereby granted to reproduce this page for client use. Duplication for any other use, including resale, is a violation of copyright law.

First Meeting Checklist

Coach _____

Phone _____

E-mail _____

Meeting time and location _____

Bring the following items to the first meeting:

- Completed Client Profile
- Personal planner/calendar and notepaper

Co-Active Coaching (2nd ed.) © 2007 by Laura Whitworth, Karen Kimsey-House, Henry Kimsey-House, and Phillip Sandahl. Permission is hereby granted to reproduce this page for client use. Duplication for any other use, including resale, is a violation of copyright law.

Corporate Client Profile

Please take time to answer the questions on the following pages. Some of the questions capture information about where you are today. Others will get you thinking about what you want from coaching, from your job, and from life in general. This information will set a good foundation and allow us to move forward.

Bring your copy to the first meeting.

General Information

Name _____

Mailing address _____

Mail stop _____

Building number _____

Department _____

Home telephone _____

Work telephone _____

Fax number _____

E-mail address _____

Work Information

Job title _____

Years with company _____

Coaching

1. What do you want to make sure you get from the coaching relationship?

_____

_____

Co-Active Coaching (2nd ed.) © 2007 by Laura Whitworth, Karen Kimsey-House, Henry Kimsey-House, and Phillip Sandahl. Permission is hereby granted to reproduce this page for client use. Duplication for any other use, including resale, is a violation of copyright law.

Corporate Client Profile cont'd

2. What do you want from me as your coach?

_____

_____

3. Other:

_____

_____

Job

1. What do you want from your job?

_____

_____

2. What projects are you leading?

_____

_____

3. What are your key job goals?

_____

_____

4. What skills or knowledge are you developing?

_____

_____

Co-Active Coaching (2nd ed.) © 2007 by Laura Whitworth, Karen Kimsey-House, Henry Kimsey-House, and Phillip Sandahl. Permission is hereby granted to reproduce this page for client use. Duplication for any other use, including resale, is a violation of copyright law.

Corporate Client Profile cont'd

5. How do your job goals support your personal goals?

_____

_____

6. What else can you do to advance the company's objectives?

_____

_____

Personal

1. What do you have to contribute that is unique?

_____

_____

2. What special knowledge do you have?

_____

_____

3. What do you believe in?

_____

_____

4. What do you do when you're really up against an obstacle or barrier?

_____

_____

Co-Active Coaching (2nd ed.) © 2007 by Laura Whitworth, Karen Kimsey-House, Henry Kimsey-House, and Phillip Sandahl. Permission is hereby granted to reproduce this page for client use. Duplication for any other use, including resale, is a violation of copyright law.

Corporate Client Profile cont'd

5. What activities have meaning and spirit for you?

_____

_____

6. What needs in the world are you moved to meet?

_____

_____

7. What two steps could you take immediately that would make the greatest difference in your current situation(s)?

_____

_____

8. When you are most "stuck," what can I say that will return you to action?

_____

_____

Co-Active Coaching (2nd ed.) © 2007 by Laura Whitworth, Karen Kimsey-House, Henry Kimsey-House, and Phillip Sandahl. Permission is hereby granted to reproduce this page for client use. Duplication for any other use, including resale, is a violation of copyright law.

Alternative Client Profile

Client Information

Name _____

Name you prefer to be called _____

Organization _____

Job title or responsibility area _____

Contact Information at Work

Address _____

Telephone _____

Cellular _____

Fax _____

E-mail _____

Contact Information at Home

Address _____

Telephone _____

Cellular _____

Fax _____

E-mail _____

Personal Information

Birthday _____

Spouse's or partner's name _____

Children (names and ages) _____

Other important information _____

_____

Co-Active Coaching (2nd ed.) © 2007 by Laura Whitworth, Karen Kimsey-House, Henry Kimsey-House, and Phillip Sandahl. Permission is hereby granted to reproduce this page for client use. Duplication for any other use, including resale, is a violation of copyright law.

Alternative Client Profile cont'd

Initial Questions

To prepare for our first meeting, please take time to ponder and then answer the following questions. They are intended to begin the process of inquiry, reflection, learning, and forward movement.

About Your Life and Career

1. What are you most proud of?

   _____

   _____

2. What has been your biggest disappointment?

   _____

   _____

3. How would you describe your satisfaction with your life direction so far?

   _____

   _____

4. What words describe how you feel about your career?

   _____

   _____

5. What is the compliment or acknowledgment you hear most often about yourself?

   _____

   _____

Co-Active Coaching (2nd ed.) © 2007 by Laura Whitworth, Karen Kimsey-House, Henry Kimsey-House, and Phillip Sandahl. Permission is hereby granted to reproduce this page for client use. Duplication for any other use, including resale, is a violation of copyright law.

Alternative Client Profile cont'd

6. What dream of yours is still unfulfilled?

_____

_____

7. What words describe you at your best?

_____

_____

8. What words describe you when you are at less than your best?

_____

_____

9. What activities have meaning and heart for you?

_____

_____

10. Imagine you can have one wish fulfilled. What one thing would you change?

_____

_____

About Coaching You

1. What will make this coaching relationship rewarding for you?

_____

_____

Co-Active Coaching (2nd ed.) © 2007 by Laura Whitworth, Karen Kimsey-House, Henry Kimsey-House, and Phillip Sandahl. Permission is hereby granted to reproduce this page for client use. Duplication for any other use, including resale, is a violation of copyright law.

Alternative Client Profile cont'd

2. What approaches encourage or motivate you?

_____

_____

3. What approaches discourage or de-motivate you?

_____

_____

4. How will you know you are receiving value from this coaching relationship?

_____

_____

5. What else would you like me to know about you?

_____

_____

Co-Active Coaching (2nd ed.) © 2007 by Laura Whitworth, Karen Kimsey-House. Henry Kimsey-House, and Phillip Sandahl. Permission is hereby granted to reproduce this page for client use. Duplication for any other use, including resale, is a violation of copyright law.

Performance Awareness Appraisal

Note below the performance skills and/or qualities your job demands of you and their relative importance both to you and to your company. At right, mark your current proficiency level for each skill with an X. Mark where you want it to be with an O.

Skill or Quality	Importance (0–10)	
	To Me	To Company
1.		
2.		
3.		
4.		
5.		
6.		
7.		
8.		
9.		
10.		

Low 0 1 2 3 4 5 6 7 8 9 10 High

Co-Active Coaching (2nd ed.) © 2007 by Laura Whitworth, Karen Kimsey-House, Henry Kimsey-House, and Phillip Sandahl. Permission is hereby granted to reproduce this page for client use. Duplication for any other use, including resale, is a violation of copyright law.

Job Performance Wheel

My Time Management

Satisfied with My Job Performance

Staying Organized

On Time with Duties and Projects

10 9 8 7 6 5 4 3 2 1

Staying on Top of My E-mail and Voice Mail

Get Along with Colleagues and Clients

Satisfied with My Team Participation

Clear About My Role and Duties

Directions: Score your sense of satisfaction with the aspects of your job performance labeled above. You may replace any of the labels with labels you believe are more appropriate for you. Use a scale of 0 to 10 to assess your performance. Identify areas you wish to improve. Determine what actions you will take to improve your scores.

Co-Active Coaching (2nd ed.) © 2007 by Laura Whitworth, Karen Kimsey-House, Henry Kimsey-House, and Phillip Sandahl. Permission is hereby granted to reproduce this page for client use. Duplication for any other use, including resale, is a violation of copyright law.

Management/Leadership Wheel

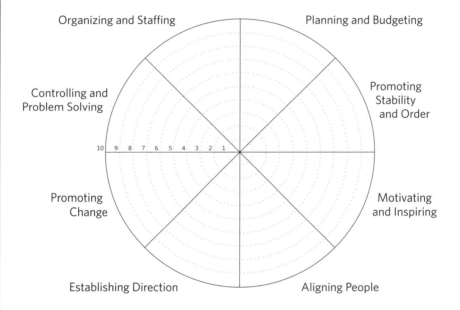

Organizing and Staffing

Planning and Budgeting

Controlling and
Problem Solving

Promoting
Stability
and Order

10 9 8 7 6 5 4 3 2 1

Promoting
Change

Motivating
and Inspiring

Establishing Direction

Aligning People

Directions: On a scale of 0 to 10, score your satisfaction with your abilities in the following areas:

- **Planning and Budgeting:** Establishing detailed steps and timetables for achieving results and then allocating the resources necessary to make it happen

- **Establishing Direction:** Developing a vision of the future, often the distant future, and strategies for producing the changes needed to achieve that vision

- **Organizing and Staffing:** Establishing a structure for accomplishing plan require-ments, staffing that structure with people, delegating authority for carrying out the plan, providing policies and procedures to guide people, and creating methods or systems to monitor implementation

Co-Active Coaching (2nd ed.) © 2007 by Laura Whitworth, Karen Kimsey-House, Henry Kimsey-House, and Phillip Sandahl. Permission is hereby granted to reproduce this page for client use. Duplication for any other use, including resale, is a violation of copyright law.

Management/Leadership Wheel cont'd

- **Aligning People:** Communicating the direction in words and deeds to all those whose cooperation may be needed so as to create a team that understands the vision and strategies and accepts their validity

- **Controlling and Problem Solving:** Monitoring results in detail, identifying deviations from the plan, and then organizing to solve these problems

- **Motivating and Inspiring:** Energizing people to overcome major political, bureaucratic, and resource barriers to change by satisfying basic, but often unfulfilled, human needs

- **Promoting Stability and Order:** Creating the potential for consistent production of key results

- **Promoting Change:** Creating the potential for production of useful change (such as desired new products)

Co-Active Coaching (2nd ed.) © 2007 by Laura Whitworth, Karen Kimsey-House, Henry Kimsey-House, and Phillip Sandahl. Permission is hereby granted to reproduce this page for client use. Duplication for any other use, including resale, is a violation of copyright law.

Assessments

Many coaches use assessment tools as part of their initial discovery work with clients. The purpose is to reveal information about the client or, in some cases, to establish a benchmark—a portrait of where the client is at the time of the assessment—based on criteria established by the assessment. Most assessments use a questionnaire format, either a paper or an online version. Assessments provide coach and client with insight into the client's strengths, inclinations, and likely actions or reactions in certain situations or in relationships. The information can help guide coach and client in the creation of goals or ways of reaching goals that have a higher probability of success.

There are far too many assessment tools and options available in the marketplace for a complete review in this book. These are a few of the main categories:

- Personality assessment: The *Myers-Briggs Type Indicator*® (MBTI®) personality inventory is well known. The DiSC® and *StrengthsFinder*™ assessments as well as assessments from Kolbe and MAPP are also widely used.

- Aptitude and interest inventories: *The Strong Interest Inventory*® assessment is a long-standing and well-respected example. Many available assessments focus specifically on leadership strengths; each assessment is built on its own assumptions or model of the important qualities of leadership.

In corporate and organizational work, it is virtually standard practice for coaches to use some form of individual assessment, and the 360-degree feedback format is the most common. The 360-degree assessment gathers feedback from co-workers, supervisors or superiors, and direct reports and provides a multifaceted picture of the client as seen through the eyes of those with whom he or she interacts daily. The LVi 360 from coach Kristie Bavaro, MBA, is a whole-life approach that includes family and friends in order to enrich the discovery process. Performance appraisal systems in the organization also provide a form of assessment and benchmarking; they reveal the evaluation criteria of the organization, a scoring system, and a way of establishing performance goals for clients.

There are also assessments available for coaches who work with teams in organizations. In most cases, these assessments combine an individual assessment with a way of interpreting the aggregate effect on the interrelationships for the team. For example, an MBTI team assessment gives the coach information about each individual on the team and, based on that, information about the dynamics of the relationships. The Belbin Team Roles fulfills a similar function. This assessment identifies which of nine Belbin roles each team member matches. According to the Belbin model, the role has certain characteristic behaviors, and by understanding the role identities on the team, the coach has a clearer picture of how the team works—where it is strong and where it will not be as strong.

The *Team Diagnostic* assessment from Team Coaching International is a different approach to team assessment. The assessment is built on the groundbreaking work of The Center for Right Relationship (see Appendix B) and a growing understanding in organizational thinking that a team is a whole system—a dynamic entity that is more than a group of individuals and their combined interrelationships. From a team coach's point of view, both the individual assessment information and a portrait of the system itself are enormously valuable. The Team Diagnostic assessment is based on a productivity/positivity model that graphically reveals a clear benchmark for the team as a system and a map for ongoing team development.

There are dozens of different assessments available to coaches. In the end, the best solution is to find one that you are comfortable working with and that provides information you find useful in your coaching.

Additional Coaching Forms

(To be used during future coaching sessions)

Co-Active Coaching

A powerful alliance designed to forward and enhance the lifelong process of human learning, effectiveness, and fulfillment

Co-Active Coaching (2nd ed.) © 2007 by Laura Whitworth, Karen Kimsey-House, Henry Kimsey-House, and Phillip Sandahl. Permission is hereby granted to reproduce this page for client use. Duplication for any other use, including resale, is a violation of copyright law.

Wheel of Life Exercise

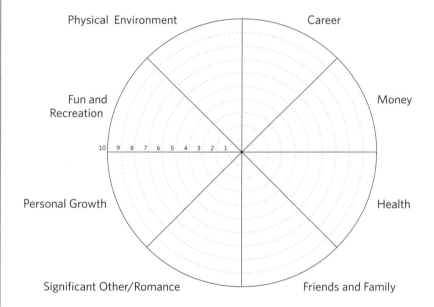

Directions: This wheel contains eight sections that, together, represent one way of describing a whole life. This exercise measures your level of satisfaction in these areas on the day you work through this exercise. Taking the center of the wheel as 0 and the outer edge as an ideal 10, rank your level of satisfaction with each life area by drawing a straight or curved line to create a new outer edge (see example). The new perimeter represents your Wheel of Life. How bumpy would the ride be if this were a real wheel? Let's start to look at areas where you want to improve your level of satisfaction and think about what you might do to accomplish that.

Co-Active Coaching (2nd ed.) © 2007 by Laura Whitworth, Karen Kimsey-House, Henry Kimsey-House, and Phillip Sandahl. Permission is hereby granted to reproduce this page for client use. Duplication for any other use, including resale, is a violation of copyright law.

Wheel of Life Exercise cont'd

Example

Physical Environment · Career · Money · Health · Friends and Family · Significant Other/Romance · Personal Growth · Fun and Recreation

10 9 8 7 6 5 4 3 2 1

Co-Active Coaching (2nd ed.) © 2007 by Laura Whitworth, Karen Kimsey-House, Henry Kimsey-House, and Phillip Sandahl. Permission is hereby granted to reproduce this page for client use. Duplication for any other use, including resale, is a violation of copyright law.

Priorities Wheel

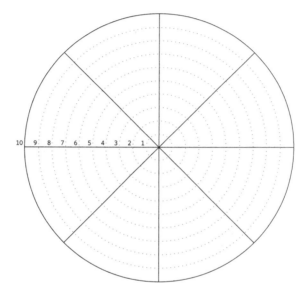

Directions: Using the Wheel of Life model, label this wheel with eight priorities in your job or life. When you complete the labeling, score your sense of satisfaction with your priorities on a scale of 0 to 10. Identify one or two scores that you want to affect immediately. What actions will you take? When will you take these actions? What support do you require to ensure that the actions occur?

Co-Active Coaching (2nd ed.) © 2007 by Laura Whitworth, Karen Kimsey-House, Henry Kimsey-House, and Phillip Sandahl. Permission is hereby granted to reproduce this page for client use. Duplication for any other use, including resale, is a violation of copyright law.

Management Competencies Wheel

Directions: This wheel contains eight sections that, together, represent a constellation of management competencies. This exercise measures your level of satisfaction in these areas on the day you work through the exercise. Taking the center of the wheel as 0 and the outer edge as an ideal 10, rank your level of satisfaction with each area by drawing a straight or curved line to create a new outer edge (see example). The new perimeter of the circle represents the Management Competencies Wheel. How bumpy would the ride be if this were a real wheel? Let's start to look at areas where you want to improve your level of satisfaction and think about what you might do to accomplish that.

Co-Active Coaching (2nd ed.) © 2007 by Laura Whitworth, Karen Kimsey-House, Henry Kimsey-House, and Phillip Sandahl. Permission is hereby granted to reproduce this page for client use. Duplication for any other use, including resale, is a violation of copyright law.

Management Competencies Wheel cont'd

Example

Decision Making · Communication · Results · Managing Change · Strategic Planning · Customer Service · Team Development · Risk Taking

10 9 8 7 6 5 4 3 2 1

Co-Active Coaching (2nd ed.) © 2007 by Laura Whitworth, Karen Kimsey-House, Henry Kimsey-House, and Phillip Sandahl. Permission is hereby granted to reproduce this page for client use. Duplication for any other use, including resale, is a violation of copyright law.

Blank Wheel
(To be labeled by coach or client)

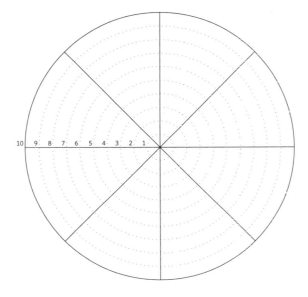

Co-Active Coaching (2nd ed.) © 2007 by Laura Whitworth, Karen Kimsey-House, Henry Kimsey-House, and Phillip Sandahl. Permission is hereby granted to reproduce this page for client use. Duplication for any other use, including resale, is a violation of copyright law.

Goals and Commitments

With a goal, there is a specific point in time by which you either have or have not accomplished it. It is measurable and specific. Either you have increased your income by 30 percent by July 31 or you have not. A commitment is different from a goal in that it is an ongoing quality-of-life shift. A commitment is not measurable. It may have to do with the state or quality of being you want to create in your life. "I am committed to making a difference in the world through my work," "I am committed to having open communication with my children," or "I am committed to a healthful lifestyle and a fit body" are all examples of commitments. Using the Wheel of Life as your guide, identify your goals (with specific due dates) and your commitments.

	Goals	**Commitments**
Career	1. _____	_____
	2. _____	_____
Money	1. _____	_____
	2. _____	_____
Health	1. _____	_____
	2. _____	_____
Friends and Family	1. _____	_____
	2. _____	_____
Significant Other/Romance	1. _____	_____
	2. _____	_____
Personal Growth	1. _____	_____
	2. _____	_____
Fun and Recreation	1. _____	_____
	2. _____	_____
Physical Environment	1. _____	_____
	2. _____	_____

Co-Active Coaching (2nd ed.) © 2007 by Laura Whitworth, Karen Kimsey-House, Henry Kimsey-House, and Phillip Sandahl. Permission is hereby granted to reproduce this page for client use. Duplication for any other use, including resale, is a violation of copyright law.

Daily Habits

Small constructive actions taken on a daily or routine basis can quickly give you a sense of accomplishment and forward momentum. These daily habits (or success practices) form the foundation on which major change takes place. Take a look at your Wheel of Life score to get ideas for habits or practices that would support you in moving forward. What action, if taken on a regular basis, would make a difference for you in one of the areas of the wheel? These practices can be related to either your professional or your personal life (e.g., process all incoming mail daily, exercise four times per week). Remember those things that will nourish you and provide you with satisfaction, such as spending twenty minutes a day with your children or taking a walk in the woods three times a week, calling one close friend each day, and so on.

1. _____
2. _____
3. _____
4. _____
5. _____
6. _____
7. _____
8. _____
9. _____
10. _____

Co-Active Coaching (2nd ed.) © 2007 by Laura Whitworth, Karen Kimsey-House, Henry Kimsey-House, and Phillip Sandahl. Permission is hereby granted to reproduce this page for client use. Duplication for any other use, including resale, is a violation of copyright law.

Daily Habits Tracking Log

New Daily Habits for the Month of _____

Habit	1	2	3	4	5	6	7	8	9	10	11	12	13	14	15	16	17	18	19	20	21	22	23	24	25	26	27	28	29	30	31
1.																															
2.																															
3.																															
4.																															
5.																															
6.																															
7.																															
8.																															
9.																															
10.																															

Co-Active Coaching (2nd ed.) © 2007 by Laura Whitworth, Karen Kimsey-House, Henry Kimsey-House, and Phillip Sandahl. Permission is hereby granted to reproduce this page for client use. Duplication for any other use, including resale, is a violation of copyright law.

Action and Planning Log

(Use this form to write down specific to-do items and long-term goals.)

To Do

Action Item

**Date Action
to Be Taken**

_____   _____

_____   _____

_____   _____

_____   _____

_____   _____

_____   _____

_____   _____

Long-Term Goals

_____

_____

_____

_____

_____

_____

Co-Active Coaching (2nd ed.) © 2007 by Laura Whitworth, Karen Kimsey-House, Henry Kimsey-House, and Phillip Sandahl. Permission is hereby granted to reproduce this page for client use. Duplication for any other use, including resale, is a violation of copyright law.

Saboteur Clarification

My Saboteur's name is _____

My Saboteur is fond of saying or often says:

_____

_____

_____

_____

_____

_____

_____

Inside my organization/community/family, we use these Saboteur comments:

_____

_____

_____

_____

_____

_____

Co-Active Coaching (2nd ed.) © 2007 by Laura Whitworth, Karen Kimsey-House, Henry Kimsey-House, and Phillip Sandahl. Permission is hereby granted to reproduce this page for client use. Duplication for any other use, including resale, is a violation of copyright law.

Saying Yes—Saying No

By saying YES to   **I am saying NO to**

1. _____ _____
                             _____

2. _____ _____
                             _____

3. _____ _____
                             _____

4. _____ _____
                             _____

By saying NO to   **I am saying YES to**

1. _____ _____
                             _____

2. _____ _____
                             _____

3. _____ _____
                             _____

4. _____ _____
                             _____

Co-Active Coaching (2nd ed.) © 2007 by Laura Whitworth, Karen Kimsey-House, Henry Kimsey-House, and Phillip Sandahl. Permission is hereby granted to reproduce this page for client use. Duplication for any other use, including resale, is a violation of copyright law.

Coaching Exercises

The exercises that follow have been referenced throughout the book. The greater detail provided here will enable the coach to better deliver these exercises to the client during the discovery session or a future coaching session.

Future Self Exercise

The following visualizations are based on a future self exercise used in a Coaches Training Institute workshop. Feel free to use these exact words. We recommend that you have the client get comfortable, perhaps lower the light level, make sure there will be no distractions, and play quiet, meditative music. When the client is grounded and ready, begin the visualization. Pause at appropriate times throughout the visualization to give the client sufficient time to be with the location or answer the questions. Allow a little time at the end for debriefing, but make continued exploration of the visualization the homework for the upcoming week. The week after debriefing the visualization in detail, do the second visualization exercise to reveal the gift the client's future self will be giving the client.

Visualization 1

Get into a comfortable position. Now allow your eyes to close and begin by focusing your awareness on your breath. Breathing in and breathing out. Breathing in easily and effortlessly. Then breathing out. Each breath allows you to become more relaxed and comfortable. Outside sounds only allow you to go deeper inside: a reminder of how good it is to leave the noise and stress of the outside world and journey into the quiet and peace of your inner world.

(Include the next paragraph only when you want the client to go to an even deeper meditative space.)

> As you allow yourself to go deeper into a state of relaxation, perhaps you can remember a time when you stood before a pond or a lake and it was quiet and peaceful. You may have tossed a pebble into the center and noticed the ripples spreading out. One ripple after another, flowing outward, farther and farther. The ripples slowing down, becoming farther apart, until the water was once again calm and peaceful. I'm going to invite you now to imagine that your body is like that body of water. And as you drop a pebble into the center of your body, you can feel ripples of relaxation rippling out. Waves of relaxation flowing through your body. Up through your torso into your chest and your back. Up through the vertebrae and spreading out into each and every muscle of your back. Through your shoulders and arms, up through your neck, your jaw, face, scalp. Feeling those ripples relax you as

Co-Active Coaching (2nd ed.) © 2007 by Laura Whitworth, Karen Kimsey-House, Henry Kimsey-House, and Phillip Sandahl. Permission is hereby granted to reproduce this page for client use. Duplication for any other use, including resale, is a violation of copyright law.

Future Self Exercise cont'd

your muscles let go and become soft and loose. Feeling the ripples of relaxation flowing down through the bottom of your torso. Flowing through your abdomen and your pelvis. Down through your thighs, calves, ankles, and toes. Know that each time you drop a pebble into the center of your body you can become more relaxed.

As you become more relaxed, you find yourself becoming more quiet and peaceful. Now bring your attention to the spot between your eyes: the third eye. Imagine a light there. What color is the light between your eyes?

Now imagine that light becoming a beam that extends out into space. Follow that beam as it leaves this building, as it travels above the city, as it continues out, so that you can view the entire area. Keep going farther and farther into outer space and notice the curvature of the earth. As you keep going farther and farther out, you find yourself enveloped by the softness and quiet of space. Notice the big blue-green ball below you with the white clouds wisping around it. Allow yourself to enjoy this perspective for a moment.

Now notice another beam of light very near to you, a different color from the one you followed into outer space. Begin to follow that beam back down to earth. The beam is taking you back to earth twenty years from now, twenty years into the future. Keep following this beam down, noticing the curvature of the earth and the geography stretched out below you. As you come closer to the end of the beam, keep noticing where you are. This is where your future self lives—you, twenty years from now. Come into contact with earth and notice where you are. Notice what dwelling or nature surrounds you. Now move to the dwelling of your future self. What does it look like? What kind of landscape does it have? Are there trees? Flowers? What kind? Get a sense of this place.

Now have someone come to the door. On the other side of the door is your future self, waiting to greet you—yourself, twenty years from now. As the door opens, what do you notice? Greet your future self and notice the way your future self returns your greeting, welcoming you into this time and place twenty years in the future. Take in this person, your future self. What does this person look like? Notice how this person stands, what this person is wearing. Get a sense of this person's essence. Notice the inside of this dwelling. What kind of person lives here? What are the colors of this place?

Co-Active Coaching (2nd ed.) © 2007 by Laura Whitworth, Karen Kimsey-House, Henry Kimsey-House, and Phillip Sandahl. Permission is hereby granted to reproduce this page for client use. Duplication for any other use, including resale, is a violation of copyright law.

Future Self Exercise cont'd

Now move with your future self to a comfortable place for a conversation. Perhaps your future self offers you something to drink. Settle in and make yourself comfortable for a talk with your future self. There are questions that you might want to ask your future self. Begin by asking: "What is it that you most remember about the past twenty years?" Take a moment now to hear the answer. *(Pause)* Now ask your future self the following question: "What do I need to know to get me from where I am now to where you are? What would be most helpful?" Listen to what your future self has to tell you. *(Pause)* Good.

Now take a moment and ask your future self your own questions. What other questions would you like to ask your future self? *(Pause)* And now ask your future self one final question before you go: "What name, other than your first name, are you called by? A special name. It could be a metaphor or a symbol of your essence. What is this name?" *(Pause)* Good. Bringing this visit to a close, thank your future self for being here with you today and sharing so much wisdom.

Now find your way back to the beam of light and journey back up the beam, watching this world of twenty years in the future grow ever smaller as you move out into space. Again, you see the ball of blue and green below you, clouds swirling around it. Notice that your beam of light has intersected with a different beam of light that will bring you back to this year and this location. Follow this beam of light back to the present time on earth. As you travel down this beam, notice the earth growing bigger and bigger. Moving farther down the beam, notice the geography of the area, the skyline and landscape of the area, and, finally, come back into the room here. Good. In a few moments, I'm going to count from three to one. At the count of one, you will be refreshed and alert, as if you've had the perfect amount of rest, knowing you can remember everything you wish of this inner journey.

When you open your eyes, please remain silent and jot down things you want to remember about your journey. *Three.* Coming back to present time, becoming more alert and refreshed. *Two.* Stretching your body, feeling the ground beneath you. And *one.* Eyes open, refreshed and alert.

Visualization 2

Just make yourself comfortable and allow your eyes to close and begin by taking long, slow, deep breaths. Breathing in through your nose and holding it . . . and breathing out through your mouth. Just allow yourself to be aware of your breathing. Easily, naturally, and freely.

Co-Active Coaching (2nd ed.) © 2007 by Laura Whitworth, Karen Kimsey-House, Henry Kimsey-House, and Phillip Sandahl. Permission is hereby granted to reproduce this page for client use. Duplication for any other use, including resale, is a violation of copyright law.

Future Self Exercise cont'd

I'm going to invite you to take a mental inventory of your body now. Beginning at the top of your head, become aware of any tension or tightness you might find. And just give that tension or tightness a color and let it drain out the tips of your toes and the tips of your fingers. Just allow that tension or tightness to drain away. And moving down your body, bring your attention to your neck and arms. Again, if you find any tension or tightness, just let it drain away. Take your awareness now down along your back, down into your abdomen and pelvic area. Again, notice any tightness you might find there and just eliminate it. Imagine it just melting away, draining out through the tips of your toes. Noticing if there is any tension or tightness in your legs or your ankles and feet and just allow it to drain out your toes. Now imagine you're like a strong and sturdy tree, putting roots down into the ground, allowing those roots to go deeper and deeper, spreading out, connecting you solidly to the earth.

Now bring your attention to the spot between your eyes: the third eye. Imagine a light there. What color is the light between your eyes? Now imagine that light becoming a beam that extends out into space. Follow that beam as it leaves this building, as it travels above the city, as it continues out, so that you can view the entire area. Keep on going farther and farther into outer space and notice the curvature of the earth. As you keep going farther and farther out, you find yourself enveloped by the softness and quiet of space. Notice the big blue-green ball below you with the white clouds wisping around it. Allow yourself to enjoy this perspective for a moment.

Now notice another beam of light very near to you, a different color from the one you followed into outer space. Begin to follow that beam back down to earth. The beam is taking you back to earth twenty years from now, twenty years into the future. Keep following this beam down, noticing the curvature of the earth and the geography stretched out below you. As you come closer to the end of the beam, keep noticing where you are. This is where your future self lives—you, twenty years from now. Come into contact with earth and notice where you are. Now move to the dwelling of your future self. You know the way. You've been here before. Your future self is waiting for you. Waiting to talk with you. As your future self greets you, notice what it is like being with this person again. Look around you. Drink up the environment. Notice the colors here.

Now is your opportunity to ask whatever questions you'd like of your future self. You might want to know your next step. Who you need to be right now in order to

Co-Active Coaching (2nd ed.) © 2007 by Laura Whitworth, Karen Kimsey-House, Henry Kimsey-House, and Phillip Sandahl. Permission is hereby granted to reproduce this page for client use. Duplication for any other use, including resale, is a violation of copyright law.

Future Self Exercise cont'd

move forward. Or ask your future self anything that feels right to you. *(Pause)* Now take a moment to listen to your future self's response. *(Long pause)*

I am going to invite you now to take a deep breath and allow yourself to step into the being of your future self. Allow yourself to merge into this person's body. Experience what it feels like to be this future self. Be aware of how you feel. Of how good it feels in your future self's body. What does the world look like through your future self's eyes? Walk around, feeling yourself move as your future self. Notice if there's one particular place in your body where you can feel your future self's power most strongly. This is the power of being your future self. Allow that feeling to expand, filling your whole body, into your very cells. You may want to touch that place on your body now in order to anchor that feeling. And know that whenever you wish to connect with your future self, you can touch that place on your body and bring forth these positive, powerful feelings. When you touch that place, these feelings and this experience will flood your body, easily and effortlessly.

Now, looking out through your future self's eyes, look at your present-day self. What do you notice about your present-day self? Looking out through your future self's eyes, what is it that you want to tell your present-day self? *(Pause)*

Now take a deep breath and shift your awareness, leaving the body of your future self and becoming your present-day self once again. Allow yourself to be fully present in the body of your present-day self.

As you look back at your future self, notice that this person has a gift for you: a special gift to remind you of who you are becoming and what you are moving toward. As your future self offers you the gift, ask if there's any meaning to it. Is there anything you need to know about it? *(Pause)*

It's time to leave now. Thank your future self for the wisdom. From now on, your future self will be an inner resource you can use whenever you need to do so. Whenever you seek guidance, whenever you need to know what your next step should be, you can contact your future self, a powerful ally and resource for you. Say good-bye now, knowing that you will remember everything you need to from this visit.

Now, find your way back to the beam of light and journey back up the beam, watching this world of twenty years in the future grow ever smaller as you move out into space. Again, you see the ball of blue and green below you, clouds swirling around it. Notice that your beam of light has intersected with the first beam of light that will bring you back to this year and this location. Follow this beam of light back to present-time earth. As you travel down this beam, notice the earth growing

Co-Active Coaching (2nd ed.) © 2007 by Laura Whitworth, Karen Kimsey-House, Henry Kimsey-House, and Phillip Sandahl. Permission is hereby granted to reproduce this page for client use. Duplication for any other use, including resale, is a violation of copyright law.

Future Self Exercise cont'd

bigger and bigger. Moving farther down the beam, notice the geography of the area, the skyline and landscape, and, finally, come back into the room here. Good. In a few moments I will count from three to one. At the count of one, you will be refreshed and alert as if you've had the perfect amount of rest, knowing you can remember everything you wish of this inner journey.

Three. Coming back now, coming back to present time, becoming more alert and refreshed. *Two.* Stretching your body, feeling the ground beneath you. And *one.* Eyes open, refreshed and alert.

Co-Active Coaching (2nd ed.) © 2007 by Laura Whitworth, Karen Kimsey-House, Henry Kimsey-House, and Phillip Sandahl. Permission is hereby granted to reproduce this page for client use. Duplication for any other use, including resale, is a violation of copyright law.

Life Purpose Exercise

We say that people are born with a life purpose. Some people never look for their purpose, and so it remains unspoken their whole lives. But it is there. The life purpose is the reason we are on this planet. It is the thing we are meant to accomplish, the gift we are meant to bring. Life purpose is not about a job or even an avocation. It is the round-the-clock, twenty-four-hour, every-day-of-your-life expression of who you are when you are reaching your full potential.

When clients are "on purpose," they are fulfilled. They are contributing and making a difference. When they are not on purpose, they feel discontented and unfulfilled. Even if a client doesn't have a life purpose statement, the life purpose is still there. Even if clients can't articulate a life purpose statement to their satisfaction, they can tell the difference between when they are on purpose and when they are not on purpose. It is very challenging for them to not act on this purpose. It feels terrible, dead, disconnected.

The coach's job is to work with clients to design a life purpose statement they can use as they clarify their purpose in the world. Such a statement allows them to connect with their life purpose easily and quickly. The life purpose statement is like a big neon sign that will help them find their way out of the swamp when they get stuck. Because it is a personal statement for the client's own use, it can be as grand and sweeping or as transformational as the client can handle. It is not open to the ridicule or judgment of others.

The process we use for finding and articulating a life purpose statement follows a series of steps.

1. The coach presents a visualization or exercise that generates impressions and allows clients to gather insight about their life purpose. (Four visualizations are included in this section.)

2. Coach and client debrief the visualization(s), looking for the impact the client wants to create. Client and coach brainstorm and collaborate. Here, the coach's job is to listen and keep encouraging all the words that come out of the visualizations. The coach listens for any repeated words or common themes. The coach also uses his or her intuition to sense the impact words or phrases. Life purpose coaching is extraordinarily intuitive. The client and coach keep listening

Co-Active Coaching (2nd ed.) © 2007 by Laura Whitworth, Karen Kimsey-House, Henry Kimsey-House, and Phillip Sandahl. Permission is hereby granted to reproduce this page for client use. Duplication for any other use, including resale, is a violation of copyright law.

Life Purpose Exercise cont'd

for the words that have the strongest resonance for the client. The coach compiles these words and replays them for the client so the client can hear them and see which ones have the strongest feeling. This forms the beginning of an impact statement.

The initial impact statement is likely to be general: "I want people to be happy," "I want people to be in better relationships." The problem with a general impact statement like this is that it is too vague to motivate the client to action. So the coaching then focuses on taking the client deeper into the impact so that it is more specific and the client has something to grab on to. The impact statement needs to be clear enough and strong enough so that the client can access it when he or she is off course. It describes the impact the client wants to have, such as to have people embrace life, act authentically, see their true selves, find their personal power, discover their creativity, experience their magnificence, or return to aliveness.

3. Once the impact statement is found, the next step is to find a metaphor that captures the essential quality of the life purpose. For example, "I am the magician," "I am the lighthouse," "I am the dynamite," "I am the rock in the shoe," "I am the alarm clock."

The metaphor can also be an action: "I wake people up," "I explode the lies," "I uncover the inner truth," "I call people home."

Note that finding a metaphor generally is not easy for clients. It is often hard for them to see themselves in the form of a metaphor or an image. Also note that finding a life purpose statement takes time. It is a process of peeling back the layers to get at the essence of a person's purpose. In this initial coaching session on life purpose, the client will likely find one version that is rough but workable. It may take months or years to refine the statement. The metaphor also may change over time. The goal is to find a version that rings true for the client, knowing that there is more work to be done.

The metaphor and impact statement should be concise and should create maximum impact for the client—in general, not more than fifteen words. The life purpose statement should follow this general format:

I am the _____(metaphor) so that
people _____ (impact statement).

Co-Active Coaching (2nd ed.) © 2007 by Laura Whitworth, Karen Kimsey-House, Henry Kimsey-House, and Phillip Sandahl. Permission is hereby granted to reproduce this page for client use. Duplication for any other use, including resale, is a violation of copyright law.

Life Purpose Exercise cont'd

The following are examples of life purpose statements:

I am the lighthouse that guides people to their dreams.

I am the dynamite that transforms people's lives.

I am the rock in the shoe that causes people to remember to be alive.

I am the alarm clock that awakens people to their magnificence.

Note that life purpose statements can be corny, grandiose, and flowery. All of that is okay. These are not for publication. They are for you and your clients to use so that they can fully feel the power of the life purpose in them. The coach needs to champion and encourage clients to create a truly big life purpose statement. The life purpose is not something they will necessarily accomplish in this lifetime, but it should have tremendous, compelling power to motivate them to be in action in their lives and to be on purpose. The visualizations are just the beginning—a place to start to collect the raw material. There are lots of additional ways to have clients envision their life purpose. They can draw pictures of their life purpose or find a piece of music to use as their theme song. Encourage clients to be creative and look for whatever inspiration they can find to help them articulate their life purpose. The coach's role is to encourage, to continue ongoing coaching in order to clarify the statement, and, of course, to use life purpose in the coaching as clients look at what will be fulfilling for them in their lives.

Visualization 1

Imagine that you're in a large group of people milling about in front of a stage. Up on the stage is your future self. Your future self begins to speak to this large group of people. Suddenly you become aware of a shift that has happened to you and the entire audience. Your future self has in some way had a profound impact on you and on the rest of the people in the audience. You are all altered or changed in some fundamental way. Aware of this impact on yourself and others, you leave the room altered for the rest of your life.

Questions:

What was the impact your future self had on you and the others?

How were you and the others transformed?

Who was your future self being to have such an impact?

Co-Active Coaching (2nd ed.) © 2007 by Laura Whitworth, Karen Kimsey-House, Henry Kimsey-House, and Phillip Sandahl. Permission is hereby granted to reproduce this page for client use. Duplication for any other use, including resale, is a violation of copyright law.

Life Purpose Exercise cont'd

Visualization 2

Turn the clock back and look at a time in your life when you felt your full power—a time when your spine, arms, and fingertips were tingling with excitement, a time when you didn't care what anyone thought of you. You were absolutely alive! *(Pause)*

Questions:

Where were you?

What were you doing?

Who was around you?

What was occurring in them at that time?

What was your impact on them?

Visualization 3

Return to the auditorium once more. The stage is there, and a large group of people is milling about. There is a buzz in the room. Everything is the same as before except this time you are on the stage. Look out over the crowd. Feel the feelings you have as you are about to address the gathering. Just as you step up to the microphone, time freezes for an instant, and you hear a voice in your ear that says your name and then says, "In the next thirty seconds, you will have a chance to have any impact you want on this entire group. It will be only one chance, one impact, but all of these people will be changed in some way; they will have a different life because of the impact you have had on them. Thirty seconds. 15 . . . 10-9-8-7-6-5-4-3-2-1."

Question:

What impact did you have? What happened to the people?

Visualization 4

You are getting into a rocket ship. The rocket ship takes off. You are on your way to an undeveloped planet in the universe. It's a fine planet in every way, but it's uninhabited. You have the power to create this planet to be whatever you want it to be. When you land, what is it that you're going to make happen—what's the impact you want to have, that's going to create the planet the way you want it to be? *(Pause)* The ship is landing on the planet. The door opens. You touch the planet and say, "It's going to be this way." What is "this way"?

Co-Active Coaching (2nd ed.) © 2007 by Laura Whitworth, Karen Kimsey-House, Henry Kimsey-House, and Phillip Sandahl. Permission is hereby granted to reproduce this page for client use. Duplication for any other use, including resale, is a violation of copyright law.

Values Clarification Exercise

Values are who we are. Not who we would like to be, not who we think we should be, but who we are in our lives, right now. Another way to put it is that values represent our unique and individual essence, our ultimate and most fulfilling form of expressing and relating. Our values serve as a compass pointing out what it means to be true to oneself. When we honor our values on a regular and consistent basis, life is good and fulfilling.

As coaches, we know how beneficial it can be for clients when they are clear about their own values. Important life decisions are easier to make and outcomes are more fulfilling when the decisions are viewed through a matrix of well-understood personal values. However, the process of clarifying values is often difficult for clients. It frequently makes people intellectualize and fantasize, whereas you want them to look into their lives and uncover the values that are already there, in their day-to-day actions and interactions. That's one of the reasons selecting values from a list seldom works: the list becomes an opportunity to vote on the most desirable or socially acceptable values, rather than serving as a mechanism to identify who we are. Selecting values from a list reinforces the intellectual urge to figure it out and get the words right. Clients' values are observable; they live in the world. Thus, they won't benefit from picking their values from a list. The coach's job is to assist clients in viewing their lives in such a way that values are revealed.

Sometimes clients can't seem to get a perspective on their values. Coaching works well in such cases because the coach can ask questions and provide scenarios that take clients into their lives rather than into their heads. Values clarification coaching allows clients to examine and articulate their values in a safe yet courageous environment. The exact wording will matter to the client in the long run, but what is most important in the short run is that the approximate label for the value resonate with the client. As a practical matter for coaches, values clarification is enormously helpful in learning to know clients, and in helping clients know themselves. Coaches and clients use values to help facilitate fulfilling choices, to strategize appropriate actions, and to recognize situations in which values are an issue.

Many clients nevertheless struggle with finding the right words. They are constrained because they feel they have to find the perfect word and the value has much more emotional meaning than the definition of a single word allows. In fact, each individual has his or her own unique meaning for each value. We may have different meanings even though we use the same word. Earlier, we mentioned

Co-Active Coaching (2nd ed.) © 2007 by Laura Whitworth, Karen Kimsey-House, Henry Kimsey-House, and Phillip Sandahl. Permission is hereby granted to reproduce this page for client use. Duplication for any other use, including resale, is a violation of copyright law.

Values Clarification Exercise cont'd

techniques that can minimize vocabulary anxiety. The first tip is to use a pencil with an eraser. Clients often experience a sense of reluctance when values have to be written in ink. The coach can emphasize the advantages of using a pencil so the client realizes that it is not important to get it right the first time. The second tip when doing values clarification is to use several words together to form a string describing the value. Separating the words with slash marks makes the string easier to read. For example:

Integrity/Honesty/Walk-the-talk

Integrity/Whole/Congruent

Leadership/Empower/Collaborative

Leadership/Decisive/Powerful

When creating the values string, ask the client to place the most significant term at the beginning, such as "Integrity" and "Leadership" in the examples above. Point out that it may take several months to come up with a fairly complete list of values. Since values show up over time in our lives, it is unlikely that we will be able to capture them accurately and completely in one sitting. Values that are fully defined and elaborated on become a powerful tool in pointing clients toward fulfilling choices as they approach a major crossroads or get off track.

The coach facilitates the process of identifying values by proposing various scenarios to the client. The following scenarios will give you a place to start. Experiment with these and continue to explore other methods for allowing clients to see their values.

A Peak Moment in Time

Ask the client to identify special, peak moments when life was especially rewarding or poignant. It's important that the time frame be quite limited—a "moment"—or there will be too much in the experience to allow the client to pinpoint specific values. When the client has a specific moment in mind, start probing: "What was happening?" "Who was present and what was going on?" "What were the values that were being honored in that moment?" Acknowledge what you are hearing and keep probing, periodically testing words to see what values resonate for this client. "That sounds important." "Is there a value of accomplishment or achievement in that experience?" or "You light up when you describe that day. It sounds like you were

Co-Active Coaching (2nd ed.) © 2007 by Laura Whitworth, Karen Kimsey-House, Henry Kimsey-House, and Phillip Sandahl. Permission is hereby granted to reproduce this page for client use. Duplication for any other use, including resale, is a violation of copyright law.

Values Clarification Exercise cont'd

honoring a value around nature and a value of connection. Does that sound right?" There will be a stronger response when the words ring true. Ask the client to expand on the first word. "What does 'accomplishment' mean to you?" "What words elaborate on your value of connection?" Keep looking at peak moments, seeking experiences the client found particularly rich and fulfilling.

Suppressed Values

Another way to isolate values is to go to the opposite extreme, looking at times when a client was angry, frustrated, or upset. This will often lead to identification of a value that was being suppressed. First, have the client name the feelings and circumstances around the upset; then flip it over and look for the opposite of those feelings. For example, the client might say, "I felt trapped, backed into a corner. I had no choices." The coach might then say, "Trapped, cornered, without choice. If we flip that over, it sounds like there might be a value around freedom or options or choice. Does that sound right?" For the coach, it's not so important that the vocabulary be right—it's important that the words feel right to the client. To further illustrate, the coach might say, "So you felt frustrated when they kept spinning their wheels, doing the same thing over and over again? Is the other side of that a value for creativity or innovation?"

Many of us have created our lives in such a way that we automatically and easily honor many of our values without even being aware that we are doing so. Therefore we may not recognize them as values until something gets in the way. The key here is to point out to the client that every upset or moment of distress is likely to signal that a value is being suppressed.

Must-Haves

Another way for clients to identify their values is to look at what they must have in their lives. Try it yourself. Beyond the physical requirements of food, shelter, and community, what must you have in your life in order to be fulfilled? Must you have a form of creative self-expression? Must you have adventure and excitement in your life? Must you have partnership and collaboration? Must you be moving toward a sense of accomplishment or success or be surrounded with natural beauty? An underlying question for the process is *What are the values you absolutely must honor—or part of you dies?*

Co-Active Coaching (2nd ed.) © 2007 by Laura Whitworth, Karen Kimsey-House, Henry Kimsey-House, and Phillip Sandahl. Permission is hereby granted to reproduce this page for client use. Duplication for any other use, including resale, is a violation of copyright law.

Values Clarification Exercise cont'd

Obsessive Expression

We are all capable of obsessive behavior—insisting on honoring a value, inflating it into a demand rather than a form of self-expression. You've probably had an experience like this in your own life, such as when your roommate's value of orderliness became an obsessive demand for perfection. Our friends and families often do us a service by pointing out the obsessive expression of our values: "You are so controlling!" "All you think about is your students." "You want all the attention." These statements might point toward a value of personal power/leadership, of learning/growth, and of recognition/acknowledgment. Have your clients examine those times when they take certain values to the extreme. "What is it that people say about you? What do you say about yourself?" "What is it that people tease you about or that drives them crazy?" There are important values here that have mutated for some reason. Look for the value, and don't focus on the mutation.

The Values-Based Decision Matrix

One of the most potent tools for making fulfilling life choices is the Values-Based Decision Matrix. This matrix is launched during the initial values clarification process. (Please note that the listing of values may take several months to complete.) After you and the client have brainstormed a list of values, ask the client to rank the top ten values in priority order. Then ask the client to score his or her sense of satisfaction—the degree to which he or she is honoring each value—using a scale of 0 to 10. Most clients find this exercise very revealing, and they are often shocked at what they learn about themselves. Generally, the coach pays particular attention when a client indicates that a score is below 7. This is a likely place for coaching, since low scores mean the client might be putting up with an intolerable situation. The coach may want to revisit this process from time to time to keep the client grounded in his or her sense of self.

Over the years, we have noted that when things are going particularly well in a client's life, the scores typically are high. When the client is struggling or is at a low point, the values matrix can help determine where corrective action is needed. When a client is facing a major decision, such as whether to make a job change or start a new business, or even to have a child, the Values-Based Decision Matrix can be particularly revealing. Ask the client to score his or her values today. Next, ask the client to project out two months, a year, or sometime in the future: "Imagine that

Co-Active Coaching (2nd ed.) © 2007 by Laura Whitworth, Karen Kimsey-House, Henry Kimsey-House, and Phillip Sandahl. Permission is hereby granted to reproduce this page for client use. Duplication for any other use, including resale, is a violation of copyright law.

Values Clarification Exercise cont'd

you did make the change. Anticipate and write down what your scores would be if you did. Next, imagine that you did not make the change and record those scores." This exercise will provide the client with useful insight about making a fulfilling choice.

The following sample Values-Based Decision Matrix represents the responses of a client determining whether or not to take on the leadership role in her company. As you can see, Leadership is not among the top ten values. Review the numbers as if these were your values and your decision. Note how provocative and revealing such an examination can be. What are not on this list of values are tangible measures, such as money and status—factors that are usually the basis for decision making yet rarely lead to fulfilling choices.

Sample Values-Based Decision Matrix

Prioritize and List Values	Date: 7/06 Score Value	Date: 7/07 Score Value	Date: 12/07 Score Value	Date: Score Value	Date: Score Value	Date: Score Value
1. Learning/Growth	9	9	6			
2. Self-Expression	7	9	8			
3. Freedom/Independence	5	7	8			
4. Innovate/Create	6	8	7			
5. Partnership/Collaborate	8	9	8			
6. Organized/Order	7	8	7			
7. Integrity/Honesty	9	9	7			
8. Fun/Humor/Play	7	6	8			
9. Connection/Intimacy	8	6	8			
10. Adventure/Risk Taking	5	8	7			

Co-Active Coaching (2nd ed.) © 2007 by Laura Whitworth, Karen Kimsey-House, Henry Kimsey-House, and Phillip Sandahl. Permission is hereby granted to reproduce this page for client use. Duplication for any other use, including resale, is a violation of copyright law.

Values Clarification Exercise cont'd

Additional Forms

Three additional forms that can be used when working with values are included in this section. They are the Values Worksheet (p. 251), to assist the client in identifying values; the Standards and Obstacles Worksheet (p. 252), to help with establishing standards and obstacles for honoring values; and the Values Action Log (p. 253), to assist in creating values-based action plans. The sample list of values (p. 254) is to be held by the coach and not provided to the client. When we are on the spot, we often forget values; using the list enables the coach to prompt clients about their values—especially when the coach senses that a client may be negating or overlooking some obvious value, such as spirituality or humor.

Co-Active Coaching (2nd ed.) © 2007 by Laura Whitworth, Karen Kimsey-House, Henry Kimsey-House, and Phillip Sandahl. Permission is hereby granted to reproduce this page for client use. Duplication for any other use, including resale, is a violation of copyright law.

Values Clarification Exercise cont'd

Values Worksheet

Rank in Priority Order	Value/Description	Score Level of Satisfaction Scale of 1 to 10 (10 = Highest)

Co-Active Coaching (2nd ed.) © 2007 by Laura Whitworth, Karen Kimsey-House, Henry Kimsey-House, and Phillip Sandahl. Permission is hereby granted to reproduce this page for client use. Duplication for any other use, including resale, is a violation of copyright law.

Values Clarification Exercise cont'd
Standards and Obstacles Worksheet

Value	Honoring Score	Standard (How is value honored?)	Obstacle to Honoring Value	Strength of Obstacle Score
1.				
2.				
3.				
4.				
5.				
6.				
7.				
8.				

Co-Active Coaching (2nd ed.) © 2007 by Laura Whitworth, Karen Kimsey-House, Henry Kimsey-House, and Phillip Sandahl. Permission is hereby granted to reproduce this page for client use. Duplication for any other use, including resale, is a violation of copyright law.

Values Clarification Exercise cont'd

Values Action Log

Value	Action to Be Taken to Increase Score	By When?
1.		
2.		
3.		
4.		
5.		
6.		
7.		
8.		

Co-Active Coaching (2nd ed.) © 2007 by Laura Whitworth, Karen Kimsey-House, Henry Kimsey-House, and Phillip Sandahl. Permission is hereby granted to reproduce this page for client use. Duplication for any other use, including resale, is a violation of copyright law.

Values Clarification Exercise cont'd

Sample Values List

The following list contains words or phrases that illustrate values. Remember as you work with this exercise that you may combine two or three values as long as critical distinctions are not lost. For example, whereas the combination "Honesty/Integrity/ Truthfulness" maintains a single distinction, "Honesty/Integrity/ Freedom" combines concepts and thereby loses clarity.

Humor	Participation
Directness	Performance
Partnership	Collaboration
Productivity	Community
Service	Personal Power
Contribution	Freedom to Choose
Excellence	Connectedness
Free Spirit	Acknowledgment
Focus	Comradeship
Romance	Lightness
Recognition	Spirituality
Harmony	Empowerment
Accomplishment	Full Self-Expression
Orderliness	Integrity
Forward the Action	Creativity
Honesty	Independence
Success	Nurturing
Accuracy	Joy
Adventure	Beauty
Lack of Pretense	Authenticity
Zest	Risk Taking
Tradition	Peace
To Be Known	Elegance
Growth	Vitality
Aesthetics	Trust

Co-Active Coaching (2nd ed.) © 2007 by Laura Whitworth, Karen Kimsey-House, Henry Kimsey-House, and Phillip Sandahl. Permission is hereby granted to reproduce this page for client use. Duplication for any other use, including resale, is a violation of copyright law.

Values Clarification Exercise cont'd

Keep Looking

Because values are such an important part of the way clients order their lives and make choices, it is essential to continue to look at this area. Values could conceivably be examined in every coaching call—either to help make a choice or to clarify and reinforce a course of action: *What is the value that would be honored if you did that?* When your clients honor their values, three things happen: one, they add additional fuel to the motivation fire and help build steam for action; two, they undermine the work of the Saboteur because action based on values is more powerful than the Saboteur's reasons for not taking action or for taking some other course of action; and three, they have fulfilling lives.

Co-Active Coaching (2nd ed.) © 2007 by Laura Whitworth, Karen Kimsey-House, Henry Kimsey-House, and Phillip Sandahl. Permission is hereby granted to reproduce this page for client use. Duplication for any other use, including resale, is a violation of copyright law.

Coaching Resources

The following resources expand on coaching skills and contexts mentioned through-out this book. These lists should be considered works-in-progress. The active professional coach will add to these lists throughout his or her career.

Powerful Questions

Powerful questions are provocative queries that put a halt to evasion and confusion. By asking the powerful question, the coach invites the client to clarity, action, and discovery at a whole new level. As you can see from the following examples, these generally are open-ended questions that create greater possibility for expanded learning and fresh perspective.

Anticipation
What is possible?
What if it works out exactly as you want it to?
What is the dream?
What is exciting to you about this?
What is the urge? What does your intuition tell you?

Assessment
What do you make of it?
What do you think is best?
How does it look to you?
How do you feel about it?
What resonates for you?

Clarification
What do you mean?
What does it feel like?
What is the part that is not yet clear?
Can you say more?
What do you want?

Elaboration
Can you tell me more?
What else?
What other ideas/thoughts/feelings do you have about it?

Co-Active Coaching (2nd ed.) © 2007 by Laura Whitworth, Karen Kimsey-House, Henry Kimsey-House, and Phillip Sandahl. Permission is hereby granted to reproduce this page for client use. Duplication for any other use, including resale, is a violation of copyright law.

Powerful Questions cont'd

Evaluation
What is the opportunity here? What is the challenge?
How does this fit with your plans/way of life/values?
What do you think that means?
What is your assessment?

Example
What is an example?
For instance?
Like what?
Such as?
What would it look like?

Exploration
What is here that you want to explore?
What part of the situation have you not yet explored?
What other angles can you think of?
What is just one more possibility?
What are your other options?

For Instance
If you could do it over again, what would you do differently?
If it had been you, what would you have done?
How else could a person handle this?
If you could do anything you wanted, what would you do?

Fun as Perspective
What does fun mean to you?
What was humorous about the situation?
How can you make this more fun?
How do you want it to be?
If you were to teach people how to have fun, what would you say?

Co-Active Coaching (2nd ed.) © 2007 by Laura Whitworth, Karen Kimsey-House, Henry Kimsey-House, and Phillip Sandahl. Permission is hereby granted to reproduce this page for client use. Duplication for any other use, including resale, is a violation of copyright law.

Powerful Questions cont'd

History
What caused it?
What led up to it?
What have you tried so far?
What do you make of it all?

Implementation
What is the action plan?
What will you have to do to get the job done?
What support do you need to accomplish it?
What will you do?
When will you do it?

Integration
What will you take away from this?
How do you explain this to yourself?
What was the lesson?
How can you make sure you remember what you have learned?
How would you pull all this together?

Learning
If your life depended on taking action, what would you do?
If you had free choice in the matter, what would you do?
If the same thing came up again, what would you do?
If we could wipe the slate clean, what would you do?
If you had it to do over again, what would you do?

Options
What are the possibilities?
If you had your choice, what would you do?
What are possible solutions?
What will happen if you do, and what will happen if you don't?
What options can you create?

Co-Active Coaching (2nd ed.) © 2007 by Laura Whitworth, Karen Kimsey-House, Henry Kimsey-House, and Phillip Sandahl. Permission is hereby granted to reproduce this page for client use. Duplication for any other use, including resale, is a violation of copyright law.

Powerful Questions cont'd

Outcomes
What do you want?
What is your desired outcome?
If you got it, what would you have?
How will you know you have reached it?
What would it look like?

Perspective
When you are ninety-five years old, what will you want to say about your life?
What will you think about this five years from now?
How does this relate to your life purpose?
In the bigger scheme of things, how important is this?
So what?

Planning
What do you plan to do about it?
What is your game plan?
What kind of plan do you need to create?
How do you suppose you could improve the situation?
Now what?

Predictions
How do you suppose it will all work out?
What will that get you?
Where will this lead?
What are the chances of success?
What is your prediction?

Resources
What resources do you need to help you decide?
What do you know about it now?
How do you suppose you can find out more about it?
What kind of picture do you have right now?
What resources are available to you?

Co-Active Coaching (2nd ed.) © 2007 by Laura Whitworth, Karen Kimsey-House, Henry Kimsey-House, and Phillip Sandahl. Permission is hereby granted to reproduce this page for client use. Duplication for any other use, including resale, is a violation of copyright law.

Powerful Questions cont'd

Starting the Session
What's occurred since we last spoke?
What would you like to talk about?
What's new/the latest/the update?
How was your week?
Where are you right now?

Substance
What seems to be the trouble?
What seems to be the main obstacle?
What is stopping you?
What concerns you the most about . . . ?
What do you want?

Summary
What is your conclusion?
How is this working?
How would you describe this?
What do you think this all amounts to?
How would you summarize the effort so far?

Taking Action
What action will you take? And after that?
What will you do? When?
Is this a time for action? What action?
Where do you go from here? When will you do that?
What are your next steps? By what date or time will you complete these steps?

Co-Active Coaching (2nd ed.) © 2007 by Laura Whitworth, Karen Kimsey-House, Henry Kimsey-House, and Phillip Sandahl. Permission is hereby granted to reproduce this page for client use. Duplication for any other use, including resale, is a violation of copyright law.

Homework Inquiries

The homework inquiry is a form of powerful question that clients use between coaching calls. Instead of looking for the one right answer, the client is in a mode of reflection, discovery, and learning. This list of homework inquiries is an excellent resource; however, active coaches will add to this list throughout their careers.

Beginning Inquiries

What do I want?

What is it to have a full, rich life?

What am I tolerating?

Where am I not being realistic?

What is integrity?

How do I operate?

What is it to live in alignment with my values?

What is it to be powerful?

What is it to be present?

What is my prevalent mood? Is that a habit?

What is choice? What is it to choose?

When do I allow myself to not be my word?

What is the difference between a wish and a goal?

Am I being nice or am I being real?

What do I use to avoid feelings? (For example, alcohol, food, work?)

Where is my attention? (On self, others, work, daydreams, my vision, values, complaints?)

What Works?

What keeps me going?

What is working?

What frees me up?

What is it to be prosperous?

Where am I too hard on myself?

What is present when I'm at my best?

What is my structure to win?

Where am I the solution?

Co-Active Coaching (2nd ed.) © 2007 by Laura Whitworth, Karen Kimsey-House, Henry Kimsey-House, and Phillip Sandahl. Permission is hereby granted to reproduce this page for client use. Duplication for any other use, including resale, is a violation of copyright law.

Homework Inquiries cont'd

Motivational
When am I unable to laugh at myself?

What do I need in order to reach my goals?

What is the distinction between feeling good and fulfillment?

Great goals are compelling; vague goals are forgotten. Which type are my goals?

What am I building? (A cathedral or a block of stone?)

Who am I becoming?

What motivates me?

What is it to be undaunted?

What am I choosing this week?

What does it mean to allow or include?

What is it to be creative?

What powerful questions can I ask myself each morning?

What is it to be tenacious?

What is it to be passionate?

What flag am I bearing?

What is it to be powerful/resilient/resourceful/empowering/determined?

What pain do I notice in people around me?

What is it to speak/act from my heart?

How have I withheld myself from life?

Is what I am doing right now life-affirming or life-numbing?

What is it to be intuitive?

What is it to be focused?

What is it to be a leader?

Stopped/Blocked Client
What is the lie?

What am I resisting?

If I were at my best, what would I do right now?

Where do I give my power away? To whom? When?

What are my false assumptions?

What do I pretend? (To know or not to know?)

What do I need to leave alone?

What is out of alignment?

Co-Active Coaching (2nd ed.) © 2007 by Laura Whitworth, Karen Kimsey-House, Henry Kimsey-House, and Phillip Sandahl. Permission is hereby granted to reproduce this page for client use. Duplication for any other use, including resale, is a violation of copyright law.

Homework Inquiries cont'd

Stopped/Blocked Client cont'd

What is needed in this situation?

What is it to be exceptional?

What will I gather evidence for this week?

What is it to generate or cause?

What are my wants versus my musts?

Where am I an automatic no or yes?

Where do I limit myself?

What are other possibilities?

Where am I too comfortable?

What is it to move toward the fear?

What does it mean to "lean into it"?

Where am I sabotaging myself? Undermining my own potential for success?

What else can I do to honor my values?

What requests can be made to get me going?

What is the powerful interpretation?

Where am I uncompromising? Where am I too flexible?

What does _____ cost me?

Where do I hold back?

What am I withholding?

What am I unwilling to risk?

What is it to surrender?

Where am I suffering?

What will free me up?

What are my assumptions?

What are my expectations?

Pleasure

How can I pamper myself today?

What am I grateful for?

Can I make someone smile this morning? Who?

What will recharge my batteries?

What is fun?

How can I contribute to my reserves of fun/leisure/balance/resourcefulness/
    patience?

Co-Active Coaching (2nd ed.) © 2007 by Laura Whitworth, Karen Kimsey-House, Henry Kimsey-House, and Phillip Sandahl. Permission is hereby granted to reproduce this page for client use. Duplication for any other use, including resale, is a violation of copyright law.

Homework Inquiries cont'd

How can I have this be easy?

Who can I get to play with me on this project?

What is it to be tickled?

What is grace/serenity?

What makes me laugh?

Do I choose heavy or do I choose light?

Since I am going to do this anyway, do I choose to have it be neutral, hard, or fun?

What can I do to my physical environment to have it nurture/relax/empower me?

What is fulfilling, what feels good, and so what?

What is pleasure?

What acknowledgment can I give myself today?

What is kindness?

What is it to go softly into life?

What is abundance?

How can I have this be playful and light?

How can I double my vitality?

What should I give myself permission to do today?

When will I take a break today?

What thrills me?

What is it to be awed?

What is it to be generous with myself?

What is it to be considerate?

What is it to be gentle with myself?

What is it to gawk/savor?

What am I grateful for today?

Provocative

What do I regret/resent?

What am I unwilling to change?

Where might I be in denial?

What am I overlooking?

Where am I slowing down?

What is the decision I have been avoiding?

Where do I stop short?

Co-Active Coaching (2nd ed.) © 2007 by Laura Whitworth, Karen Kimsey-House, Henry Kimsey-House, and Phillip Sandahl. Permission is hereby granted to reproduce this page for client use. Duplication for any other use, including resale, is a violation of copyright law.

Homework Inquiries cont'd

Provocative cont'd
What is a big enough game?
What have I wanted to do and haven't?
What keeps me from winning?
Where have I denied myself/others?
Why bother?
What am I being right about?
What complaint/fear/bad habit/discomfort can I do something about today?
Where am I asleep at the wheel?
What am I settling for?
What will this goal get me?
What am I overlooking?
How do I sabotage myself?
What is it to transcend my sense of failure/sense of resignation/feelings of "I can't"?
Where am I selling out on myself?
What am I willing/unwilling to change?
What am I stepping over?
What is my reputation?
What do I expect of myself?
What is grace/enthusiasm/prosperity/abundance?
What is it to be proactive?
What is it to be centered/optimistic/supportable/non-attached?
What is it to be fluid/flexible?
What is it to be compassionate?
What is completion? Where am I incomplete?
If my whole attention is focused on producing the result, what will I have to give up?
Why am I taking this action?

Completion
What is it to be complete?
What's next?
What territory have I taken?
How far have I come?
What valuable learning am I taking away?

Co-Active Coaching (2nd ed.) © 2007 by Laura Whitworth, Karen Kimsey-House, Henry Kimsey-House, and Phillip Sandahl. Permission is hereby granted to reproduce this page for client use. Duplication for any other use, including resale, is a violation of copyright law.

Homework Inquiries cont'd

Who have I become?
What have I built?
What did it take to get here?
What have I learned about myself?
What does it take to maintain?
What is momentum?
What will keep me on track?
What is it to be filled with loving kindness?
What is it to live life fully?
What is it to love deeply?
What values require my constant attention?
What will I be giving away?
What is my contribution to the world going to be?
Who did I have to be to reach this place?
How will I know to ask for support?
What acknowledgment would I like to give myself?

Assignments

Forgive yourself once a day.
Count the number of times a day you notice the Saboteur.
Laugh/smile twenty-five times a day.
Cite twenty-five things that make you proud of yourself.
Be present for fifteen minutes straight three times a day.
List your five most prevalent Saboteur conversations.
What is the most insidious side of your Saboteur?
List your justifications.
List your expectations.
Design a challenge for yourself that takes your breath away. Then do it five times.
Eliminate _____ words from your vocabulary this week.
Add _____ words to your vocabulary this week.
Do the hard thing first each morning and after lunch.
Say no _____ times a day.
Make _____ mistakes a day.

Co-Active Coaching (2nd ed.) © 2007 by Laura Whitworth, Karen Kimsey-House, Henry Kimsey-House, and Phillip Sandahl. Permission is hereby granted to reproduce this page for client use. Duplication for any other use, including resale, is a violation of copyright law.

Homework Inquiries cont'd

Assignments cont'd

Take _____ risks this week.

Ask _____ people out for coffee this week.

Say "So what?" _____ times a day.

Ask and answer the question "Why bother?" with every new action.

Count the times you speak powerfully.

Only speak powerfully this week (not positively, but powerfully).

Catch yourself growing (making mistakes).

Acquire evidence of some new ability. (Using the "bushel basket" metaphor, gather evidence of accomplishments, compassion, being proactive, going for it, and so forth.)

Choose what you have in every moment.

Enjoy two big belly laughs each day.

Co-Active Coaching (2nd ed.) © 2007 by Laura Whitworth, Karen Kimsey-House, Henry Kimsey-House, and Phillip Sandahl. Permission is hereby granted to reproduce this page for client use. Duplication for any other use, including resale, is a violation of copyright law.

Structures

A structure is a method for helping people remember and take action on what is designated as important. For example, putting a note in the client's calendar is a simple structure for jogging the memory and getting that person to take a desired action. But a structure will work only if people notice it. Whether or not they do what the structure indicates, the structure will lead to learning. The number of structures to get people into action is unlimited. Here we cover some of the basic categories.

Basic Structures

Here are some structures that have worked:

- Call your coach's voice mail or your own voice mail every day when a certain task is done. Or send an e-mail.

- Wear a rubber band on your wrist when you want to remember to do something, such as breathe deeply, speak powerfully, sit up straight, turn complaints into requests, or tell someone something positive.

- Throw a dinner party once a month. This can be a structure for cleaning house or keeping up relationships with friends.

- Find an exercise partner.

- Devise an intentionally fabricated deadline on the day you start a project—such as scheduling a meeting to show a colleague or friend your completed project in two weeks.

- Schedule appointments with one friend a week for two months.

- Put a chair in front of the door when you come in at night to remind yourself to take along important documents tomorrow.

- Send yourself an e-mail or voice mail to request that a certain task be done.

- Ask a friend to send you a pre-designed postcard once a month to encourage you to . . .

    Counting is a structure. When you want to pay attention to a certain behavior—when your Saboteur shows up, for example, or when you acknowledge others—

Co-Active Coaching (2nd ed.) © 2007 by Laura Whitworth, Karen Kimsey-House, Henry Kimsey-House, and Phillip Sandahl. Permission is hereby granted to reproduce this page for client use. Duplication for any other use, including resale, is a violation of copyright law.

Structures cont'd

simply count how many times you do it in any given day. This is a structure that focuses your attention on noticing. You can also count the number of cigarettes smoked, the number of calories consumed, the number of sales appointments, the number of times you apologize, and the like. Counting does not require you to do anything other than notice. But noting every time you do something heightens your awareness.

A talisman can be a structure. A toy lion by the phone can remind the client to be ferocious in pursuit of a goal.

A coach is one of the best structures. Coaching is a relationship of accountability and a place where clients stop everything while they look at their lives, at how they are doing, and whether they are headed in the direction they want.

Time Management

This category includes any kind of calendar, day timer, or to-do list. It can be paper, computer based, store-bought or handmade, rigorously designed down to the quarter hour, or just an overview. The key to its effectiveness is how well it fits the client. There is a mistaken belief that there is just one right way. For all the evolution in format and technology, from pencil and paper to palmtop, the appropriate system is what works for your client.

Money Management

For most people, about the only structure they have for managing this significant area of their lives is the register in their checkbooks. Other structures might include computer programs, a monthly budget, regularly scheduled money management discussions with a spouse, or the services of a financial planner or home budget consultant. This is by no means an exhaustive list; it merely gives you a sense of the variety of options available.

Using the Senses

For clients who are highly visual, any structure that appears in their daily field of vision is likely to work—sticking notes to their computer, the cabinet above the desk, or the refrigerator door, for example. Postcards or pictures cut from magazines are

Co-Active Coaching (2nd ed.) © 2007 by Laura Whitworth, Karen Kimsey-House, Henry Kimsey-House, and Phillip Sandahl. Permission is hereby granted to reproduce this page for client use. Duplication for any other use, including resale, is a violation of copyright law.

Structures cont'd

another good structure. Repainting a room to change the visual space might be an important new structure for a client, or simply changing a chair position so that the client is forced to look at the world from a different perspective. Any structural device that engages these clients visually is likely to be powerful and effective.

Think about how you could use the other senses as well. Auditory structures, like music or an audiotape of affirmations, and even particular fragrances can be very powerful structures. Religious ceremonies and rituals have used fragrance for thousands of years because it's a structure that works. How could you use the structure of smell creatively in your clients' lives?

Some of the best structures come from your intuition and may not seem to make sense at first. Place watermelon seeds on the kitchen window sill . . . carry a flashlight in your briefcase . . . wear mismatched shoes today. One reason structures work is because they interrupt the ordinary mind-flow and grab your attention. The more outrageous they are, the more likely it is that they'll interrupt the semiconscious way we often glide through our days.

You may have a whole catalog of structures you have used with clients. That's handy and a great source of ideas. But it's also very effective to let clients create their own structures. Then the structure will be even better suited to the client.

Co-Active Coaching (2nd ed.) © 2007 by Laura Whitworth, Karen Kimsey-House, Henry Kimsey-House, and Phillip Sandahl. Permission is hereby granted to reproduce this page for client use. Duplication for any other use including resale, is a violation of copyright law.

Sample Co-Active Coaching Skills List

Accountability

Acknowledgment

Articulating what's going on

Asking permission

Bottom-lining

Brainstorming

Challenging

Championing

Clarifying

Clearing

Confidentiality

Creating trust

Dancing in the moment

Forwarding the action

Goal setting and planning

Holding the client's agenda

Holding the focus

Inquiry

Intruding/taking charge

Intuiting

Listening

Metaphor

Meta-view

Powerful questions

Reframing

Requesting

Self-management

Structures

Visioning

Co-Active Coaching (2nd ed.) © 2007 by Laura Whitworth, Karen Kimsey-House, Henry Kimsey-House, and Phillip Sandahl. Permission is hereby granted to reproduce this page for client use. Duplication for any other use, including resale, is a violation of copyright law.

Organizational Impact of Co-Active Coaching

In the years since the first edition of *Co-Active Coaching* was published, coaching has taken on a more significant role in the workplace.

ORGANIZATIONAL LEADER AS CO-ACTIVE COACH

Numerous studies now exist that provide evidence for the claim that coaching in the workplace is an effective strategy for boosting productivity, morale, job satisfaction, and profitability (Bolch 2001; Thach 2002; Luthans and Peterson 2003; Wales 2003; Wilson 2004). Coaching in organizations is no longer the territory of just human resource professionals, trainers, or externally hired coaches; it is an essential leadership attribute. The expectation that leaders in organizations apply coaching competencies in interactions with employees and colleagues has grown by leaps and bounds and is likely to continue to grow in years ahead.

Although we know that coaching in general can provide a positive return on investment, what indicators do we have that the co-active coaching model *specifically* works well for leaders in organizational settings? What distinguishing features of co-active coaching *in particular* align with what we know about how adults learn and perform in organizations? This appendix addresses these questions by considering how key aspects of the co-active coaching model (the cornerstones, the designed alliance, and specific competencies) may contribute to a leadership coaching style that serves to support learning and performance in organizations.

CORNERSTONES OF CO-ACTIVE COACHING

The cornerstone of people being *naturally creative, resourceful,* and *whole* is a fundamental premise that underlies co-active coaching. Research from fields including health care, education, and business management shows that when leaders hold the assumption that the other's capability is high, performance tends to be high (Rosenthal and Jacobson 1968; Livingston 1969; King 1971; Eden and Shani 1982; Eden 1992). This positive self-fulfilling prophecy, known as the *Pygmalion effect*, has a reverse cousin known as the *set-up-to-fail syndrome*: employees who are perceived as mediocre by managers tend to perform at a lower level than their counterparts (Manzoni and Barsoux 1998). It is reasonable to expect that as managers and professional colleagues within organizations apply co-active coaching skills and view others as being naturally creative, resourceful, and whole, the impact on productivity will be positive.

When adopted in organizations, the other three cornerstones of co-active coaching (following the client's agenda, dancing in the moment, and including the client's whole life) create a climate in which employees are valued and encouraged to focus on development that is most relevant and meaningful to them. In such an environment, employees are viewed as multifaceted human beings with whole lives, and interactions within the organization reflect this perception. These cornerstones form a foundation of co-active coaching that may be distinct from other approaches and that may contribute to an organizational climate that is most conducive to strong employee satisfaction and high performance for both the individual and the organization.

This contention is supported by several areas of research. Contrary to common perceptions, when organizations can include and make explicit the links between the personal lives of employees and business goals, the company generally benefits as well as the employees (Bailyn, Fletcher, et al. 1997). Similarly, in its landmark 1998 study, the Gallup Organization identified core factors that contribute the most to creation of a strong workforce and measured the links between employee satisfaction and business unit results (Buckingham and Coffman 1999). Several factors align closely with the co-active coaching cornerstones, such as the degree to which employees have a sense of being valued as whole people, the opportunity to excel at work that is meaningful and in alignment with organizational purpose, and the knowledge that one's development is important.

In the book that resulted from the study, author Marcus Buckingham describes a great manager in a way that is quite similar to our characterization of a co-active coach. He advises managers to "do everything you can to help each person cultivate his talents. Help each person become more of who he already is" (p. 141).

RELATIONSHIP: THE DESIGNED ALLIANCE

The co-active coaching model places explicit emphasis on the *designed alliance* that is formulated between coach and client. This co-created relationship forms a container in which coaching occurs, similar to what is described by developmental theorists as a "holding environment" (Winnicott 1965; Kegan 1982; Daloz 1999). Research indicates that results from coaching in organizations occur *most* when the quality of the relationship between coach and client is strong (Wales 2003). This holding environment created by the alliance provides a climate of trust between the leader or coach and the learner. Describing strong learning partnerships characterized by deep trust, adult educator Laurent Daloz (1999) says:

> To *engender trust* is central to any strong, nurturant relationship. But although the trust that characterizes an early relationship owes much of its strength to the ascribed authority of the teacher, more mature trust is sustained increasingly by the shared commitment of each partner. It must be constantly recreated. (p. 176)

The importance of a trusting and confidential relationship with a coach is especially important for organizational leaders at executive levels who may experience increasing isolation and the absence of confidantes as they rise to higher organizational levels (Bolch 2001; Rider 2002).

Within the container of the coaching relationship, the co-active coach uses skills that *support* the client (such as listening, acknowledgment, and championing) as well as skills that *challenge* (for example, articulating what's going on, championing, and challenging). The ability to balance providing support with creating sufficient challenge for learners is a fundamental skill of powerful adult educators, mentors, and leaders (Brookfield 1990; Heifetz 1994; Daloz 1999). When this type of alliance exists, individuals are able to stretch beyond their current level of capability. In her research of highly creative partnerships, Vera John-Steiner (2000) refers to this co-created relationship as the *emotional scaffolding* that provides "the gift of confidence, and the leaning on that gift by creative people during periods of self-doubt and rejection by those in power" (p. 128).

CO-ACTIVE COACHING AND EMOTIONAL INTELLIGENCE

Coaching skills, particularly coaching approaches that are nondirective in nature, correspond closely to the skills of emotional intelligence identified by psychologist Daniel Goleman (1997). Numerous studies have found the competencies of emotional intelligence, organized in the clusters of *self-awareness*, *social awareness*, *self-management*, and *relationship management,* to be an important factor in leadership effectiveness (Jay 2003; Wasylyshyn, Gronsky, et al. 2004).

Several key skills and contexts emphasized in the co-active coaching model are particularly important in the repertoire of the emotionally intelligent leader—examples include *intuition, self-management,* and *Level II and Level III listening.* The ability to trust intuition, to listen to one's "gut feelings," has gained new respect as more neurological studies indicate links between our emotional responses and the ability to find meaning in data and make good decisions (Damasio 1999). The competency of self-management enables transparency, "an authentic openness to others about one's feelings, beliefs, and actions—allows integrity, or the sense that a leader can be trusted" (Goleman, Boyatzis, et al. 2002). Listening at Levels II and III contributes to what Goleman refers to as *social awareness* and *empathy* and is crucial to a leader's ability to respond appropriately to the feelings of others in a given moment and to sense the shared values and priorities that guide a group.

SUMMARY

Broadly speaking, coaching methodologies are either directive or nondirective in approach (Bacon and Spear 2003). A directive coaching model provides specific direction and may be most useful in situations of high risk or when correction for specific problems is needed. It is the leadership and coaching style that is most familiar and developed in Western business. Nondirective approaches such as co-active coaching place greater emphasis on the learning process, with the leader or coach acting as a catalyst for new awareness, and may be most appropriate when the focus of coaching is developmental. What sets co-active coaching apart from other methodologies is the strong emphasis placed on the leader's fundamental *perspective* of the learner and the *relationship,* as represented by the foundational cornerstones and designed alliance of the model. Generally speaking, these are among the underdeveloped muscles of leaders in today's organizations, particularly as organizations become flatter and more reliant on bringing forth the creative talent and individual leadership capability of employees.

References

Bacon, T., and K. Spear. (2003). *Adaptive Coaching: The Art and Practice of a Client-Centered Approach to Performance Improvement.* Mountain View, Calif.: Davies-Black Publishing.

Bailyn, L., J. K. Fletcher, et al. (1997). "Unexpected Connections: Considering Employees' Personal Lives Can Revitalize Your Business." *Sloan Management Review* 38(4): 11–19.

Bolch, M. (2001). "Proactive Coaching." *Training* 38(5): 58–66.

Brookfield, S. (1990). *The Skillful Teacher: On Technique, Trust, and Responsiveness in the Classroom.* San Francisco: Jossey-Bass.

Buckingham, M., and C. Coffman (1999). *First, Break All the Rules: What the World's Greatest Managers Do Differently.* New York: Simon & Schuster.

Daloz, L. A. (1999). *Mentor: Guiding the Journey of Adult Learners.* San Francisco: Jossey-Bass.

Damasio, A. R. (1999). *The Feeling of What Happens: Body and Emotion in the Making of Consciousness.* New York: Harcourt.

Eden, D. (1992). "Leadership and Expectations: Pygmalion Effects and Other Self-Fulfilling Prophecies in Organizations." *Leadership Quarterly* 3: 271–305.

Eden, D., and A. B. Shani. (1982). "Pygmalion Goes to Boot Camp." *Journal of Applied Psychology* 67: 194–199.

Goleman, D. (1997). *Emotional Intelligence.* New York: Bantam Books.

Goleman, D., R. Boyatzis, et al. (2002). *Primal Leadership: Realizing the Power of Emotional Intelligence.* Boston: Harvard Business School Publishing.

Heifetz, R. A. (1994). *Leadership Without Easy Answers.* Cambridge, Mass.: Belknap Press of Harvard University Press.

Jay, M. (2003). "Understanding How to Leverage Executive Coaching." *Organization Development Journal* 21(2): 6.

John-Steiner, V. (2000). *Creative Collaboration.* New York: Oxford University Press.

Kegan, R. (1982). *The Evolving Self: Problem and Process in Human Development.* Cambridge, Mass.: Harvard University Press.

King, A. S. (1971). "Self-Fulfilling Prophecies in Training the Hard Core: Supervisors' Expectations and the Underprivileged Workers' Performance." *Social Science Quarterly* 52: 369–378.

Livingston, J. S. (1969). "Pygmalion in Management." *Harvard Business Review* 47(4): 81–89.

Luthans, F., and S. J. Peterson. (2003). "360-Degree Feedback with Systematic Coaching: Empirical Analysis Suggests a Winning Combination." *Human Resource Management* 42(3): 243.

Manzoni, J.-F., and J.-L. Barsoux. (1998). "The Set-Up-to-Fail Syndrome." *Harvard Business Review:* 101–113.

Rider, L. (2002). "Coaching as a Strategic Intervention." *Industrial and Commercial Training* 34(6/7): 233–237.

Rosenthal, R., and L. Jacobson. (1968). *Pygmalion in the Classroom: Teacher Expectations and Pupils' Intellectual Development.* New York: Holt, Rinehart & Winston.

Thach, E. C. (2002). "The Impact of Executive Coaching and 360 Feedback on Leadership Effectiveness." *Leadership & Organization Development Journal* 23(3/4): 205.

Wales, S. (2003). "Why Coaching?" *Journal of Change Management* 3(3): 275.

Wasylyshyn, K. M., B. Gronsky, et al. (2004). "Emotional Competence: Preliminary Results of a Coaching Program Commissioned by Rohm and Haas Company." *Human Resource Planning* 27(4): 7.

Wilson, C. (2004). "Coaching and Coach Training in the Workplace." *Industrial and Commercial Training* 36(2/3): 96.

Winnicott, D. W. (1965). *The Maturational Processes and the Facilitating Environment.* New York: International University Press.

Arthur Shirk, EdD, PCC, CPCC, is a faculty member of The Coaches Training Institute and leader of the Co-Active Leadership Program. He received his doctoral degree in organization and leadership from Teachers College at Columbia University. Leadership roles he has held in organizations include Vice President of Learning and Communications at Fidelity Investments and Senior Director of Learning and Leading at Princeton University. He holds an MBA degree from Boston University and leads a consulting and coaching practice in Natick, Massachusetts. Contact: www.artshirk.com.

APPENDIX B
Faith Fuller, PhD, CPCC
Marita Fridjhon, MSW, CPCC, PCC

Coaching the Team, the Organization, or the Relationship

Coaching a group is different from coaching an individual, and the difference goes well beyond the added complexity of numbers. A team, an organization, even a partnership or intimate relationship exists as a living system, not simply a collection of individual parts. A human system can be thought of as a group of interdependent members with a common focus. The behavior of the system emerges out of the interaction of its players and is greater than the sum of its parts.

The system itself is alive, has needs, strengths, weaknesses, values. It can be robust or fragile. In organization and relationship systems coaching, we refer to the system as the "third entity." Every system has a constantly changing climate or emotional field. Anyone who has been on a winning team knows the living spirit that imbues and influences every team member—a spirit that can inspire the whole team to extraordinary levels of performance. Anyone who has been in an organization with sinking morale knows the way that atmosphere can demoralize even the most motivated individuals. In our model, the focus of the coaching is on coaching the system, this third entity, rather than the individuals it comprises.

While there is clearly a role for coaching individuals who are part of a team, it is important to recognize that this is still individual coaching. Executive or leadership coaching for team members or key individuals will likely improve their performance and can have secondary impact on the team, but the coach is still interacting with an individual. Coaching the system as a whole leverages the power of the coach to impact the entire team or group. Experience shows that when there is individual coaching for team members, the system may resist, sometimes even reject, the individual change like an unwanted transplant. The system has its own homeostasis. The preferred approach is to have both one-on-one coaches as well as a team coach to provide optimal value to the system.

In today's organizations, the perception frequently is that the team is composed of functional parts (team members) and that repairing or replacing a broken part will fix the team as a whole. But the theory and reality of living systems are different. Every individual has an impact on the system, but it is also true that the system has an impact on individuals. The coach's job is to keep a soft focus on the players and maintain a powerful awareness of the third entity—that morphic field that exists *between* players and is more than the sum of the individuals. Given the unique nature of the system as a living entity, the question is, how do we coach a system? What is different and what is the same?

THE MODEL

The core skills of co-active coaching apply to relationships and teams in the same way they apply to individuals. Powerful questions are still powerful questions; challenging is still challenging except that it is now the partners or the group reacting to the coach's challenge. The contexts too are just as relevant here: coaches use listening, intuition, self-management, curiosity, and commitment to forwarding and deepening. We also find parallels between the cornerstones of co-active coaching and the cornerstones of organization and relationship coaching.

Hold the System Naturally Creative, Resourceful, and Whole

For example, we hold the system, as we hold the individual, as naturally creative, resourceful, and whole—even in breakdown.

Relate to (or Coach) the Whole Relationship System

Just as the individual coach coaches the client's whole life, the systems coach coaches the whole system. Like the conductor of an orchestra, the systems coach must hold the focus of the whole system at all times while occasionally singling out subsections of the system for special attention.

It Is the Clients' Agenda, and the *System* Is the Client

A systems coach needs to be clear that the client is the system itself. This eliminates any tendency to take sides or support one individual over another. The coach's alliance and allegiance are with the needs of the third entity, the system. System coaching trains the coach to be curious about what is trying to happen, and provides skills to facilitate that. The systems coach can succeed in this by being alert and listening for the voice of the system.

Reveal the System to Itself

This fourth cornerstone is unique to relationship systems coaching. It is the assertion that a system is naturally self-correcting when it becomes aware of itself and its functioning. The role of a systems coach is to help the system become aware of its strengths and weaknesses—to hold up a mirror. This shifts the focus from "Who is doing what to whom?" to "What is trying to happen here?"

The Designed Partnership Alliance

The container that surrounds and supports coach and client is equally as important in relationship and systems coaching as in individual coaching. However, while the individual coach has one alliance to create with the client, the systems coach has two designed alliances to shape: one between the partners being coached, so that they are in alignment regarding the coaching goals and expectations, and the other between the clients and the coach.

The Dimensions

In the relationship systems coaching model, there are three dimensions within which relationships play out: relationship intelligence, systems geography, and relationship path. Each dimension provides access points for working with the system, and each has its own set of skills.

- Relationship intelligence plays out in the flow and expression of emotion and meaning. In this dimension, coaches unfold the emotional flow and dynamic fluidity of relationship. This is key, because emotions are the currency of relationships, and systems coaches must be comfortable working with the full range of emotions in order to be effective.

- Geography is the dimension in which to explore the impact and interaction of roles. These include functional and informal roles, ghost roles that haunt the system, and hidden selves whose appearance may be triggered by certain events. This dimension of systems coaching also includes valuing and empowering differences rather than feeling threatened by them.

- Relationship path focuses on the generative processes of relationship. It examines ways of releasing the creative vision and power of possibilities available in all relationships.

BASIC RELATIONSHIP SYSTEMS COACHING SKILLS

Working with a system requires a special set of skills, beyond the fundamental coaching skills. Some of these are listed below and illustrate theory and mental models from the different dimensions.

Listen for the Voice of the System

In order to coach the system, the coach must be able to discern the voice of the third entity. What does the system want and need beyond the needs of the individuals? Specific skills such as reading the emotional field and constellating the system train the coach to keep a broad focus on the overall dynamics of the relationship system.

MetaSkills™ (Dimension: Path)

All coaching has an aspect of *being* as well as *doing*. A MetaSkill is a skill, an attitude, or a stance that creates an intentional space in which the coaching occurs. MetaSkills are infinite, but several that are most useful to relationship include respect, heart, collaboration, deep democracy, curiosity, and commitment.

MetaSkills provide an underlying context for the way individuals interact in the system. The systems coach learns not only to read the emotional field but also to actively generate an emotional field. Each MetaSkill is like a room, which coach and clients step into, that informs the coaching. Coach and clients experience the topic of the coaching within the MetaSkill of Curiosity, for example, which is different from the same topic experienced within the MetaSkill of Commitment.

For example, Deep Democracy is a MetaSkill, and it holds that every voice in the system must be heard in order for reality to be accurately represented. Each voice in the team, even if unpopular, is like a piece of the puzzle and holds critical information. The systems coach promotes the free and safe exchange of viewpoints and information as an important component for the vitality of the organization.

Work on All Three Levels of Reality (Dimension: Path)

All relationships exist on three levels: the Sentient Essence level, the Dreaming level, and the Consensus Reality level.

- The Sentient Essence level is the almost inexpressible energetic signature of the system. This could be called "chemistry" or the essential spirit of the relationship. In organizations, it is the experience of inspiration or vision.
- The Dreaming level involves the emotional flow of the relationship or organization. It includes feeling states, hopes, fears, projections, and dreams. This is the level of emotional experiences between people.
- The Consensus Reality level is where those dreams, hopes, and

fears become concrete and real. This is the world of figures, facts, and measurable events.

Relationship systems, whether intimate or organizational, need to exist effectively on all three levels in order to be healthy. Too much Consensus Reality and the system feels heavy and dragged down by "reality." Too much Dreaming or Sentient Essence and the system cannot successfully manifest anything. If one member of the team is focused on the mission of the organization and another is focused on getting the budget finished by noon, the system is being pulled in more than one direction. Both the long-term vision work and the more immediate budget work are real and important to the system. All three levels are critical for effective functioning. The systems coach's job is to help support fluidity between all three levels so that the system can be fully expressed.

Lands Work (Dimension: Geography)

Differences are an unavoidable aspect of any group or family. How often have you heard two people or two departments lament, "You don't understand what you're asking for." Marketing and engineering . . . doctors and hospital administrators . . . children and parents . . . sales staff and manufacturing. We live in different worlds, with different rules and expectations and sometimes vastly different priorities. Each person or department is like an individual land, separate and distinct, with its own beliefs, needs, challenges, and gifts. If the system can learn to appreciate the creativity brought from these different lands, then diversity can be a powerful ally to the relationship, not a threat to it. The systems coach works with the system to recognize "joy in the difference" and develop an appreciation for the richness to be found in diversity.

Increase Positivity

Negativity is a toxin that saps the life from a system and can become fatal. We have probably all experienced negativity at some level on a team, in an organization, or in a relationship. The antidote is positivity—ways to help ensure a healthy atmosphere for growth. This doesn't mean "just be happy," but it does mean creating a positive, encouraging, and honest environment. The systems coach works actively with clients to develop and maintain structures for recognition, appreciation, and celebration of the system.

Work with the System

This approach to coaching the system is a contribution to the leading edge of applied general systems theory and field theory. The model includes adaptations from the Process Work of Arnold Mindell, Alternative Dispute Resolution, general systems theory, and other sources. When we survey the coaching landscape, we see that there is a growing demand for coaches with the skill and know-how to work with relationships, teams, and organizations. In our view, the technology to address that demand will be built on the knowledge of how to work with the system and the competencies that go with it.

Faith Fuller, PhD, CPCC
Marita Fridjhon, MSW, CPCC, PCC
Center for Right Relationship
www.therelationshipcoaches.com

Ethics and the Professional Coach

One of the very best resources for the coaching profession is the International Coach Federation (ICF). The ICF is a multifaceted source of support and information for professional coaches worldwide, whether you are building a private practice or coaching inside an organization; whether you are looking for a coach or simply want to learn more about coaching. The Web site (www.coachfederation.org) offers a wealth of resources and contact links along with information about upcoming conferences around the world.

We believe in coaching as a powerful means of change and fulfillment. Our experience over the years has been that we meet within this profession people of integrity, vision, and commitment to the highest of human ideals. At gatherings of coaches, there is a feeling that we are embarked on a common mission, a calling. We believe that the strength of the profession is as strong as its ethics and the integrity of the people in the profession. Included here is the current ICF Code of Ethics.

THE ICF CODE OF ETHICS

Part One: The ICF Philosophy of Coaching

The International Coach Federation adheres to a form of coaching that honors the client as the expert in his/her life and work and believes that every client is creative, resourceful, and whole. Standing on this foundation, the coach's responsibility is to:

- Discover, clarify, and align with what the client wants to achieve
- Encourage client self-discovery
- Elicit client-generated solutions and strategies
- Hold the client responsible and accountable

Part Two: The ICF Definition of Coaching

Professional coaching is an ongoing professional relationship that helps people produce extraordinary results in their lives, careers, businesses, or organizations. Through the process of coaching, clients deepen their learning, improve their performance, and enhance their quality of life.

In each meeting, the client chooses the focus of conversation, while the coach listens and contributes observations and questions. This interaction creates clarity and moves the client into action. Coaching accelerates the client's progress by providing greater focus and awareness of choice. Coaching concentrates on where clients are now and what they are willing to do to get where they want to be in the future. ICF member coaches and ICF-credentialed coaches recognize that results are a matter of the client's intentions, choices, and actions, supported by the coach's efforts and application of the coaching process.

Part Three: The ICF Standards of Ethical Conduct

Professional Conduct at Large

As a coach:

1. I will conduct myself in a manner that reflects positively upon the coaching profession, and I will refrain from engaging in conduct or making statements that may negatively impact the public's understanding or acceptance of coaching as a profession.

2. I will not knowingly make any public statements that are untrue or misleading, or make false claims in any written documents relating to the coaching profession.

3. I will respect different approaches to coaching. I will honor the efforts and contributions of others and not misrepresent them as my own.

4. I will be aware of any issues that may potentially lead to the misuse of my influence by recognizing the nature of coaching and the way in which it may affect the lives of others.

5. I will at all times strive to recognize personal issues that may impair, conflict, or interfere with my coaching performance or my professional relationships. Whenever the facts and circumstances necessitate, I will promptly seek professional assistance and determine the action to be taken, including whether it is appropriate to suspend or terminate my coaching relationship(s).

6. As a trainer or supervisor of current and potential coaches, I will conduct myself in accordance with the ICF Code of Ethics in all training and supervisory situations.

7. I will conduct and report research with competence and honesty and within recognized scientific standards. My research will be carried out with the necessary approval or consent from those involved and with an approach that will reasonably protect participants from any potential harm. All research efforts will be performed in a manner that complies with the laws of the country in which the research is conducted.

8. I will accurately create, maintain, store, and dispose of any records of work done in relation to the practice of coaching in a way that promotes confidentiality and complies with any applicable laws.

9. I will use ICF member contact information (e-mail addresses, telephone numbers, etc.) only in the manner and to the extent authorized by the ICF.

Professional Conduct with Clients

10. I will be responsible for setting clear, appropriate, and culturally sensitive boundaries that govern any physical contact that I may have with my clients.

11. I will not become sexually involved with any of my clients.

12. I will construct clear agreements with my clients and will honor all agreements made in the context of professional coaching relationships.

13. I will ensure that, prior to or at the initial session, my coaching client understands the nature of coaching, the bounds of confidentiality, financial arrangements, and other terms of the coaching agreement.

14. I will accurately identify my qualifications, expertise, and experience as a coach.

15. I will not intentionally mislead or make false claims about what my clients will receive from the coaching process or from me as their coach.

16. I will not give my clients or prospective clients information or advice I know or believe to be misleading.

17. I will not knowingly exploit any aspect of the coach-client relationship for my personal, professional, or monetary advantage or benefit.

18. I will respect the client's right to terminate coaching at any point during the process. I will be alert to indications that the client is no longer benefiting from our coaching relationship.

19. If I believe the client would be better served by another coach, or by another resource, I will encourage the client to make a change.

20. I will suggest that my clients seek the services of other professionals when deemed appropriate or necessary.

21. I will take all reasonable steps to notify the appropriate authorities in the event a client discloses an intention to endanger self or others.

Confidentiality/Privacy

22. I will respect the confidentiality of my client's information, except as otherwise authorized by my client or as required by law.

23. I will obtain agreement from my clients before releasing their names as clients or references or divulging any other client-identifying information.

24. I will obtain agreement from the person being coached before releasing information to another person compensating me.

Conflicts of Interest

25. I will seek to avoid conflicts between my interests and the interests of my clients.

26. Whenever any actual conflict of interest or the potential for a conflict of interest arises, I will openly disclose it and fully discuss with my client how to deal with it in whatever way best serves my client.

27. I will disclose to my client all anticipated compensation from third parties that I may receive for referrals of that client.

28. I will only barter for services, goods, or other non-monetary remuneration when it will not impair the coaching relationship.

Part Four: The ICF Pledge of Ethics

As a professional coach, I acknowledge and agree to honor my ethical obligations to my coaching clients and colleagues and to the public at large. I pledge to comply with the ICF Code of Ethics, to treat people with dignity as independent and equal human beings, and to model these standards with those whom I coach. If I breach this Pledge of Ethics or any part of the ICF Code of Ethics, I agree that the ICF at its sole discretion may hold me accountable for so doing. I further agree that my accountability to the ICF for any breach may include loss of my ICF membership and/or my ICF credentials.

Glossary

Accountability. Accountability is having your clients account for what they said they were going to do. It stems from three questions: (1) What are you going to do? (2) When will you have this done? (3) How will I know? Accountability does not include blame or judgment. Rather, the coach holds clients accountable to their vision or commitment and asks them to account for the results of their intended actions. If need be, holding clients accountable includes defining new actions to be taken.

Acknowledgment. Acknowledgment addresses the self and who clients had to be in order to accomplish the action they took or the awareness they achieved. It is the articulation of your deep knowing of the other.

> *"I acknowledge the courage it took for you to show up for this session, knowing that you had difficult things to share with me today."*

Agenda: Big-"A" Agenda. The Big-"A" agenda is the meta-view, or how clients' choices and actions relate to their big-picture agendas. This is where clients learn more deeply about how they operate. At its core, the Big-"A" agenda consists of the three principles of co-active coaching: fulfillment, balance, and process. It assumes that clients want these three things: (1) to live fulfilling lives, (2) to be in balance about those lives, and (3) to be present in the process of life. The coach interacts with clients holding this Big-"A" agenda at all times.

Agenda: little-"a" agenda. The little-"a" agenda consists of the small picture, the circumstances in the client's life, his or her agenda of the moment. This agenda is focused on a particular event, on the client's choices around that event, or on the actions the client will take related to that specific event.

Articulating what's going on. This skill involves telling clients what you see them doing. It may be what you're hearing with your Level II listening, or you may tell them what they have not said based on your Level III listening and awareness. Sometimes, it is powerful to simply repeat their words back to them so they can really hear themselves.

> *"Debbie, I know how much you want to change your relationship with your dad, yet I hear you are interacting with him the way you always have." "You're annoyed that your manager didn't consider your workload when she assigned you to this new project."*

Asking permission. This skill enables clients to grant the coaching relationship access to unusually intimate or sometimes uncomfortable areas of focus.

> *"May I tell you a hard truth?" "Is it all right to coach you on this issue?" "May I tell you what I see?"*

Bottom-lining. This is the skill of brevity and succinctness on the part of both the coach and the client. It is also about having clients get to the essence of their communication rather than engaging in long descriptive stories.

Brainstorming. Using this skill, coach and client together generate ideas, alternatives, and possible solutions. Some may be outrageous and impractical. This is merely a creative exercise to expand the possibilities available to clients. Neither coach nor client is attached to any of the ideas suggested.

Challenge. A challenge is a request that stretches clients way beyond their self-imposed limits and shakes up the way they see themselves. A challenge, like a request, includes three things: (1) a specified action, (2) conditions of satisfaction, and (3) a date or time of completion. Clients will respond to a challenge with a yes, a no, or a counteroffer. Frequently, the counteroffer is greater than the concession they initially intended to make.

> *A client wants to make cold calls to increase his business. He thinks he can make only one call a day. You challenge him: "I challenge you to make fifty calls a day!" The client counteroffers with "I'll make seven."*

Championing. Championing clients means standing up for them when they doubt or question their abilities. Despite their self-doubt, the coach knows clearly who they are and that they are capable of much more than they think.

Clarifying. When clients are unable to articulate clearly what they want or where they are going, the coach clarifies their experience. Clarification may be used in response to the client's vague sense of the desired outcome, confusion, or uncertainty. This skill represents a synergistic application of questioning, reframing, and articulating what is going on. It is particularly useful during the discovery process.

Clearing. Clearing is a skill that can benefit either the client or the coach. When clients are preoccupied with a situation or a mental state that interferes with their ability to be present or take action, the coach assists by being an active listener while they vent or complain. Both client and coach hold the intention of clearing the emotionality from the situation. This active listening allows clients to temporarily clear the situation out of the way and focus on taking the next step. When a coach gets hooked by a client interaction or is preoccupied with issues that do not pertain to the client, the coach can clear. The coach clears by sharing his or her experience or preoccupation with a colleague or a friend in order to show up and be fully present with the client.

Dancing in the moment. Coaches are dancing in the moment when they are being completely present with the client, holding the client's agenda, accessing their intuition, letting the client lead them. When coaches dance in the moment, they are open to any steps the client takes and are willing to go in the client's direction and flow.

Designed alliance. Coaches and clients begin designing their alliance during the discovery session. Both client and coach are intimately involved in designing the coaching relationship that will be most beneficial to the client. Designed alliances tend to shift over time and need to be revisited regularly.

Goal setting. Clients live their Big-"A" agendas by setting goals and following through. Goals keep clients focused and on track toward the people they are becoming. Goals are not the same as action; they are the desired results of action. In co-active coaching, goals should be specific, measurable, accountable, resonant, and thrilling (SMART).

Granting relationship power. The coaching relationship is separate from the client and the coach. Since the power of coaching resides in the relationship between coach and client, not with either of the two individuals, both coach and client take responsibility for creating the coaching relationship that will most fully serve the client, thereby granting power to the relationship.

Holding the client's agenda. Holding the client's agenda is both a philosophical stance and a cornerstone of the co-active coaching model. When coaches hold the client's agenda, they let go of their own opinions, judgments, and answers in support of facilitating the client's fulfillment, balance, and process. Coaches follow the client's lead without knowing the right answer, giving solutions, or telling the client what to do. Holding the client's agenda requires coaches to put their whole attention on the client and the client's agenda, not on their own agenda for the client.

Holding the focus. Once clients have determined a direction or a course of action, the coach's job is to keep them on track and true to that course. Clients frequently become distracted by events in their lives, strong feelings elicited by the Saboteur, or the wealth of other options available. The coach consistently reminds clients of their focus and helps redirect their energy back to their desired outcomes and life choices.

Homework inquiry. When the coach gives the client a powerful question as homework, the intent is to deepen the client's learning and provoke further reflection. Clients are asked to consider the inquiry between sessions or over a longer period of time and to see what occurs for them. The inquiry is usually based on a particular situation that clients are addressing at the time. An inquiry has multiple answers, none of which are "right."

"What are you tolerating?" "What is it to be undaunted?" "What is challenge?"

Intruding. On occasion, the coach may need to intrude, to interrupt or wake up clients who are going on and on or who are kidding themselves. The coach does this for the sake of the client's agenda, often pointing the client in a specific direction:

"Stop a moment. What's at the heart of this?"

Intrusion is considered rude in some cultures. In co-active training, however, intrusion is viewed as being direct with the client, allowing the client to honestly assess and immediately deal with the situation. Sometimes the intrusion is a hard truth, such as *"You are kidding yourself."* Or the intrusion could simply be a statement about what is going on, such as *"You're skirting the issue."*

Intuiting. Intuiting is the process of accessing and trusting one's inner knowing. Intuition is direct knowing, unencumbered by the thinking mind. The process of intuiting is nonlinear and nonrational. Sometimes the information received through intuiting does not make logical sense to the coach; however, it is usually quite valuable to the client. Intuiting involves taking risks and trusting your gut.

> *"I have a hunch that . . ." "I wonder if . . ."*

Listening. The coach listens for the client's vision, values, commitment, and purpose as expressed in words and demeanor. To listen for is to listen in search of something. The coach listens with consciousness, with a purpose and focus that come from the alliance designed with the client. The coach is listening for the client's agenda, not thinking about his or her agenda for the client. In co-active coaching, when coaches listen to their own thoughts, judgments, and opinions about the client's story, they're listening at Level I; listening that focuses on the client is Level II, and global listening is Level III.

Making distinctions. One way to help clients see a situation from a fresh perspective is to help them distinguish between two or more concepts, facts, or ideas. For example, the client may have blended two facts together into one disempowering belief. The belief appears to be a fact of life, but it's not.

> *"Since I failed, I am a failure"* (equating failing with failure). *"If I make money, that means I'm successful"* (equating money with success).

Metaphor. Metaphors are used to illustrate a point and paint a verbal picture for the client.

> *"Your mind is like a ping pong-ball bouncing between one choice and the other." "You're almost at the finish line. Go for it! You can win the race!"*

Meta-view. The meta-view is the big picture or expanded perspective. The coach pulls back (or asks clients to pull back) from clients' immediate issues and reflects back to clients what he or she sees through the clarity of that expanded perspective.

> *"If your life were like a road, and we were to take a helicopter ride up above it, what would we see?"*

Perspectives. Perspective is one of the gifts that the coach brings to the coaching relationship—not the "right" perspective, but simply other points of view. Part of coaching is inviting clients to see their lives or certain issues from different angles. When clients see things from only one perspective, they are less resourceful and may be victimized by their circumstances. When they are able to reexamine their viewpoints, look at their lives or certain issues from different angles, they are able to see possibility and change.

Planning. The coach helps clients articulate the direction they wish to take and actively monitors their progress. Clients frequently benefit from support in planning and time management as the coach helps them develop their skills in these areas.

Powerful questions. A powerful question evokes clarity, action, discovery, insight, or commitment. It creates greater possibility, new learning, or clearer vision. Powerful questions are open-ended questions that do not elicit a yes or no response. They are derived from holding the client's agenda and either forwarding the client's action or deepening his or her learning.

> *"What do you want?" "What's next?" "How will you start?" "What does that cost you?" "What's important for you to remember?"*

Reframing. With reframing, the coach provides clients with another perspective by taking the original information and interpreting it in a different way.

> *A client has just been informed that she was selected as second choice for a high-powered position in a very competitive market. She is disappointed and is questioning her professional competence. The coach reframes the situation by pointing out that being selected as second choice in such a competitive market indicates the high quality of the client's expertise and experience.*

Requesting. One of the most potent coaching skills is that of making a request of the client. The request, based on the client's agenda, is designed to forward the client's action. The request includes a specified action, conditions of satisfaction, and a date or time for completion. There are three possible responses to a request: (1) yes, (2) no, or (3) a counteroffer.

Saboteur. The Saboteur concept embodies a group of thought processes and feelings that maintains the status quo in our lives. It often appears to be a structure that protects us, but in fact it prevents us from moving forward and getting what we truly want in life. The Saboteur will always be with us. It is neither good nor bad; it just is. The Saboteur loses its power over us when we can identify it for what it is, notice our options in the situation, and then consciously choose the action we really want at that time.

Self-management. This skill involves the coach's ability to put aside all opinions, preferences, judgments, and beliefs in order to hold the client's agenda. Self-management also includes managing the client's Saboteur. The coach can aid clients in identifying their Saboteur and then provide tools for managing it.

Structures. Structures are devices that remind clients of their vision, goals, or purpose, or the actions they need to take immediately. Collages, calendars, messages on voice mail, and alarm clocks can serve as structures.

Taking charge. The coach chooses and directs the path of the coaching in order to serve the client's agenda. Sometimes clients become lost in their circumstances and forget what matters most to them. That's when the coach needs to take charge and direct the coaching back to what is most meaningful to them.

Values. Values represent who you are right now. They are principles that you hold to be of worth in your life. People often confuse values with morals, but they are not the same. Values are not chosen. They are intrinsic to you and are as distinctly yours as your thumbprint.

Vision. This is a multifaceted mental image that personally defines and inspires the client to take action and create that picture in his or her life. A powerful vision is sensuous, exciting, and magnetic, constantly inspiring the client to try to bring it to fruition. Vision provides clients with direction and meaning in life.

Witnessing. Witnessing means being authentically present with the client. This skill creates the space for clients to fully express themselves. When the coach witnesses the client's learning and growth, the client feels seen and known at a very deep level.

About the Authors

Laura Whitworth is an early pioneer in the field of professional coaching. She has been an active coach for executives, entrepreneurs, and other professionals since 1988 and is viewed by many as the "godmother" of the coaching profession. Laura is cofounder of The Coaches Training Institute, The Executive Coaching Summit, The Personal and Professional Coaches Association, the Association of Coach Training Organizations, the Time To Change Prison Project (a nonprofit organization), and The Bigger Game Company, a leadership and advanced coaching training company.

Karen Kimsey-House has been coaching people to excel in their personal and professional lives since 1987 and is a cofounder of The Coaches Training Institute and the CTI Leadership Program. A successful entrepreneur, she founded the Learning Annex San Francisco adult education program in 1986 and helped develop it into one of the most admired programs among Learning Annex city programs.

Karen specializes in working with entrepreneurs and start-up companies, helping them with innovative business practices and no-nonsense strategies for moving forward quickly. She is a founding member of the Personal and Professional Coaches Association and is also a well-known keynote speaker.

Henry Kimsey-House has been a successful coach and workshop leader since 1981. Widely recognized as an innovator in experiential learning and creative course design, he is a cofounder of The Coaches Training Institute and The Co-Active Leadership Program. An actor since age nine, Henry brings that experience and understanding of human process and development to CTI. His acting career includes appearances in Woody Allen's *Stardust Memories*, soap operas, and regional theater productions. Today, Henry continues to refine and expand training curriculum options for CTI, leveraging his creative insights and experience and his background as an actor and a highly regarded creative designer in experiential learning.

Phillip Sandahl is cofounder of Team Coaching International (TCI), which helps organizations worldwide excel through the power of teams. TCI works with teams in organizations and trains team coaches in a leading-edge model of effective team performance. Phillip and cofounder Alexis Phillips are also developers of the *Team Diagnostic*™ assessment, an online tool to provide teams with a portrait of their team as it is today and a map for ongoing team development. Phillip is also a senior faculty member of The Coaches Training Institute, where he leads the professional coaching curriculum and the Organization and Relationship Systems curriculum. He can be reached at Phillip@TeamCoachinginternational.com or through www.teamcoachinginternational.com.

Index

The Coaches Training Institute

An Industry Pioneer Since 1992

CTI is the first ICF-accredited and largest coach training organization in the world, conducting trainings in numerous cities in North America, Europe, Africa, Asia, and Australia. CTI's curriculum includes Co-Active Coaching, Co-Active Leadership, and Organization and Relationship Systems Coaching.

In addition to its public trainings, CTI offers extensive leadership development programs custom tailored to organizations. It has trained employees from close to 100 of the Fortune 500 companies. CTI's trainings span the entire range of emotional intelligence competencies, proven through research to comprise the majority of competencies that distinguish great leaders. Co-active leadership and individual and team coaching have dramatically affected both the performance and the job satisfaction of leaders and teams in a variety of functions, from sales and customer service to engineering, manufacturing, finance, and operations.

What Is Unique About CTI?

CTI's passion is about creating change that is both substantial and sustainable. Most leadership trainings have been shown to fizzle out in effectiveness within a short period of time. To create both substantial and sustainable change, CTI's training enables participants to discover and shift deep underlying paradigms and beliefs that feed behavior and competencies. Since coaching and leadership competencies reside mostly in the emotional intelligence rather than the analytical domain, our training employs pioneering methods for engaging and expanding those competencies experientially and through action. Recognizing the critical need for practicing new competencies, we create learning communities that practice and support the new competencies in action. And, finally, we incorporate powerful learning about relationship systems to which the individuals belong, as these systems affect individual behavior and need to be addressed in order for new competencies to take hold.

The Coaches Training Institute
4000 Civic Center Drive
San Rafael, CA 94903
Telephone: 415-451-6000
Toll-free: 800-691-6008
Web site: www.thecoaches.com
E-mail: CTIinfo@thecoaches.com